What to Read on Love, not Sex

Freud, Fiction, and the Articulation of Truth in Modern Psychological Science

Perspectives in Medical Humanities

Perspectives in Medical Humanities publishes peer reviewed scholarship produced or reviewed under the auspices of the University of California Medical Humanities Consortium, a multi-campus collaborative of faculty, students, and trainees in the humanities, medicine, and health sciences. Our series invites scholars from the humanities and health care professions to share narratives and analysis on health, healing, and the contexts of our beliefs and practices that impact biomedical inquiry.

General Editor

Brian Dolan, PhD, Professor of Social Medicine and Medical Humanities, University of California, San Francisco (UCSF)

Recent Titles

Paths to Innovation: Discovering Recombinant DNA, Oncogenes and Prions, In One Medical School, Over One Decade
By Henry Bourne (Fall 2011)

Clowns and Jokers Can Heal Us: Comedy and Medicine
By Albert Howard Carter III (Fall 2011)

The Remarkables: Endocrine Abnormalities in Art
By Carol Clark and Orlo Clark (Winter 2011)

Health Citizenship: Essays in Social Medicine and Biomedical Politics
By Dorothy Porter (Winter 2011)

Darwin and the Emotions: Mind, Medicine and the Arts
Edited by Angelique Richardson and Brian Dolan (Fall 2012)

mh

www.medicalhumanities.ucsf.edu

This series is made possible by the generous support of the Dean of the School of Medicine at UCSF, the Center for Humanities and Health Sciences at UCSF, and a Multicampus Research Program Grant from the University of California Office of the President.

For SYM
in memoriam
and EHM

What to Read on Love, not Sex

Freud, Fiction, and the Articulation of Truth in Modern Psychological Science

Edison Miyawaki, M.D. | Foreword by Harold Bloom

University of California Medical Humanities Press
2012

First published in 2012
by UNIVERSITY OF CALIFORNIA MEDICAL HUMANITIES PRESS
in partnership with eScholarship | University of California
SAN FRANCISCO – BERKELEY – LONDON

UNIVERSITY OF CALIFORNIA
MEDICAL HUMANITIES CONSORTIUM
3333 California Street, Suite 485
San Francisco, CA 94143-0850

Cover Art: Leonardo da Vinci, *Virgin and Child with Saint Anne and a Lamb* (unfinished),
Louvre, © Getty Images, with permission
Design by Margaret N. Miyuki and Agnes T. Miyuki

Figures on page 171:
Mona Lisa–Portrait of Lisa Gherardini, wife of Francesco del Giocondo/Leonardo da Vinci/The
Bridgeman Art Library/ © Getty Images
Virgin and Child with St. Anne/Leonardo da Vinci/The Bridgeman Art Library/ © Getty Images
St. John the Baptist/Leonardo da Vinci/The Bridgeman Art Library/ © Getty Images

Library of Congress Control Number: 2012934221

ISBN 978-0-9834639-5-5 (paperback)
ISBN 978-0-9834639-6-2 (hardback)

Printed in USA

Contents

Foreword

I TAUGHT DR. Edison Miyawaki at Yale both when he was an undergraduate and graduate student of literature. His long-gestated book on Freud moves and delights me.

Sigmund Freud's hope that psychoanalysis would make a contribution to biology was mistaken. Instead, Freud became the Montaigne of his age, a great moral essayist who attained the literary eminence of Proust, Joyce, Kafka, Beckett.

The science of love, for secularists, finds its authentic sages in Plato, Dante, Shakespeare, Tolstoi, and Proust. Freud, at his subtlest, is a sixth in that visionary company.

The vulgar misunderstanding of Freud, still too prevalent, regards him as a mere sexologist. Miyawaki's enterprise is to correct this undisciplined view, so as to restore our sense of the Freudian Speculation.

Ludwig Wittgenstein thought he deprecated Freud's theory of mind by calling it a speculation, not a philosophic venture, but to me that mode of wonder is the great strength of psychoanalysis. Edison Miyawaki would agree. Like Wittgenstein, he too shows that love is not a feeling. Love, unlike pain, is put to the test. We do not say: "that was not a true pain, because it passed away so quickly."

Like Freud, Miyawaki is both a neurologist and a literary humanist. If we are to continue our creative apprehension of Freud, we require an understanding that literature is a way of life. Freud, as literature, is a guide to love as the summit of life. Edison Miyawaki joins himself to that quest in this heartening and lucid study of much that still matters most in Freud.

— Harold Bloom

Introduction

A MONG PSYCHOLOGICAL WRITERS in the last two centuries, Sigmund Freud's fundamental originality, as this book argues, had to do with the stories and art he chose to describe our greatest emotion. He used a great deal of clinical material in his writing, as one would expect from a doctor in practice, but he referred often and strategically to works of the imagination, because they were repositories of knowledge as useful as anything he learned from his patients. He once wrote, in a stark irony, that "only rarely" is a psychoanalyst compelled to study art. Yet throughout his career, Freud stole from stories and art like a proud thief, always in the name of science.

Today, courses in psychology and psychiatry address brain science; professionals obsess over their "basis in evidence." Why should a modern psychologist venture away from the lab or clinic, into non-science? The simple answer is that there is data to be found there, especially if one reconsiders Freud's all-but-forgotten claim that every day, speaking psychologically, we rehearse stories and themes articulated long ago in works that are canonical in the Western tradition.

Consider "love," scientifically. If we aren't precise about what it is, then a "science of love" will be difficult to conduct. Love is complex (it is not *a* complex), yet we all claim to know what it is, intuitively and intimately. So why can't we understand it with thoroughgoing empiricism? If we examine Freud's career with more charity than some have exhibited in recent years, we might understand at least one very important—and possibly unavoidable—impediment to knowledge. Sometimes, in studying a phenomenon, we do violence to the very thing that we study, maybe because theory (like Freudian theory) gets in the way. What follows is not a book about the psychoanalysis of anything. It is a new look at a lesson buried in the depths and sources of Freud's writings. We will learn about an issue that is acute today: at what point do we approach a limit in articulating what the subject of our scientific study *is*? Regarding human love, a line of crossing lies somewhere between calling it a biological drive to perpetuate the species by sexual encounter on the one hand, and, on the other, some greater, vaguer, and more beautiful complexity involving many affects—call it "love," which is the best word we have for love. I'll build a case that a real science of the emotions (actually, any human emotion), is a problem of finding an adequately intricate language to describe the subject in question. It is a writerly conundrum and an artistic one as well, and it's a problem at the core of modern psychology and psychiatry.

Freud had some ideas about whom we might consult on the subject of "adequate" language, and his suggestions aren't bad—in fact, he offers an extraordinary reading list. I think a new discussion of his sources is worth a short book, intended mainly but not exclusively for psychiatrists and psychologists. I also have in mind my own students (I teach at a medical school), who not infrequently ask about what books to read to be "better rounded." In what follows, there's a manageable bibliography and a few paintings to consider. Perhaps if students and other readers consult those sources, they would be better grounded—and they'd be better rounded, too—in the subtleties of psychology with which all clinicians contend.

₿

From at least the early twentieth century to this day, an explanation of the mind's mechanisms couldn't be more desirable—and wanting. There have been many attempts at it, from Freud to behaviorism to evolutionary psychology. Especially in recent years, some believe that we approach, at last, a serviceable explanation of the brain and mind. Let's think about two contemporary examples: from neuropharmacology, a field linked to what we know about how nerve cells communicate with each other by way of molecules, and, second, from neurogenetics, a field in which we've seen progress in understanding the genetic information expressed in brain development. By studying these topics, respectively, we begin to understand mood and attention as a function of chemistry (serotonin is a well known neuro-molecule today) and the origin of brains. Investigations in both areas have brought forth revelations and results: the treatment of mood and anxiety disorders using serotonergic drugs, for example, from Prozac (or fluoxetine) to new generations of Prozacian drugs. From neurogenetics, we learn that brain development wasn't reinvented for humans (nature conserves genetic information across species, and "evolution rarely throws out anything," as Frans de

Waal has nicely observed). Brain development isn't altogether different in a human being than in a worm; a worm is intricate, a human more so, but genetics will always apply either way. Investigators justifiably claim progress in understanding the chemistry of mental states and the biological information processing of early life.

Here we might recall that, early in his career, Freud thought he could produce a great synthesis, as profound in his time as pharmacologic or genetic developments today. At the time of an unfinished manuscript which he entitled "Sketch of a Psychology" (known to English readers by the title *Project for a Scientific Psychology* from 1895), he thought to explain psychological mechanisms as a function of the activity of nerve cells. The work obsessed him; during his project, he found himself "alternately proud and happy and abashed and miserable;" in private correspondence, he confided a haunting doubt:

> the mechanical explanation is not coming off, and I am inclined to listen to
> the still, small voice which tells me that my explanation will not do.

As described by one of Freud's best intellectual biographers, Frank Sulloway, we hear an echo of the same, still voice more than twenty years later, at the time of *Beyond the Pleasure Principle* (1920):

> Freud did not abandon the hope . . . that his psychoanalytic ideas would
> someday find a firmer basis in neurophysiology. As he himself later insisted
> . . . "The deficiencies in our description [of the mind] would probably vanish
> if we were already in a position to replace the psychological terms by physi-
> ological or chemical ones."

Then or now, can science, triumphantly based in chemistry, genetics, or physiology, disappoint our desire for the most complete description possible? I'd argue that there should be second thoughts regarding any espoused truth in psychology, whether in 1895, 1920, the twenty-first century, or in the future.

No one in a right mind today would claim that we fully understand neurochemistry and neurogenesis (in the worm or human), never mind a relationship between nerve-cell physiology and everyday psychology. The good news is that we are within our province as scientists—or, just as savvy readers—to ask countless, good questions and, importantly, we shouldn't assume that the ever-expanding database of our neurosciences is tantamount to a complete psychology.

Rather, we might reiterate Freud's concern about the "deficiencies of our description," whether or not we happen to be scientists. As a point of clarification, to ask about *how we are wrong* couldn't be more scientific: the best scientists I know are the ones with the most clear-eyed skepticism; usually— gently, among the wisest—they ask the kinds of questions that would cause any thoughtful person to rethink. The mental process involved—to call it "insight" is not too strong—can be gleaned in other ways than doing science at a laboratory bench or in a hospital. In fact, repeated and incessant questioning has been described many times previously, in different, non-scientific idioms with excellent story lines. These fictions have engaged readers in diverse cultures for a long time.

Freud didn't complete his *Project for a Scientific Psychology*. Some say that he abandoned the project as a failure; others contend he could never let it go, for a lifetime. All that we know with certainty is that he took up other reading as his career evolved. Two questions of ongoing interest might be: What were those books (at least, some of them)? and Why and how could they be considered serviceable in a science of human love?

Let's consider Sigmund Freud's most infamous reference first.

₿

In the romantic life of both men and women, is it really true that we live the story of Oedipus in many variations, whether we realize it or not? *Oedipus the King* by Sophocles, dating to twenty five centuries ago, is anything but an obvious choice for a love story. The play doesn't appear to say much at all about love. Freud could have chosen countless dramas, but this particular selection provided a foundation for his study of human intimacy. Why? A word to the wise: even if Freud himself answered (he might talk about how men "really" feel about their mothers and fathers), we wouldn't necessarily understand why a tragedy describes love. Maybe a better answer happens if we read Sophocles for ourselves.

Oedipus, King of Thebes, was not an indecisive sort. He suffered no complex about loving his biological mother and killing his biological father. He probably truly loved his Jocasta—who, in fact, "did it all" as his wife, his actual mother (unbeknownst to Oedipus), and the mother of his children. He didn't hesitate for a moment at the infamous crossroads, where he dispatched his father. His fundamental discovery—tragic, triumphant, and pathetic—

was simply that his life was not what he thought it was. Perhaps when we talk about the Oedipus complex, we really should think about the shock and tragedy of the unexpected. In Freud's conception of the mind, there is *always* the shock and tragedy of what we don't know, especially in families.

So, in what sense is *Oedipus the King* a story of love? It is a dangerously mature fiction, as relentless as the person who truly seeks anything in love or in life. The poet and novelist D. H. Lawrence, for whom love, sex, and the mind were always related, thought that we "never quite get used to our own minds" at our intellectual best or lascivious worst, and that, as a result, we are always in the throes of desperate discovery. The comment applies directly to Freud as a psychologist. Freud was Sophoclean, because he believed, too, that self-discovery can be hazardous. *Oedipus the King* is a kind of love-as-horror story, not a confirmation of Freudian theory.

Naturally there are those who would take issue with the last sentence, but I'd argue that when we study Freud's sources, there's a tendency to get lines of influence confused. It's not that Freud explained Oedipus, but the other way around: read *Oedipus the King* carefully, and a person might "get" human psychology more subtly and powerfully than if one were to slog through all twenty-odd volumes of *The Standard Edition of the Psychological Works of Sigmund Freud*. To Freud's credit, he invited us to re-examine not only Sophocles, but also a handful of other works examined in what follows. If we study Freud's sources next to Freud's writing, I suggest that we gain a simple insight: regarding love, just when you think you know something, inevitably, you realize you haven't the foggiest, and *that* was the deep lesson all along. Our modern psychology, including the physicians who treat us chemically (or, in the future, genetically), should heed an implicit warning. Do psychological doctors know their patients when it comes to love in a personal life? Can they fathom what the essayist Montaigne described as the pleasure "inflamed by difficulty" that love truly represents?

⊜

In my first chapter, I begin with a story (partly a joke) I heard in my psychiatric training that surely was not an inspiration for Freud. It's about the faulty perceptiveness of psychiatrists and psychiatry, and I use it to introduce what I take to be a compelling antecedent for Freud's ideas in general. Plato once told a story about the origins of love. It's a good story, and Freud used it. Plato maintained that love was both a form of memory and of madness.

In the late essay *Beyond the Pleasure Principle*, in one of the few sustained references to Plato in Freud's works, he refers to a Platonic myth in which men and women were once a single being, a pure union of two bodies, with four hands and feet, two faces, and two "privy parts." Eventually, the gods decided to cut these beings in half, and after the division (here is Freud paraphrasing Plato): "the two parts of man, each desiring his other half, came together, and threw their arms about one another eager to grow into one."

Plato elaborates an idea of love as a return to a former state of affairs—love as a type of memory—in two famous dialogues, the *Symposium* and the *Phaedrus*. I will concentrate on the *Phaedrus*, which addresses issues central to all the chapters that follow in my book. In what sense is psychiatry, like love, a mad exercise, a "psychic analysis" (as someone once quipped), with all the dubiousness of the word "psychic"? Why is fiction so powerful a means of expressing psychological workings? In what ways is psychiatry, especially after Freud, a mix of the very "blessings of madness" that Plato discusses in the *Phaedrus*—that is, a bit of prophecy, religion, love, and poetry—all in one modern discipline?

A natural follow-up question is whether we really need psychiatrists and psychologists, if we have access to religion, love, and poetry. The short answer is that we may not, but neither do we need to throw away our Freud.

That the past reveals the future is a part of Freud's world view. Plato lyrically elaborates a myth in the *Phaedrus*: a lover falls in love; the beauty of the person she loves overwhelms her; the disappointments or enjoyments that she will experience in her love will be a function of her past, as if she were rediscovering what she had quite forgotten. The plot is Freudian only to the degree that he stole it outright; it was Plato's invention.

⁜

I address *Oedipus the King* in detail in my second chapter. I'm curious, to start, about the association between tragedy (whether Sophoclean or not) and love. Is love tragic? Need it be? We know that the term "Oedipus complex," which describes the intricate links between children, men, and women, refers to a king whose family history is dramatized in three important plays from antiquity. So if we read Sophocles, do we learn what Freud's Oedipus complex is and how it operates? Answer: yes, sort of, but the real work lies in understanding Oedipus as a human being, fictional though he may be.

A great misuse of literature in intellectual history has been to read *Oedipus the King* as confirmation that we have murderous and adulterous links to our parents. That statement might characterize the Oedipus complex as discussed by Freud's followers, but the Theban plays of Sophocles are a different matter. They are dramas about ignorance and knowledge; decisions by heroes and heroines have consequences that stun, because the human will and intelligence seem powerful and powerless at once.

In a famous passage from *The Interpretation of Dreams*, Freud alludes to the real utility Sophocles had for him. I discuss this passage to make the point that, in depicting the mind as it moves towards some logical, if tragic resolution, Sophocles anticipated the kind of mental work that Freud wanted to accomplish in his discipline of psychoanalysis. While interesting that a play about patricide and incest should have become a central drama in the Western tradition, the truly disturbing news is that the Theban plays paint so rich a picture of "mental work" that "an Oedipus complex" doesn't do justice either to Sophocles or to any psychology-in-depth. Sex, as Henry James once said, is what we think about when we have nothing else to think about; when we stop thinking about Freud's sexual Oedipus complex, then we have the pleasure of thinking about Sophocles, by felicitous default. Freud learned from Sophocles that a "tragedy complex" exists: tragedy says more about love than, perhaps, any of us care to hear. Yet, we love our tragedies.

⁂

In one of his most provocative if convoluted statements, Freud said that a person can love one of four things: what he is himself; what he once was; what he would like to be; or someone who was once part of himself. It's true, he goes on to say in his characteristically deadpan way, that a person could love someone else "for the sake of mere attachment"—say, because the lover provides either food or protection. But Freud never concedes the simple possibility that "I" can love "you." No real story is that simple, he seems to say. Following my discussion of parents and children in *Oedipus the King*, it seems natural to discuss the varieties of self-love–forms of what Freud called "narcissism." The legend of Narcissus, as I hasten to point out in chapter three, is actually several myths.

The most famous version, which had the greatest influence on Freud, belonged to the often off-color and occasionally pornographic poet of *The Metamorphoses*. Here is a summary of Ovid's legend: a nymph named Echo protests to the gods because Narcissus, who is very beautiful to her as he is to other nymphs, does not return her love. Actually, he returns no one's love, and all are unrequited and miffed as a result. The god Nemesis arranges that Narcissus see himself in a stream one day. Narcissus, who immediately falls in love with the face he sees in the water, seeks everywhere for the same vision. He dies along the river Styx as he gazes at his own reflection, and in that spot a flower grows.

In another classical version, rarely discussed, Narcissus has a twin sister, but she dies. In mourning, Narcissus sits next to a stream and thinks that he sees his sister in the water.

In a third variation, almost never discussed, a man named Ameinias loves Narcissus, but Narcissus promptly rejects him and (suggestively) sends him the gift of a sword. Ameinias, not failing to perceive the message in this gift, kills himself with it, and as he dies he curses Narcissus. Later, Narcissus sees himself in water, and oddly kills himself in a grisly *quid pro quo*. In all three versions of the myth, the slender stem and delicate flower of the Narcissus plant grows where Narcissus dies.

I'm not aware of a convincing scientific argument as to why we love ourselves as much as we do. Maybe the evolutionary biologists would say that it was good for survival of the species to look out for ourselves, but such a statement about the self—that it would prefer, all things considered, to survive—is a nominal rather than interesting truth. The lack of a real difference between love and self-love is a more interesting but disturbing view, especially when we consider that, in the world of Narcissus, a brutal formula applies: where love is, there death shall be.

But death has its nuances—its flowers of immortality, as it were. In all three changelings or versions of the Narcissus myth, there is an intricate truth about selfhood that Freud examines in "On Narcissism: An Introduction," from 1914. This paper (central in Freud's long career) is best read alongside the myth(s) to which he refers. The myths describe, maybe better than Freud himself, the relationship, essentially, between what we want and what we get. When we read Freud and the myths together, I think we approach the conclusion that in a narcissistic universe, when we want something very badly, we usually get it one way or another. In fact, we change the world to get it, creating and destroying ourselves and others in the process. Such is the fate of Narcissus, whose story resonates with what people in the world and in the consulting room call "suffering" (a synonym might be "ambition").

⊜

In my fourth chapter, I draw attention to a throwaway comment in Freud's great late essay, *Civilization and its Discontents*. (Freud preferred a more literal translation from German for the monograph's title; he suggested *Man's Discomfort with Civilization*, which was promptly nixed by editors.) In the context of a discussion of "loving thy enemies" in that book, Freud borrows from Heinrich Heine, a poet whom he often quoted: "I possess the most peaceable disposition. My wishes are: a modest cottage, a thatched roof, but a good bed, good food, very fresh milk and butter, flowers before my window, a few handsome trees before my door; and if the good Lord wants to make me completely happy, he will let me live long enough to have the pleasure of seeing some six or seven of my enemies hanged on those trees." I think of Heine's list of wishes as a general epigraph to Freud, especially in his later, more brooding works, like *Civilization and its Discontents*.

Heine and even Freud's beloved poet Goethe, as often as both are cited throughout Freud's writings (especially in *Civilization*), don't quite express what Freud means by "discontent." It is a lack of ease affecting both individuals and whole cultures; it arises because two great forces, love and death, are inextricably linked, just as love and the past are bound together in Freud's conception of love.

Almost twenty years before he wrote *Civilization*, the groundwork and foundation for his thinking about discontentment can be found in a rich and brief discussion of Cordelia, the third and most beloved of the daughters of Shakespeare's King Lear. I will examine Freud's "Theme of the Three Caskets" (1913) as it anticipates the great works of Freud's middle and late periods, *Beyond the Pleasure Principle* (1920) and *Civilization and its Discontents* (1930). "Theme of the Three Caskets" addresses a constellation of star-like and beautiful women, including Portia in Shakespeare's *Merchant of Venice*, Aphrodite, Psyche, and even Cinderella, but the central heroine is Cordelia.

Freud contemplates the most pathos-filled stage instruction in the history of drama,

Enter Lear with Cordelia dead in his arms . . . ,

to conclude that "Cordelia is Death." Wisdom, he goes on to say, "bids the old man [Cordelia's father, King Lear] to renounce love, choose death and make friends with the necessity of dying."

The argument in "Theme of Three Caskets" anticipates *Beyond the Pleasure Principle* and *Civilization*, because of what we understand in Shakespeare's *King Lear* to the point of pain, that love is as strong as death.

⊜

Freud is the central figure in this book because he invited us to read, not just anything, but a few items off his chosen list. Unfortunately, a well-known effect of Freudianism has been to over-read literature and art in the wrong way. In my next chapter (five), I address a common problem in so-called psychiatric readings of Shakespeare's *Hamlet*. Basically, I wonder why the Prince of Denmark has always been considered a patient of some sort. I think there is only one correct diagnosis for Hamlet, and it has to do with an anxiety of anticipation. As philosopher Bertrand Russell observed, the Prince's deepest and quite understandable fear was that, someday, he might be psychoanalyzed. Without question, Hamlet has been so analyzed over time that we no longer know *Hamlet*.

We should dispense quickly with observations like "Ophelia really means O Phallus" to inspect the more interesting influences of *Hamlet* on Freud's thinking. While true that Freud and others after him tried to psychoanalyze the Dane by tagging him with an Oedipus complex, I think we must take these presumably Freudian views to be wrong. *Hamlet* teaches us to turn the tables on those who would analyze us, if (and only if) we are smart enough to do so.

Hamlet had complicated relationships with his ghostly father in the play, no less than with his uncle the king, his mother the queen, and Ophelia. (Hamlet's cry "I loved Ophelia" is perhaps the most complicated statement of love that Hamlet could possibly proclaim.) But to say that the dramatic action in *Hamlet* is governed by Oedipal issues is to make *Hamlet* into a mere appendix of Freud's *Totem and Taboo*. Worse, it makes for a lousy reading of the play. In *Hamlet*, every relationship that involves the Prince is an interpersonal whirl or vortex, and any analysis of the transactions between him and other individuals becomes, in the words of the hapless Polonius in the play, "a springe to catch a woodcock." Many illustrations from the play could be cited in corroboration, but I'll examine only one, from act II, scene ii.

For me as a clinician, Rosencrantz and Guildenstern working like two therapists on the difficult case of Hamlet is painfully funny, and the scene in question serves as a precise critique of psychiatry or psychology, whenever it tries to dissect our emotional lives. The suspect duo is guilty of what could be charged against any unimaginative psychiatrist: he "pathologizes" Hamlet. It is an unusual verb, so let me explain myself.

To "pathologize" is to decide someone else is the problem. The diagnosis of Drs. Rosencrantz and Guildenstern, that Hamlet is ambitious, is diagnostic vanity, a gross instance of incompetence. They are unsurprised by Hamlet's "bad dreams," as if they could understand Hamlet's dreams. I confess that of all the people Hamlet kills in the play, I understand his motivation to do away with Rosencrantz and Guildenstern best of all. What should a psychiatrist or psychologist learn from even this small part of *Hamlet*? What did Freud learn from the play as a whole? He learned, as we should, not to underestimate difficulty.

⊜

Freud is at his best when his sits and merely stares at art, as he did most famously with the *Moses* of Michelangelo and *Hamlet* (works that he discussed next to each other), transfixed by either as by a riddle. His answers to the riddles are often far less interesting than the degree to which he could be transfixed. "[W]orks of art do exercise a powerful effect on me," says Freud in "The Moses of Michelangelo"; "This has occasioned me, when I have been contemplating such things, to spend a long time before them trying to apprehend them in my own way, i.e., to explain to myself what their effect is due to. . . . Some rationalistic, or perhaps analytic, turn of mind in me rebels against being moved by a thing without knowing why I am thus affected and what it is that affects me."

"Rebels against" is a very precise choice of words, though one could wonder why all the fuss over some piece of art that should either inspire awe or, simply, give pleasure. In a different context, we again encounter the embattled urge to explain and understand in the figure of Leonardo da Vinci. Freud's "study in psychosexuality" regarding Leonardo is my interest in chapter six.

Here is Leonardo talking about what motivates him to love in his *Treatise on the Art of Painting*: "great love springs from great knowledge of the beloved object, and if you little know it, you will be able to love it only little or not at all." And here is Freud's curt response: "There is no psychological value in these utterances of Leonardo. What they maintain is obviously false, and Leonardo must have known this as well as we do. It is not true that people refrain from loving or hating until they have studied and become familiar with the nature of the object . . . *On the contrary they love impulsively*; they are guided by emotional motives which have nothing to do with cognition [my emphasis]."

Love isn't an act of scientific knowledge or cognition, says Freud, but if we put "The Moses of Michelangelo" and *Leonardo da Vinci* next to each other, he seems confused on the subject: Freud's proclivity to "cognition" was as intense as Leonardo's, so what is the psychological value in the utterances of Freud the analyst?

Freud characterizes da Vinci as largely an asexual being, profoundly gifted, probably gay; his sexual drive was "sublimated" into ceaseless, but (according to Leonardo) never-completed work. In a remembrance that Freud thinks explains Leonardo's work habits and sexuality, there was a large black bird, as Leonardo reported in the *Codex Atlanticus*, which descended upon him in his crib.

"[A]nd it seemed to me," said Leonardo, "while I lay in the cradle, as though a kite had come down to me, opened my mouth with its tail, and struck me with it several times between my lips." Once we understand that story, Freud says, we come to understand what motivated Leonardo to transcend sex (or embrace men) and why we are so moved by his art, particularly the haunting smiles of the Mona Lisa, the Virgin, and Mary's mother, St. Anne, in two representative works of his immortal art.

Now: do we really believe Freud in the lengthy discussion that takes up five of six chapters in his *Leonardo da Vinci*? We could believe him, or we might reconsider his raw material.

In the last chapter of his book, Freud talks about how psychoanalysis really can't explain the nature of Leonardo's artistic accomplishment. To borrow from the nineteenth-century literary critic Walter Pater (as Freud does repeatedly in his book), the affective power of Leonardo's art is beyond words, because it is "an image defining itself on the fabric of a dream." I am uncertain what an image on a dream fabric is, but I do know that *Leonardo da Vinci* is a strong over-interpretation of a kind that the author himself viewed as dubious.

Freud has rightly been criticized for his sexualism, regrettably in evidence when he describes the tail of Leonardo's black bird (the "kite") as an amalgam of the male penis and the mother's breast, with the black bird's flight as a kind of sexual sublimation into air. Gratifyingly, there has been progress in Western intellectual history since Freud: fewer stock "Freudian readings" have seen the light of publication. If "psychosexuality" is understood as *just* covert erotic tendency, then one misses what Freud tried to accomplish in his exploration. Freud wanted to articulate the suggestiveness and evocativeness of a childhood memory. In his last paragraphs in *Leonardo da Vinci*, we hear Freud refer to Nature's "countless causes" [*ragioni*, Leonardo's word]—causes which are infinitely difficult to capture in a theory of personality no less than in art.

"The psychology that is taught in the schools gives us but very inadequate replies to questions concerning our mental life," Freud wrote in "One of the Difficulties of Psychoanalysis" (1917); in that paper and in *The Introductory Lectures on Psycho-analysis* published between 1916 and 1917, he wonders whether the inadequacies of our academic theories might relate to something that students have observed probably since the beginning of all schools—namely, the tendency for teachers to congratulate themselves far too eagerly. In the history of science, Freud goes on to say, we have observed "severe wounds" to human self-love, which is hardly restricted to the academy. We have learned that the earth holds no privileged position in the universe and that man holds no privileged position in nature. In the aftermath of the Copernican and Darwinian revolutions, respectively, a new psychology announces that, "*the ego is not master in its own house*" (Freud's italics). The take-home point isn't that Freud was insufferably tendentious to include himself in a pantheon with Copernicus and Darwin. The teacherly lesson is that a theory (any theory) has no inherently privileged position. While surprising to consider that Sigmund Freud, of all people, would believe in theoretical fallibility, he did so believe, in the name of both science and (covertly) art.

⊟

Let's return to basics: a meditation on psychology is, for Freud, always a contemplation of the past, and the past has to do with parents, specifically (and curiously) the fatherly presence of Moses in his works, as I discuss in chapter seven.

What story about Moses most motivated Freud? In his late book *Moses and Monotheism*, Freud argues that Moses wasn't a Jew raised in Egypt; he was an Egyptian who gave rise to the Jews. With the prophet Hosea in mind, he further subscribes to the idea that the Moses's own people killed him in the manner of cannibalistic stories (described in his *Totem and Taboo* from 1913) in which fathers were ceremoniously killed and consumed.

Critic Kenneth Burke wisely suggested that in reading Freud, we should avoid subscribing to a psychology of cannibalism, mainly because most of us aren't cannibals, and because we should avoid reducing our thinking to the level of *New Yorker* cartoons about missionaries in African pots. True, but in *Moses and Monotheism*, the central theme is inescapably cartoonish: it's too bad that we ate father, but now, thank God, we believe in him.

"The dramatic murder and incorporation of the father is, if rarely a reality, a recurrent and virtually universal fantasy," writes the Freudian scholar Peter Gay in a reemphasis of standard thinking—that fantasy often substitutes for reality in psychological life. Gay subtly misrepresents Freud in blurring the fantasy/reality distinction. A real murder of an Egyptian gave rise to real religions (Judaic and other monotheistic faiths), according to the argument of *Moses and Monotheism*. Freud refers not only to normative Judaism, but also the faith of Paul the evangelical Christian (Saul of Tarsus), who sadly observed that "it is because we killed God the Father that we are so unhappy." Because the murder really happened, religion is more real to us. In Christian terms, unless we believe that Christ as god really died for man, then faith is suspect.

Freud's story of Moses—which, to repeat, he thinks is both true and absolutely believable—drives his understanding of faith. In many ways, given the resoluteness of his argument in *Moses and Monotheism*, it surprises the reader that he viewed organized religion with any skepticism at all. If the guilt over Moses is real, then faith as expiation makes perfect sense. In short: the Moses story Freud liked best was his version; his closest friends urged him not to publish *Moses and Monotheism*, yet he did. What lesson can be gathered from the stubbornness?

Freud was interested in stories of great complexity and allusiveness, because theory cannot achieve that complexity and allusiveness by itself. When he describes his Moses, he refers to the power of a story or legend to dominate one's own thought so completely that we feel as if we could genuinely know something greater than our understanding.

‡

Freud loved vignettes, and one in particular speaks much about him. He describes a visitor from the provinces who spent a night in a modern urban hotel—a rustic's first experience in the big city. The man liked to read in his bed at night. That particular night, in unfamiliar surroundings (a very different bed and the night stand with an unusual light source on it), when he was ready for sleep after reading, he spent an inordinate amount of time trying to blow out the light. Freud asks us: don't you see the problem he encountered? Sometimes, one needs to look for the switch.

The works that I call Freud's sources (my list, though incomplete, might suffice), were "switches" for him, allowing him to think beyond the idea that all light must come from burning candles.

Freud contemplated the stark separation between what we live and see in the emotional life and how we understand its vicissitudes. Art offered him a view, as if from a great height, on the possibility of bridging experience and understanding. Such perspective is one thing he retrieved from the imaginative genius of the past. But as I discuss in my concluding chapter, Freud's sources also teach that all theories of the mind are dubious, including Freud's. A brand-new scientific psychology of love—even the one that will appear tomorrow or next century—will be no less suspect. Freud invites us to re-read past genius as an exercise in true psychological science. I suggest that we follow his lead, with pragmatic intent and hope. Perhaps we might become more skeptical, critical, and (as happens from time to time, always incompletely) more capable of thinking as deeply as the world around us is complex.

One

Plato's Memory

I N PSYCHIATRIC TRAINING, I heard a joke that I've never quite forgotten. Once there was a soldier who spent all his free time outside his barracks picking up scraps of paper. He would inspect each scrap, say "that's not it," discard it, and proceed to any other trash he could find. As a soldier, no bad word could be said about him. He followed every order, conducted himself honorably, and had no flaw, except his unusual free-time activity. Eventually, his superiors became concerned, and referred him to the psychiatrist, who said that the soldier was only interested in a section eight and should return to duty. The soldier did so without complaint, but, whenever he had the chance—whether on break or on leave—he'd return to his ceaseless business of picking up scraps, inspecting each one, and deciding "that's not it."

Many months passed, and now thoroughly dismayed, his superiors again consulted the psychiatrist, who admitted him to a hospital for observation. The soldier participated in every scheduled activity on the ward; he seemed quite sane. But, in his free time, in the courtyard of the hospital or in the corridors, he could be found picking up scraps of paper, turning each in his hand, and arriving at his inevitable conclusion. Additional experts were consulted, and after weeks of observation, they concluded that no one could behave in such a way unless deeply troubled. Despite the fact that as a soldier nothing could be said against him, his behavior merited a discharge under section eight of Army Regulation 615-360 "on the grounds of insanity or an inability to adjust to army life." The soldier responded to the news indifferently. He packed his belongings. On the day of discharge, he was handed his section eight, at which time he looked at the paper, then at the person who handed it to him, and said, "that's it."

The tendency is to think the joke is about psychiatrists, but I have always liked the part about how he was a good soldier, except that he seemed to be crazy. The section eight, or the classification of madness, is also part of the joke. Was he crazy? The business of studying another mind is at issue, and there's a trap in that work, as has been acknowledged by good minds more than once. William James, for one, arguably the best scientific psychologist of his time, wrote in 1890 (his italics): "The *great* snare of the psychologist is the *confusion of his own standpoint with that of the mental fact* about which he is making report." What he called the psychologist's fallacy can be stated simply: when a psychologist, or anyone else for that matter, tells you what is on your mind, it's entirely possible that all you hear is what's on his mind, projected onto yours. James implores us to guard against our own bias, but he stops short of stating the logical consequence, that the corruption can't be escaped, only continually evaded. If a person believes that the soldier was sane all along, the joke works because of that bias.

The crazy or cunning soldier, for me, captures everything that is problematic about a depth psychology. Freud once said if an explanation is too good, if it explains too much, then there is something wrong with the explanation. I think his comment is deeply wise, but what about psychoanalysis, which arguably tried to explain all mental phenomena? In the late, unfinished *Outline of Psychoanalysis*, Freud said that success in therapy required a patient's honesty and a therapist's discretion, that the relationship was like a pact with a confessor. But there is an additional, extraordinary characteristic to that relationship, which lends it the quality of love more than religious confession, that the patient expresses not only what he doesn't tell others, but also what he doesn't know of himself. I remain stunned at Freud's characterization: I will sit here and listen, he assures us, and we (his patients) will reveal ourselves.

Says who? Say there is someone who believes that a perfectly intimate knowledge of another person is not just possible, but altogether vital to happiness and health, that in this relationship there is no psychologist's fallacy, only the transparency of one mind to another. So transparent is this relationship, in fact, that we discover what we hadn't previously realized—and we accept what we learn as psychological truth. Is it crazy to think that way? Whenever I hear, usually (but not exclusively) in the context of love, that someone "knows" another person, I think to myself that the knowledge can seem quite real: two people can know each other astonishingly well, despite what James has to say and without Freudian analysis. But in love, psychotherapy, and most friendships, one often hears a private Iago whispering in the ear to the point of annoyance, "Do I know this person? Does that person know me?" It would be crazy if we didn't have such doubts from time to time.

We could shortcut through much conceptual trouble if we observed that psychology simply is not the study of other minds; it is the study of someone trying to study other minds. Returning to the *Outline of Psychoanalysis*, we read that Freud's answer to the psychologist's fallacy was to use it. What makes psychotherapy work is a "surprise," as Freud calls it, built into the experience. "The most remarkable thing is this," he writes. "The patient is not satisfied with regarding the analyst in the light of reality as a helper and adviser who, moreover, is remunerated for the trouble he takes and who would himself be content with some such role as that of a guide on a difficult mountain climb." The mountain-climb analogy is simply funny, because in therapy (especially of Freud's type), it's the patient who must take the lead and who should probably pay himself. But Freud goes on, without pause, to describe the most remarkable thing: "On the contrary, the patient sees in him the return, the reincarnation, of some important figure out of his childhood or past, and consequently transfers on to him feelings and reactions which undoubtedly applied to this prototype." He describes the so-called "transference," but we shouldn't be too technical or wedded to his terminology in reading him. He refers to a subspecies of love, with all the joys and dangers of love built within it.

When I finished my basic psychiatric training, I thought that, at best, I could be a reluctant therapist. I was so reluctant that the idea of more advanced training in psychoanalysis, which would involve many more years, struck me as both unattractive and dubious. The above passage from the *Outline* stuck in my head as much as the joke about the soldier, and the upshot was that I decided to remain undecided about psychotherapy, either giving or receiving it. Wasn't being a therapist just a bit presumptuous and possibly, as James would say, a stock-in-trade fallacy? When I expressed this concern to my supervisors–my teachers were "supervisors," ominously enough—they told me that I could "work through it" in my own personal psychotherapy. In fact, investigating my "resistance" was just the work I needed to do.

I remember thinking that psychiatry was not just an "impossible profession" (Freud's own words) but a professional impossibility. (Karl Kraus, a contemporary of Freud's, once told his psychiatrist to kiss his ass, at which point they discussed his "fixation," to Kraus's shock and dismay. I understood Kraus.) In short, my future in psychiatry appeared quite grim, until one of my teachers said that the real work in anything in science or art was the systematic cleaning out of cant. After much therapy with that teacher, I still resist therapy, but perhaps I am able to articulate my skepticism, and love, of psychiatry more clearly.

The patient sees in him the return, the reincarnation, of someone important from the past, Freud said. Philosopher Ludwig Wittgenstein's suggestion to "hold on to one's brains" when reading Freud should be applied as quickly as we read that line. There is no reason to believe, nor would Freud contend, that the transference happens only in the context of analysis or Freud-inspired therapy. In fact, there is nothing unique in the therapeutic experience, except that it is a paid experiment in love, in which we watch ourselves in psychological action, sometimes even falling in erotic love with a therapist. That is hardly a desired outcome, but it is precisely the danger that therapy courts. In the end, what happens in therapy is less interesting than the assumption behind it. If I think about my shrewd soldier one last time, perhaps I need to reformulate my approach to him in light of Freud: maybe he was he looking for something he genuinely lost or forgot, which he thought belonged to him in the first place. Maybe everything is a recollection or rediscovery, whether in madness or in love. The soldier found what he sought; I will leave it at that. But to say that love, wherever and whenever it happens, is a form of memory is as profound an observation about human nature that I know. The idea wasn't Freud's originally, but he made extensive use of it. What was his source?

I

One tends to forget, but should not forget, how radical the most ancient answers to the "other mind" problem were, from the so-called Archaic period of Greece, roughly three centuries before Plato. Then, the problem of another mind was not much of one, and if it was madness to think that others could reveal themselves in the full light of an early day, then madness was not a terrible thing, and certainly not something to be cured. If we believe today that interpersonal knowledge is possible and that the psychologist's fallacy, however oppressive it might seem, can still yield to an understanding that is like love in its intellectual and emotional rewards, then we look back to a very early time indeed, well before all discussions of psychologists' fallacies. Someone once said that the problem with progress was its ridiculous insistence that it move forward rather than backward. Freud's transference was no modern discovery; he moved quite backwards in time to the oldest story-telling and Plato's troubled reaction to it.

"I must speak out, I said, though a certain love and reverence for Homer that has possessed me from a boy would stay me from speaking. For he appears to have been the first teacher and beginner of all these beauties of tragedy. Yet all the same we must not honor a man above truth, but, as I say, speak our minds." That is Plato's Socrates in a famous diatribe against poetry (the poetry of Homer) and drama (that of Sophocles and Euripides, among others) in *The Republic*. Socrates objects to what might be called the plain sense of the mind as the poets depicted it.

Critic Erich Auerbach has characterized that plain sense, in Homer specifically, by contrasting Book 19 of the *Odyssey* with the story of Abraham's near-sacrifice of Isaac in Genesis 22. Since the time of Homer in the eighth century BCE and the early Judaic tradition, the strangeness of others and the otherness of the gods have been perpetual subjects of discussion. Auerbach's choices are not random. In general, he says, the ancients told one of two types of story about otherness, as the *Odyssey* and the Old Testament attest.

In Book 19 of the *Odyssey*, when a disguised Odysseus arrives home after his many years of travel, his housekeeper, the faithful Euryclea, recognizes him by a scar on his leg that signifies who he must be. Euryclea marvels at how the stranger's face reminds her of her master; she welcomes him by washing his feet. Once she sees the scar, she remembers the history of his injury (a tussle with a wild boar). As if to indicate what she now realizes beyond doubt, that the stranger couldn't be anyone else but her master, she touches the scar.

By contrast, in Genesis, when God asks Abraham to sacrifice his son Isaac at a specific place and time, we hardly know what Abraham thinks. In context, Yahweh's request follows His earlier promises that it will be through Isaac that the covenant will be fulfilled. One modern biblical scholar, reflecting on this paradox, has said that perplexity is Abraham's only rational response. Yet Abraham isn't obviously perplexed. We mainly have an eerie silence to interpret: father and son barely talk to each other over three days' travel to Moriah, where the sacrifice is supposed to occur. Abraham says "here am I" first to his god, then to his son, who finally gears up to ask a few questions after they arrive in Moriah. A sacrifice is supposed to occur, as Isaac knows, but where is the animal? Why have they traveled all this way? Abraham says, "here am I" without further explanation—the statement captures the burdens of faith and fatherhood as well as the befuddlement that both can cause. "Far from seeking, like Homer, merely to make us forget our own reality for a few hours, [the author of Genesis] seeks to overcome our reality," Auerbach says. A single utterance, "here am I," overwhelms by what it does and does not reveal.

We observe in Homer, Auerbach continues, "fully externalized description, uniform illumination . . . all events in the foreground, displaying unmistakable meanings." Far more darkly in the case of Genesis, we have the "suggestive influence of the unexpressed, 'background quality,' . . . and preoccupation with the problematic." Translating these observations into psychology, are people transparent despite their guises? Or does one think more about background and shadow in contemplating a psychology? It hardly matters that Odysseus speaks to Euryclea, who is very human, whereas Abraham speaks primarily with God. The gods in Homer are as human as the humans, and, if we compare Homer and Genesis on the matter of communication with gods, Genesis simply wins in terms of uncanniness. Is Auerbach's distinction useful or does it mislead us into thinking that the world of other people's psychologies is a grand either/or, *just* a question of plain or problematic?

Although Homeric description is lucid, it is not free of difficulty, if one stops to think about it as Plato did, almost four centuries after Homer. In his dialogue about love called the *Phaedrus*, he directs our attention away from poems and speeches to their effect on the listener. The starting point for the *Phaedrus* is a speech on love by someone named Lysias. Phaedrus has gone to the trouble of transcribing the speech; he keeps a copy of it close to him, and as he recalls it to Socrates, we sense that he has swooned over every word, like a youngster before a media star. Later in the dialogue, it is Socrates who rhapsodizes in his own hymn to love that is among the most poetical of Plato's works. It's hard not to see a bit of Homer in both Lysias and Socrates, if only because of the effect on the young Phaedrus.

I should mention a bit more about the experience of Homeric poetry (I suppose we don't really know what it was like to hear it, but we do have some scholarly suggestions). It was spoken or chanted aloud in a mesmerizing stream of information; each line took the same amount of time to read; about 600 lines were chanted in an hour. If the poem were read aloud from beginning to end at one stretch, a full day and night would pass. The Greek alphabet and thus the written word didn't appear until roughly the seventh century BCE, and so all communication was orally transmitted in the age of Homer to some time after Hesiod, but before Plato. In the *Phaedrus*, Plato suggests that the audience's experience of poetry is like love–one without love letters or documentation of any kind, a love stored only in memory and communicated face to face.

Today, as one reads either Homer or the Old Testament in print, one learns a great deal about other human beings—call it a psychological knowledge, though I'm certain that the Greeks understood "psychology" more simply and more beautifully as a love of stories. At those moments when an audience finds itself in the rapture of a poet's incantations, Plato seems to suggest, there is a dilemma having to do with the emotions blinding us to our critical faculties. But that is a tiresome way of describing the effect of poems: they don't merely touch us emotionally, and sometimes poems make us think very critically. Plato is subtler in his characterization and critique.

In the *Phaedrus*, when he famously refers to the "blessings" of prophecy, religion, poetry, and love as forms of divine madness, he acknowledges—but doesn't defer to—the overwhelming effect of those modes. If Plato had had the chance to read some version of Genesis (perhaps he did; in the nineteenth century, Arthur Schopenhauer would maintain "[a]s regards Plato, I am of the opinion that he owes to the Jews the theism that periodically comes over him"), I wonder whether Plato would think Homer was more like the Old Testament than meets the eye or ear. Today, the personal preference of the *Odyssey* over Genesis or vice versa largely reflects how a person likes to be affected, since one can be moved by either the mystery or the plain sense of things.

That a poet can allow us to forget our reality temporarily is part of Plato's grand complaint against Homer in *The Republic*, but it would be a mistake not to observe his fascination for a state of mind in which a person can be consumed by some otherness, whether that of a poet, prophet, priest, or paramour. More shrewdly than William James, Plato recognizes that human beings once could happily transcend the psychologist's fallacy rather than accept its logical necessity. Nor have we quite forgotten that naïve time, he suggests, since it would appear that we willfully seek such transcendence on a regular basis. Plato felt surprisingly at ease with the idea that two people could be as one through the stories they shared. Long before Freud talked about how our choices in life were always erotic choices, Plato talked about our natural tendency to fall into a madness that went by many names, chief among these being love.

II

Regarding any intimacy between people (whether a "transference" in psychoanalysis or an "alliance" in so-called insight-oriented psychotherapy or in any heart-to-heart conversation), Plato offers as good a commentary as any, put in the form of a question: what is the wisdom of understanding special types of human communication as subspecies of madness or love? Madness (*mania* or *theia mania* in the Greek, variously translated as "divine madness," "frenzy," or "enthusiasm") is not necessarily bad, says Plato. It would be simplistic to argue that way, since:

> We owe the greatest blessings to madness, provided it comes as a gift from the gods. In their madness, the prophetess at Delphi, and the priestesses at Dodona, do much that is good for Greece–both for individuals and states. When sane they do little or nothing. And then there's the Sibyl and others, who with their inspired gift of prophecy have made many predictions for many people, and given them good guidance for the future.

We need a more detailed sense of all types of madness (Plato describes four types). He discusses prophecy first, as if it had an inherent priority. *When sane the prophets do nothing* means that a certain kind of insanity makes sense and could even be practical. Plato's point seems to be that divine inspiration was not suspect because it presumed to tell the future or because of some relationship with invisible gods. Instead, he appreciated *mania* in the Greek sense as royal road to the mind or, at least, the mind of his fellow Greeks. Stories of such madness were his introduction the psychology and philosophy of love, and those tales could serve much the same purpose today.

⏚

The woman named Pythia was the central figure at the Delphic Oracle. Most accounts of what regularly happened there rely on Plutarch, who famously described an episode in which Pythia suffered some terrible paroxysm, like a seizure. I suspect that somewhere a medical doctor has built a case that Pythia had epilepsy, but such attempts to explain away the experience at Delphi seem to me to miss the point. Classicist E. R. Dodds is more helpful in suggesting that her trance, witnessed by untold numbers who flocked to the Oracle for centuries both before and after Plato, was the result of self-hypnosis–a state, in other words, of profound meditation or absorption. What we should mainly appreciate is that Pythia, who was said to be a farm girl with little education (in Plutarch's time), and who was therefore presumably ignorant of the social and political problems about which she often wisely prognosticated, had a presence of pure mind, just as her ceremony had surreal charm. Though her predictions could be perfectly incomprehensible at times (like speech in tongues), she herself was a reliable embodiment of mystery. Mystery interests Plato in all four types of madness.

Why believe Pythia? There are scholars who have argued that the Oracle was a mouthpiece for propaganda. Many of the Delphic pronouncements seemed quite politically motivated: the Oracle often advocated Greek colonization throughout the Mediterranean, for example. But I would focus, as have most, on the "knowledge aspect" of the Oracle—its power to inspire reflection, if not self-knowledge, that could endure over time. "Know thyself," of course, were the words inscribed at the Delphic temple itself, next to a proviso that one shouldn't do anything to extremes (perhaps the greatest wisdom is that a person shouldn't know himself too well). Socrates' version of the Delphic advice, often confused with it, was that he knew absolutely nothing. He comments on prophecy and madness from the perspective of a cognitive emptiness or ignorance, but one senses a deep respect, if not a longing, for prophecy's facile and inspired knowledge. Many centuries later, the poet Virgil spoke of the "breathing into" the great mind and soul of Pythia: he meant that she was inspired in a way that poets and philosophers have longed to be. French critics have referred to the *transport prophétique* that happened at Delphi as a way beyond cares.

The mix of sensuality and spirituality at Delphi has moved scholars to their own kind of frenzy. Pythia's ceremony has been variously described, but Dodds is authoritative, and I borrow a description from his *Greeks and the Irrational*: she would silently bathe, drink from a spring, and, in the manner of Themis in the vase paintings of the fifth century, hold a laurel branch, sometimes chew its leaves, or otherwise burn them in small pyres, thereby enshrouding herself in vapors. Dodds delightfully tells the story of a classicist, who, in the hope of recapturing her inspiration, ate a number of laurel leaves himself, calling his experiment "scientific." It failed.

Plato says very little about the religious rights that have to do with his second form of madness, though religious and prophetic forms of mania are clearly related. His specific comments have vexed the critics–the Platonist von Wilamowitz-Moellendorf called Plato "incomprehensible" on the subject–but our interest should focus on the one aspect that seems somewhat clear: madness of the religious type was healthful. Religious enthusiasm could dispatch evil and mitigate a guilt that whole families bore:

> there are those great afflictions and hardships suffered by some families, arising perhaps from some long-standing guilt. Madness appears where it must, with prophetic power, and finds a way out, taking refuge in prayers to the gods and divine services. Finding in these its rites of purification, it puts its possessor out of danger, both for the present and for the future, discovering a release from present troubles for him who is maddened and possessed in the right way.

A few paragraphs later, Plato talks about rhetoric as a kind of medicine or therapy in much the same way that religion is characterized as a refuge. If we wonder why Plato would bother at all with the odd matter of prophecy and the often bizarre rites of purification in Greek religion, all as a prelude to his discussion of love, we might guess that the Greeks believed in madness, not because they were superstitious fools, but because they believed that mind, God, and love were as fundamentally related as a trinity. In addressing such abstract matters, what recourse is there except to a mad, possessed, and privileged language?

In Plato's first two forms of madness, the participant in Delphic ceremony or the religious acolyte is taken up by a greater power, and is somehow made, if not whole, then mysteriously better. Although classicists have studied the religious rituals of archaic Greece as if they were anthropologists inspecting a primitive society, the wisest have strictly avoided calling either the rituals or the Greeks primitive. Among the best stories I have encountered is, again, from Dodds, reflecting on Greek wildness as revealed not by historical accounts from the fifth or sixth centuries BCE, but by way a story from a mining town in twentieth-century Kentucky as described in *The Picture Post* of Leslie and Perry counties from 1938. Several key elements of Greek religious purification, inspired by the cults of Dionysus and Orpheus, were present in the Kentucky experience: an animal (in this case, a rattlesnake), frenzied dancing followed by physical exhaustion, and then a ceremony that involved placing the rattlesnake into a person's clothing and allowing it to wriggle to the ground in whatever way it saw fit. The wriggling had to do, I read, with the union of god and the worshiper in a strangely literal rendering of Mark 16:18: "They shall take up the serpents." Religious snake handling, I learn further, was ancient even in Plato's time, and the god Dionysus is well known to have been represented as a snake.

In what sense is all of the above healthful or psychologically helpful? Scholars have routinely observed that Plato revered myth and mysticism to a degree that even Socrates himself did not, perhaps as a result of Plato's exposure to Dionysian cult in Sicily in the decade after Socrates' death and before he established the Academy in Athens. (The Pythagoreans of Sicily thought themselves under the divine influence of Dionysus and Orpheus. To participate in their culture, one had to be purified so as to contemplate personal truth; one disavowed notions of communal or familial guilt in favor of individual responsibility and individual mind.) Presumably, then, the healthfulness of religious ceremony was a function of becoming pure once more, perhaps becoming "truly" oneself. But everything depends on pure faith, whether in Kentucky or anywhere else.

Religious faith, as a sacred text has it, "makes us certain of realities we do not see." Religious ritual might or might not purify us, but it probably helps most when we are uncertain of realities that we don't or can't see. To understand Plato on the subjects of personality, individuality, and love is to understand his preoccupation with a hidden reality of religious flavor, a secret information which places one in the vicinity of the divine and makes one complete.

Such knowledge did not merely come from a God or from peculiar ceremonies. Plato on madness begins to read like a meditation on that knowledge which makes us who we are, and I begin to agree with those dissenters who feel that a madman out for a walk is as good a model of the mind as a neurotic lying on a couch—in other words, that modern neurosis explains less about man than a good psychosis. Here is a religious scholar talking about the knowledge that makes us who we are, in what amounts to a reasonable synopsis of Plato:

> the reality that makes one divine must neither be regarded an impersonal force that, as in ancient Dionysiac ecstasy and Apolline prophecy, penetrates the individual and expels the individual ego . . . nor must it be interpreted, in terms of modern depth psychology and the blandishments of currently dominant subjectivism, as . . . attainable by a simple act of inner reflection.

The Gods will not give us information as if it were a separate reality to be taken in; nor can we look only into ourselves to find it. "To know" is "to identify with," but such knowledge is neither purely objective nor subjective. From the standpoint of any religion in which revelation plays a role–and it has been said that religion without such knowledge is no religion–revelation isn't merely a function of some extraordinary event in the world, as in the experience of miracles. As in ancient ecstasy and prophecy, one must proceed quite beyond oneself, in a process that is neither purely revelatory nor introspective.

⇔

Poetry, Plato's third type of madness, also necessitated such participation and transcendence. Plato's own lyricism, so much in evidence throughout the *Phaedrus*, cannot be ironic; it is usually (and always to my surprise) erotic, as in his description of how the muse ravishes the poet: "Taking hold of a soft, virgin soul, it rouses it to a state of poetic ecstasy, in lyric or some other form, and so educates later ages . . . . But as for the man who arrives at poetry's door without the Muse's madness, in the belief that technical skill will make him a good poet, he remains incomplete, himself and his works, and disappears before the poetry of madness." Plato, as mentioned before, reviled poets and storytellers in *The Republic*, but in the *Phaedrus* the poets are "educators" in the progress of love. Interestingly, Plato admits that unless a poet is mad, he's just a technician. And we are not interested merely in technique, but rather in what experience like Pythia's might be our own.

III

Modern psychiatry, we hope, does not involve erotic love between doctors and patients. But sooner or later in any psychological career, a person must decide his or her stance towards love in the complex Platonic sense. The *Phaedrus* is the finest expression of the concept called Platonic love, though Diotima's speeches in Plato's *Symposium* are a close second, especially when she tells Socrates that knowledge without love is "merely useful." In response to the question "under what circumstance do people know each other without psychological fallacy?" Plato provides not one answer, but four answers in one (the divine madnesses). Love, which we now address, is the fourth madness, perhaps the greatest. To be clear, it is not a love without eroticism.

Platonic love must mean something other than an intellectual's celibacy, a sublimated or un-carnal love. The *Phaedrus* is obsessed by sex, and while there are those who might be dismayed by its homoeroticism, the fourth madness is hardly just gay love or the love of under-aged boys. Rather, and here is the important point, love is a type of memory, sometimes very sexual in nature, in which experience in this world reminds us of a prior and truly beautiful state of being:

> When a man sees beauty here, in this life, he is reminded of true beauty. He grows wings, and stands there fluttering them, eager to fly upwards, but unable to do so. Yet still he looks upwards, as birds do, and takes no notice of what is below; and so he is accused of being mad. My conclusion is quite different. Of all forms of divine possession, this is the best–and has the best origins–both for him who has it and for him who shares in it. It is this madness which the lover of beauty must experience if he is to be called a lover.

The passage is part of a grand saga, passionately told, in which the memory of true beauty is proof, if proof were necessary, that man was once divine. And we are further told that the soul, once fallen, can be divine yet again. The wings tell the story: a soul's divinity relates to the state of those wings, which grow, are lost, and regrow in the seasons of a soul's life across much time. Even the chariots of gods have wings, says Plato's Socrates; but wings can be lost if one is weighed down by forgetfulness and weakness; the regrowth of wings can take thousands of years. There is far more to Plato's mythology that I won't discuss in detail: among psychological writers, a great deal has been made of the chariot, the charioteer, and the horses; there's an obedient horse and a wild horse. I cringe whenever Plato's chariot is mentioned as a precursor to Freud's picture of the mind, with the wild horse representing the Unconscious and the good horse the conscience or super-ego. The mind as a chariot, like the universe as a timepiece or the brain as a computer, is just one of a long line of mechanical metaphors for the abstract. A relationship to the past ("When a man sees beauty here, in this life, *he is reminded. . .* ") should be the aspect of interest for us, since love as memory is an idea replete with psychological significance.

One might reasonably ask, Love is a memory of what or whom? "Often we hear it said that in Platonic love, when it is *you* I think I am in love with, I shall find at the end of the day that it was something else that I really loved all along," writes Platonist Graeme Nicholson, who echoes the venerable complaint that in Platonic love it would seem that we don't love people, just abstractions. A purely intellectual love—whatever that might be—is not, I think, what Plato has in mind. Plato's Socrates understands love as a powerful and transforming knowledge between human beings—powerful when erotic; profound and still powerful when not just erotic. As in prophecy, religion, and poetry, the madness in love takes us quite outside ourselves and transforms us in the process. Plato says that we love what we once were, even when we love erotically.

⁊

He is so close to Freud on the subject of love as memory that I can only conclude that Freud stole from him better than anyone, and rewrote the story of Platonic love with an intensely sexual imagination. Love as a function of what we forget (and try to recollect) is a depth psychology if there ever was one, notwithstanding the differences between Plato and Freud as theorists of mind.

Philosopher Søren Kierkegaard, who was enraptured but always troubled by Socrates, summarizes the argument of the *Phaedrus* in this telegraphic way: "Successively the object of love is: beautiful bodies–beautiful souls–beautiful observations–beautiful knowledge–the beautiful." In Freud, especially in his work with the conversion disorders (or hysterias), we have this progression: sexual symptom, sexual transference, sexual interpretation, sexual truth. The beautiful, in Plato, is a memory of a primordial past that could only be described in a mythology. The sexual, in Freud, is a memory of an infantile past that could only be described by the mythology we call psychoanalysis.

We shouldn't be too wedded to terms like "symptom," "transference," or even "sexual." Both in Freud and Plato, the issue is love, and love is memory. In what amounts to an organizing principle for him, Freud famously said that the hardest thing for a person to give up is a pleasure he or she has once known. We can still long for the pleasures we have forgotten, as he describes in a central passage from his *Three Essays on the Theory of Sexuality* (I have edited to rid Freud of his technical terms, though we get at the essence—keep the passage in mind, because we return to it in the next chapter):

> At a time at which the first beginnings of sexual satisfaction are still linked
> with the taking of nourishment, the sexual instinct has a sexual object out-
> side the infant's own body in the shape of his mother's breast. It is only later
> that he loses it. . . . [There are] good reasons why a child sucking at his
> mother's breast has become a prototype of every relation of love. The find-
> ing of an object is in fact a re-finding of it.

The "first beginnings of sexual satisfaction" is a classically Freudian phrase,
outrageous in its unique way. Only a Sigmund Freud could look at an infant,
who has just fed at the mother's breast, now sated and happy, and conclude
that the child was experiencing something sexual, like the afterglow of a
consummation. To see sexuality going back as far as infancy was a landmark
Freudian interpretation, offensive in his time.

Today, we are less outraged to see sexuality where it might or might not
be, and since Freud has been absorbed into our thinking, we more or less
concede that sex must be everywhere, as modern advertisers seem to understand implicitly. Reading Freud against Plato invites a different obsessive
concern, however, one quite separate from the tedium of looking for sex in
usual and unusual places. What is the role of memory in understanding or
loving other people? When Freud says that the finding of an object is in fact a
re-finding of it, he invites no end of heavy-handed interpretations, as the history of Freudian readings of most anything illustrates. If the past is so dominant and inescapable, then everything has a meaning located in the past, and
the Freudian interpreters have a field day, usually with a sexual emphasis.

One doesn't have to go far to find someone raising a sound objection:

> Everything has a meaning. When, [before Freud] . . . if a man moved his leg
> up and down while he was talking to his wife, and an onlooker asked what
> the meaning of this leg movement could be, no one would have taken the
> question seriously. The movement was something that just happened. We
> have different ideas now. Not much imagination is needed to suspect that
> the man with the moving leg has a grudge against his wife; he is kicking her
> out of the room, even if he reduces his kicks to very modest, and, to the
> uninitiated (are there any left?), innocent dimensions.

The author is J. H. van den Berg, a psychiatrist, whose comments are refresh-
ing, because he's not parroting Freudian interpretation. He wrote at a time,
in the 1950s, when over-interpretation of legs moving up and down (and

other such data) was at its best or worst, depending on one's point of view. I think he speaks for many people (lay and professional) in the above paragraph: maybe the leg moving up and down is precisely random information. Randomness is no solace, as van den Berg goes on to say:

> Who can feel at ease with all this? Life is full of trivialities—which appear always to have a meaning. And what a meaning! This meaning always escapes *us*; it almost seems a law that it is always somebody else who discovers the apparent meaning of our actions. . . . To deny it does not help, for the meaning is essentially unknown, it is subconscious. We cannot possibly feel at ease with it. And yet—I am convinced—we accept the idea that everything has a meaning so eagerly because more than almost any other formula, it makes us feel at ease.

The ancient formulas for ease were different, as we have seen. The Greeks believed in their oracles, religions, poems, and eroticism not because they were superstitious, foolish, soft, or depraved. The four madnesses offered meaning that Plato embraced. Through the persona of Socrates in the *Phaedrus*, he suggests that philosophy is an alternative to *theia mania* or "enthusiasm"—a more perfect form of it, so to speak:

> According to what we have said, every human soul, by nature, has seen the things that are, or else it would not have entered into this [human] creature. But it is not easy for every soul to be reminded of them by the things that are here–not for those who then saw what was there only briefly, or those who by some misfortune were cast down here and through keeping bad company have committed unjust deeds, quite forgetting the holy things they once saw. Just a few remain who still retain sufficient memory.

> And we ourselves were whole then as we made our celebration, not afflicted by the evils that were in store for us in the time to come; whole and simple and serene, we were initiated into the most joyful mysteries, witnessing them in the pure light, for we ourselves were pure, not entombed as we are now in what is called a body, fettered like an oyster in a shell.

The beautifully complex language, as translated by Graeme Nicholson, is evocative as poetry is: *every human soul has seen the things that are; it is not easy for every soul to be reminded of the things that are; we ourselves were whole then as we made our celebration . . . whole and simple and serene.* The whole and simple and serene time was golden before the glory of Greece, a magnificent *former* time. If only we could recall it, we might be cured of ills. Freud's Unconscious is like Plato's soul: it, too, has "seen things that are." In a psychoanalysis as in Platonic recollection, it is rarely easy to recall what once was. "Entombment" is real, because we rarely disclose ourselves to any other human being in the world of shadows and fetters where we live now (one wants to say, a world with the quality of Genesis 22).

Freud never stopped believing that his psychology was the best alternative to all previous ways of viewing the mind. If we listen to van den Berg, the power of Freud's psychology, the ease it affords, has to do with "meaning in everything." The search for meaning pushes us further and further back in time:

> In psychiatry, and afterward in everyday philosophy, the conclusion that human phenomena have a meaning which is located in the past came to have another, an exceptional and far-reaching, significance. The past soon was regarded as a past of long ago, that its owner could not be expected to know it. As far as the owner was concerned, the meaning of the phenomena was unknown or subconscious.

In the emotional life, we can believe amazing things, like a transparency between persons—a poetical idea that dates to Homer, though revised by the Judaic tradition, by Plato, and certainly by Freud. Plato and Freud substituted stories of recollection for the fiction of minds transparent to other minds, thus giving rise to Plato's philosophy and Freud's depth psychology, respectively.

Although I am deeply moved by Homer's Euryclea seeing through Odysseus's disguise, I have my doubts about the touching of scars, just as I am dubious of ceremonies involving snakes, snake-oil psychotherapy, and even the prescription of our modern drugs, which depend on our sometimes desperate faith in them. My doubts aren't the consequence of some mid-career crisis (I don't think so, at least); I'm merely forced to admit what experience teaches, that human transparency is the exception not the rule, both in the clinic and, much more so, in affairs of the heart.

"How do we know people?" is not a useful question when you are a doctor or a lover. A person necessarily sidesteps such perplexity in order to practice medicine or to love, but Freud would say that it's surprising and interesting that our attempts at answering "how do we *really* know?" involve old stories, whether Homeric, Patriarchal, or Platonic. We'll consider in the next chapter how an ancient tragedy (Oedipus) takes on the moniker of "a complex"—Freud makes his story sound like a universal diagnosis. If he had described a "Plato complex," it would be a syndrome in which we search the hallways and wards of memory in search what we have misplaced: it wouldn't be un-Freudian to say that all of us suffer from the deep need to re-member and refind a time, as described in Plato's grand mythology, when we were whole. Regarding Freud's "Oedipus complex" and the sad family story to which it refers, I'm especially curious why *a tragedy* becomes the central fiction for his science.

Two

Oedipus

IN CHAPTER FIVE of *The Interpretation of Dreams*, on the subject of King Oedipus of Thebes, we read:

> His destiny moves us only because it might have been ours—because the oracle laid the same curse upon us before our birth as upon him. It is the fate of all of us, perhaps, to direct our first sexual impulse towards our mother and our first hatred and our first murderous wish against our father.

Our dreams convince us, Freud says, that the fate of Oedipus is our tragedy in love and life. If such were not the case, the tragedy of Oedipus would not move us to the degree that it has since antiquity.

Let's pause—in fact, let's come to a full stop. In a work of tragedy, Freud finds corroboration for many clinical observations in his *Interpretation of Dreams*, including material from his own dreams. If we put to one side the "typicality" of dreams about sex with one parent and the death of the other, what is to be made of the terms "destiny," "oracle," "curse," "fate," and, most of all, *tragedy* in the experience of love? I suggest a short digression, because it isn't immediately apparent to me why a psychology of love and the mode of tragedy should be related to one another.

In a minor thought experiment, what if we chose a different story as an archetype for human intimacy? The alternative should be familiar to all of us and still within the genre of tragedy; we would discuss it without preconceptions about lovers, families, and incest. Would a concept of the tragic be just as crucial, if not more so than sexuality, to Freud's argument about unconscious determinants for emotion?

I

My vote for an alternative would be Shakespeare's *Romeo and Juliet*, which has inspired many renditions or adaptations of its apparently universal theme. As we know, the play has to do with young, ill-destined love in an unforgiving world, but it's not merely about immature love or a love that older people wouldn't indulge in their wizened maturity. It's a play, also, about how we fall, or rather *accelerate*, into love.

> ROMEO
> When, and where, and how
> We met, we wooed, and made exchange of vow,
> I'll tell thee as we pass; but this I pray,
> That thou consent to marry us to-day.
>
> FRIAR
> Holy Saint Francis! What a change is here!

Juliet is circumspect:

> Although I joy in thee,
> I have no joy of this contract to-night:
> It is too rash, too unadvis'd, too sudden,
> Too like the lightning, which doth cease to be
> Ere one can say 'It lightens.'

But just a few lines later, we realize that speed has always been the essence, that Juliet (more than immediately) answers Romeo's questions *before* he asks them, and that she is oceanically in love:

> My bounty is as boundless as the sea,
> My love as deep. The more I give to thee
> The more I have, for both are infinite.

It's not Sophocles, but surely it is love that we can appreciate, or wish we had for ourselves. One could be skeptical about Juliet's affection, but then one would miss a very lovely emotion and the playwright's insight, which is true

(I hope) at any age: when love happens, it can be astonishing in its ineluctable power over us.

"Cynics are fond of saying that if Romeo and Juliet had lived their love would not have 'lasted.' Of course it wouldn't—in the cynic's sense," wrote Harold Goddard in *The Meaning of Shakespeare*. As we read *Romeo and Juliet*, we can try to have a sense of humor about the proceedings (a wickedly cynical Mercutio in the play instructs us in this effort), but, finally, people die and tragic necessity prevails.

A reader who has followed me thus far would say, "Of course 'tragic necessity prevails.' It's a tragedy." Let me return to Goddard's remark: "If Romeo and Juliet had lived" is an impossible subjunctive. Goddard knows as much; he adds that we can no more expect Romeo and Juliet "to last" than we can expect the month of April not to end. Two people fall in love; it's a tragedy: why must it be so? Goddard says it just *is* so, like the ephemerality of April and of Spring.

Replace *Romeo and Juliet* for the Oedipus story, and we don't substitute a star-crossed-lover's complex for an Oedipal one; we merely ask about the interrelationship between tragedy, necessity, and love. Freud saw little disparity between these three ideas; they were perspectives on and of each other, as he learned directly from ancient tragedy.

Freud's debt to Sophocles was not solely the "discovery" of patricidal and incestuous wish.

II

"Things that have to do with love," Freud wrote in 1915, "are incommensurable with everything else; they are, as it were, written on a special page on which no other writing is tolerated." At any given time in his writing, we should be interested to decide whether he discusses sex or "the special page." But often it's difficult to decide a difference; it is a pivotal problem when we read him. Here he is on October 15, 1897, writing to Wilhelm Fliess (somewhat breathlessly) as he worked on *The Interpretation of Dreams*:

> A single idea of general value dawned on me. I have found, in my own case too, [the phenomenon of] being in love with my mother and jealous of my father, and I now consider it a universal event in early childhood, even if not so early in children who have been made hysterical. (Similar to the invention of parentage [family romance] in paranoia–heroes, founders of religion). If

this is so, we can understand the gripping power of *Oedipus Rex,* in spite of all the objections that reason raises against the presupposition of fate ... but the Greek legend seizes upon a compulsion which everyone recognizes because he senses its existence in himself.

In this letter, often quoted because it is Freud's first rough articulation of the Oedipus complex, the vast conceptual leaps—from "my" case to a "universal event"; from childhood to psychopathology; from family relations to religions; from Greek drama to compulsive behavior—have been discussed at length by Freud's detractors and advocates. The upshot of the commentaries seems to be: if you think Freud is a genius, the leaps are brilliant; if you think he's daft, the letter cinches the case. The greatest leap is implied. We have already seen how his "single idea of general value" develops in his *Three Essays on the Theory of Sexuality.* To recite a key phrase from that book, the "first beginning of sexual satisfaction" *is* the phenomenon of "being in love" to which Freud refers in the above passage. First attachment to mom is erotic in Freud's view (for boys and girls) whether or not we agree with his description. He wants to broaden our idea of sexuality and demystify what we too romantically call "being in love."

Freud's jealousy is also a type of love. We shouldn't mystify love when we use the word; we also shouldn't mystify it when we talk about a feeling very different from love. What Freud feels for his dad is tinged by jealousy, fear, paranoia, or perhaps frank hate, but it still could be love. Describing exactly what he feels requires some acknowledgment of "complexity" (or, at least, of paradox: a mix of love and hate) whether or not we happen to know about Oedipus.

Dream interpretation or just raw waking experience teaches that an acknowledgment of complexity is fundamental to the psychological explanation of normalcy and abnormality. Put differently, it isn't pathological to think that the person you love most is also the person you could hate most. But so complicated a sentiment could easily be pathological in its manifestations, as we surmise when we hear about bizarre crimes of passion in the tabloids or on the evening news.

Freud alludes to Sophocles in *The Interpretation of Dreams* as in his letter to Fliess. When he mentions "a legend that come down to us from antiquity," he refers us, again, to the love children feel for their parents and the corroborating evidence of the Oedipus legend:

Being in love with one parent and hating the other are among the essential constituents of the stock of psychical impulses which is formed [in childhood] . . . It is not my belief, however, that psychoneurotics differ sharply in this respect from other human beings who remain normal—that they are able, that is, to create something absolutely new and peculiar to themselves. It is far more probable—and this is confirmed by occasional observations on normal children—that they are only distinguished by exhibiting on a magnified scale feelings of love and hatred to their parents which occur less obviously and less intensely in the minds of most children.

This discovery is confirmed by a legend that has come down to us from classical antiquity: a legend whose profound and universal power to move can only be understood if the hypothesis I have put forward in regard to the psychology has an equally universal validity. What I have in mind is the legend of King Oedipus and Sophocles' drama which bears his name.

What does Sophocles' *Oedipus the King* prove or confirm for all of us, whether abnormal or normal? (Regarding the meaning of "psychoneurosis," note Freud's suggestion that there isn't much difference between any of us, whether we suffer psychopathology or not, in terms of the origin of love.) If our answer runs along the lines of, "well, the play validates the Oedipus complex," then we confuse ourselves. Sophocles proves and confirms nothing Freudian.

In *Oedipus the King* Sophocles paints the picture of a person who: 1. thinks he knows about X; 2. finds he doesn't know as much about X as he had thought; 3. inevitably comes to grief because of 1. and 2. In Sophocles, X is "the personal history of Oedipus, king of Thebes;" in Freud, X is "love in one's personal history."

A take-home point, articulated by classicist J.-P. Vernant with brilliant understatement, would be: "If [Oedipus] kills his father and sleeps with his mother it is not because, in some obscure way, he hates the former and is in love with the latter." Oedipus kills his father and sleeps with his mother without murky fuss about how he feels or why he loves; he operates without any psychological complex regarding his behavior. On this view, *Oedipus the King* is a lousy case-in-point for Freud, except that there is a separate matter about the tragedy's "profundity" and "universality." A description of love should be no less profound and universal in its power to stimulate and disturb our thinking, as Freud clearly believes.

The actual term "Oedipus complex" appears a decade after *The Interpretation* in "A Special Type of Object Choice Made by Men" (1910). In that essay, Freud sounds tentative; he talks about how people come "under the sway" of the Oedipus complex, as if one could deftly swerve to avoid it. Psychoanalysts Jean Laplanche and J.-B. Pontalis in *The Language of Psychoanalysis* assure us that Freud was convinced of the universal validity of the Oedipus complex early in his psychological career, even when he wrote to Fliess. The "universal validity" depends, however, on how we think Freud *might be* valid. In *The Interpretation*, Freud thought to describe the complex of emotions that all children feel (and what they feel could be very complicated, so his point could be valid), but it is rather different to say that the Oedipus complex describes universal urges, whatever they might be. We could discuss any number of other complexes with no less validity. Indeed, when it comes to the Greeks, one could choose among many flavors of complexes based on one's taste for this or that tragedy. In Aeschylus's *Oresteia*, Clytemnestra kills her husband Agamemnon because he sacrificed their daughter Iphigenia as he prepared for war; his case wasn't improved by the fact that he slept with the siren named Cassandra. Someone has offered that since all wives desire—unconsciously, of course—to murder their husbands for myriad good reasons, perhaps the power of Aeschylean tragedy relates to a tacit identification with Clytemnestra: thus, we have a "Clytemnestra complex." If one thinks that the desire to kill one's spouse is not universal, nevertheless, life between Agamemnon and Clytemnestra is like an apocalyptically bad day in marriage.

What explains the power of marital tragedy in Aeschylus? Clytemnestra kills Agamemnon, but she has a paramour as well (the hapless Aegisthus). Her son Orestes and daughter Electra do away with both Clytemnestra and Aegisthus; Orestes feels tormented after the deed. In the end, only an act of god fixes the mess. (Sophocles and Euripides would write their own versions of the Electra story in which the daughter eerily starts to resemble her mother.) If we felt strongly motivated to do so, we could think about how Aeschylean tragedy needs at least several psychological complexes to account for its power: a Clytemnestra complex if you hate your husband, an Orestes complex if you hate your mother, a very dangerous Electra complex in which you start to resemble the people you most despise, and so on. No one today seems to be busy identifying new psychological complexes, and that is for the better. The exercise leads us nowhere, and it dilutes Freud's idea that in a truly immortal tragedy, its insights into the human condition are absolutely inescapable. Deciding in what way an insight is inescapable is a more difficult matter.

⊜

By 1919, in the essay "A Child is Being Beaten," the Oedipus complex is an "actual nucleus" and "true determinant" for most, if not all, psychological problems, according to Freud. He does not describe hate separate from love (he is not saying that we *only* hate one parent and love the other); he describes the complexity of an emotion, especially the paradoxes built within it. If, for whatever reason, we aren't capable of dealing with a dense mix of sometimes violently contrary feelings, then it's likely that some type of problem (either clinical psychopathology or "normal" psychological difficulty) will manifest later. The Oedipus complex describes this emotional mix for both men and women. Freud and all psychiatrists after him have invited us, therefore, to inquire how we feel about our fathers and mothers, if only to begin the long work that reveals how confused we really are.

There is a fascinating illogic in Freud's argument. The Oedipus complex cannot be proved wrong, like any statement whose irrefutability is built into how one makes the statement. Similar self-referential validity is common: "living in a violent age encourages violence" (in violent times, yes, one would expect violence); "love will keep us together" (if it doesn't, it wasn't love); or "all past beliefs sooner or later turn out to be false" (I'd italicize *past* belief; what one believes now must be true); and we could cite many other instances. If we read *Oedipus the King* with an eye towards its psychological significance, then, certainly, murder and attraction are themes to address, especially if we already believe that hate and love are important in an infant's (and the adult's) emotional world. But the "profound and universal power" of a legend does not relate to, and does not impart, "universal validity" of a theory, which requires a different kind of validation, as Freud knows perfectly well. Freud hedges his discovery regarding the role of conflicting emotions in mental life by way of a literary allusion to the "perfect" tragedy, as Aristotle described *Oedipus the King*.

Philosopher of science Sir Karl Popper has said that Freud's irrefutability didn't make him scientific. Science, Popper said, is much more flawed, and it needs to be fallible, because discovering how science errs is part of the scientific process. In Freud's time and to a greater degree now in our science-dominated time, it is unusual that any imaginative work should corroborate a supposedly scientific argument. Consider the matter of behaving "out of love": it would be bizarre if a psychiatrist suggested regular viewing of *Casablanca* to understand the heroic Rick syndrome, an Ilsa complex, or a dreaded Victor Lazlo disease. A Casablanca school of psychology might never be a science, but one suspects it would have its adherents. To read Sophocles is a profounder business, not unimportant for not being scientific.

Mainly, Freud is curious to explain why *Oedipus the King* affected him. Today, maybe the only people who brood over Sophocles are undergraduates under duress of an assignment or scholars in a long and fruitless search to find something original to say about it. But Freud believes that the tragedy is a text of psychology and should be read as such, for our ongoing psychological edification. He thinks that we identify emotionally with the hero, and in fact I think we do, but, as with any serious private reading, the question to ask is why a story matters, and in what sense it is personally relevant. It comes as a bit of a surprise, as J.-P. Vernant suggests, that the depth of Oedipus as a character has little to do with the psychological complex the play supposedly illustrates.

⊟

What is the play about? We answer the question best by understanding its dramatic context, which extends beyond *Oedipus the King*. To say it is about patricide and incest is a misrepresentation; it is about a family, and the story actually begins with Oedipus's daughter. Sophocles produced *Oedipus the King* as the second of three plays about the family history of a king of Thebes. Sophocles' audience would already have been familiar with the legend of family Oedipus; they would have known the play's essentials as one is familiar today with a stock plot in advance of a contemporary rendering. *Antigone*, the first of the Theban plays, which dates to about 440 BCE, addresses the end rather than the beginning of the family's demise. Sophocles always relies upon—and often toys with—the audience's familiarity with basic plot. Unlike the tragedies of Aeschylus, who was a bit older than Sophocles and whose *Oresteia* was intended specifically as a trilogy, Sophocles' three "Theban plays" stand as three independent perspectives on a well-known saga.

Antigone is one of four children by King Oedipus and Queen Jocasta. In *Antigone*, she and her sister, Ismene, contend with the death of their two brothers, Eteocles and Polynices. After Oedipus's self-banishment from Thebes (as will be described in *Oedipus the King*), Jocasta's brother, Creon, assumes power together with Eteocles and Polynices. The triumvirate is unsettled from the start; the brothers bicker regarding succession to the throne. Creon and Eteocles assume joint power. Polynices, now without an ally, leaves Thebes to build an army abroad. When he returns, backed by new forces against Thebes, he and Eteocles kill each other. Creon becomes sole ruler.

As *Antigone* begins, we learn that she intends to violate Creon's royal edict that Polynices' corpse will not be buried. Her crime, which she promptly commits (actually, she tries to bury him not once, but twice), is punishable by death. To complicate matters, Antigone is betrothed to Creon's son, Haemon. Creon and Haemon offer a frightful Punch-and-Judy show that counterpoints Antigone's defiance of law. Creon nags at Haemon; Haemon pleads with Creon on behalf of Antigone; Creon gets enraged on cue. (Haemon plays psychiatrist, "If you weren't my father, I would say you were insane"; Creon spits back that Haemon is weak and should die; Haemon concedes, "you will never see me again," and adds with particular venom, "Rage your heart out, rage with friends who can stand the sight of you.") Haemon wanted his father to stay Antigone's death sentence; Creon acquiesces only after a tragic delay, during which time Haemon, viscerally angry beyond appeasement, goes to Antigone's tomb, where he meets his father a last time, spits in his face, and then commits suicide.

From the very start of the play, Ismene implores her sister to avoid tragedy by thinking about all the grief that has already visited their family, not only the brothers' mutual murders, but also their mother's suicide by hanging and Oedipus's own death, which she mentions rather incidentally. *Oedipus the King* culminates in Jocasta's death and the king's self-blinding; *Oedipus at Colonus* ends with the exiled Oedipus's death, but both are later Theban plays. *Antigone* exemplifies the Sophoclean idea of heroism long before we first meet Sophocles' Oedipus.

"I will bury him myself," Antigone tells Ismene (referring to Polynices, though she will also attend her father's burial at Colonus), "And even if I die in the act, that death will be a glory." Her very next sentence (here translated by Robert Fagles) articulates the subject of all the Theban plays: "I will lie with the one I love and loved by him—an outrage sacred to the gods." David Grene's translation is clearer perhaps: "I shall lie by his side, loving him as he loved me. I shall be a criminal—but a religious one." But the phrase "sacred outrage" (more than religious crime) is useful, especially if we think of the root meaning of "sacred": "to cut, cleave, or sever." *Antigone* is more than a play about whatever outrage she engenders by her actions, just as *Oedipus the King* is more than a play about outrage over the violation of sexual taboos.

Antigone's quiet rage sets her apart, quite severs her from human company, including Haemon's or Ismene's. *Oedipus the King* is also a play about how Oedipus sets himself apart as a kind of fearful example for all men and women; outrage in his play is a hero's lamentation over how he has been terribly singled out by fate.

Old, blind, and exiled, the Oedipus in the last of Sophocles' Theban plays, *Oedipus at Colonus*, ends his homeless wandering. Colonus is a sacred grove inhabited by the Eumenides, or "kindly" furies, who both punish and protect. Antigone is her father's tireless companion, his set of eyes, guide, and protector. Ismene shows up with news from Thebes, and prepares offerings to the Eumenides on her father's behalf. The city of Athens, which is visible on the horizon past Colonus, accepts Oedipus and will protect him, by mandate of the kind Theseus, King of Athens. Ismene brings news from Thebes about the internecine conflict over who will rule after Oedipus. Oedipus laments that his sons have an "Egyptian" taste for war, and he prophecies that the two will kill each other. Although there is great kindness in the play (Antigone's and Theseus's), there is also an Oedipal fury for retribution.

On meeting the old king, Theseus says, "I know all about you"—i.e., about the story of Oedipus. But he doesn't quite know the changed person before him. Oedipus in his last days becomes a more furious and enigmatic figure than he is at any other time in his life.

According to prophesy, the locale where Oedipus dies will be protected from all aggression by foreign force. It becomes clear, after Creon makes his appearance at Colonus, that Thebes will be punished and Athens spared because Oedipus will die near Athens. Creon invites Oedipus back to Thebes, because the exile's return would be in Creon's best interest. Creon seeks protection for Thebes; his transparent insincerity outrages Oedipus, and Creon doesn't help matters when he kidnaps Antigone and Ismene (Theseus summarily stops Creon). Thebes will pay dearly because of Oedipus's death at Colonus, but the retribution is an irony, since Oedipus's lifework has been the protection of Thebes.

At the start of Oedipus at Colonus, Oedipus famously says (I pause at the words, because there is beautiful resignation in them) that acceptance is what suffering teaches. But "acceptance," like the kindness of the Eumenides, is a mix of emotions, only some of which are beneficent. Oedipus at

Colonus, like *Antigone*, depicts what has been called Sophoclean "heroic temper," both in the sense of a heroic character who transcends circumstance and the intricate rage of someone who has fallen from grace.

⊜

Writing about the origin of tragedy in Greece, a young Friedrich Nietzsche (at the time, he was an academic philologist) offers the best one-sentence perspective on Sophoclean heroism, whether in the person of Antigone, old Oedipus, or Oedipus the king: "we immediately delude ourselves that we have looked into the innermost depth of their essence, with some surprise that the bottom of these depths lies so near the surface." "Delude" is the problematic and important word: we think, if we now return to *Oedipus the King*, that it is a story with a simple premise—the investigator of a crime discovers that he is the perpetrator. We also think that Oedipus is relentless in sounding the depths of his history. Certainly he does not yield in finding out who killed Laius, the previous king of Thebes. But Nietzsche correctly surmises that there is no shock in the knowledge that Oedipus has committed deep, dark crimes. (Nor is there shock in *Antigone* that the heroine will commit a crime. She announces it in the first lines of *Antigone*, and, later, she admits it with gusto.) To peer into the depth of Oedipus is, in part, to miss a premise of his tragedy–that his temper, temperament, and curse are plain for all to see. Antigone was a heroine of the obvious ("I don't deny a thing," she tells Creon, to his utter consternation). Oedipus is tragic partly because he is so obviously oblivious.

I don't refer to "unconscious" motivations that become "clear." The point of the Unconscious in Freud is that the Unconscious is not obvious, that much is hidden by a process called repression, which is a type of forgetting. A great oddness in the history of psychology is that we now seem to know all dark unconscious corners as a result of textbook renditions of Freud. Using *Oedipus the King* as a primary textbook, we know, just as an Attic audience would have known, that he killed his father, Laius, and slept with his mother, Jocasta. These are edgy issues of course, but maybe less so these days, because we have heard too much about the Oedipus complex. "Freud argues," says Jonathan Lear in a thoughtful survey of Freud, "that on the right interpretation, [*Oedipus the King*] describes us all, man and woman, boy and girl. But he [Freud] calls his interpretation a 'simplification,' a 'schematization,' which he admits does not likely occur as such in human beings. . . [Regarding the] familiar structure of the Oedipus complex. . . *Freud basically admits that it never occurs*" (Lear's italics). J. Lear means that, as a general rule, we don't kill dad, have children by mom, eat our parents or offspring, etc.

The Oedipus complex describes a complex mix of love and hate; the complexity—or "ambivalence," in Freudian terminology—operates whether we talk about either love or hate. Likewise, Sophoclean heroism is an uneasy mix of many emotional ingredients, but Sophocles' Oedipus doesn't seem emotionally ambivalent. As said, he is virtually straightforward (Nietzsche: "so near the surface"), and, in all the Theban plays, the audience, like the prophets and choruses in those plays, seem to know more about him than he knows of himself. The possibility of delusion is ever present, however, for hero and audience alike. All that we really know is that any clarity in the Oedipus saga (at any point in his family's saga) comes at a severe price. Could the same statement be true for the condition we call love?

III

A British writer once remarked that at a certain time of year in her country, in August, a person can take a long walk in fine weather and feel that "for some reason everything seems dangerously simple." She deftly adds, in what I also take to be germane to the study of Sophocles, "There is something truly or falsely spiritual about this state. . . which if prolonged may easily lead to disaster." In *Oedipus the King*, it seems dangerously simple to think, for example, that Oedipus saved Thebes by answering the riddle of the Sphinx—or, in the language of the play, that Oedipus was a "sword of thought" to save a dying army of his citizens. Much has been made of the hero's intelligence in the play, and we know that Freud identified with Oedipus, probably enamored by his talent at solving riddles (Freud also affectionately called his daughter Anna "his Antigone"). But one recalls the first line of prophet Tiresias in the play (from the Bernard Knox translation), "wisdom is a dreadful thing when it brings no profit to its possessor." Wisdom can also be dreadful as one gains it, as *Oedipus the King* amply shows.

J.-P. Vernant has observed, based on a study of puns and double meanings throughout *Oedipus the King*, that maybe the answer to the famous riddle of the Sphinx was straightforward, that its solution couldn't have been plainer to Oedipus. Before citing exactly how the Sphinx's riddle was obvious, we should understand some background about the questioner. The Sphinx in Sophocles and in Attic Greece was always female, a Gorgonic amalgam of woman, lion (some think dog), bird, and serpent's tail. According to the *Theogony* of Hesiod, she sat on a promontory or "Sphinx mountain" outside of Thebes, asking questions of visitors like some guardian at a gate. She differs from the Sphinx represented in Egypt, though the Egyptian Sphinx was the archetype for later Mycenaean and Greek versions. The Egyptian Sphinx is male, typically with a pharaoh's head (like Khafra, Pharaoh when the second Pyramid was constructed), as we see today in the worn face of the Sphinx at Giza.

In *Oedipus the King*, the "harsh, brutal singer," as the chorus describes the Theban Sphinx, doesn't immortalize and memorialize a king. She reminds a future king of who he is—at very least, of his unique name. There is a passing comment in the play, spoken by Creon, that Thebes would have investigated the death of King Laius more carefully at the time of his murder, had it not been for the Sphinx. She "persuaded" Thebes to forgo all investigation of the king's possible murder and to concentrate on "what lies at the feet" of the citizenry. Ancient lore has it (Sophocles alludes to this myth, later described in the so-called *Library* attributed to Apollodorus) that, after killing all those who hadn't guessed an answer to her riddle, the Sphinx hurled herself to her death once Oedipus came along with his idiosyncratic knowledge.

Here is Vernant on her famous query: "The baleful songstress' question is: who is the being that is at the same time *dípous, trípous, tetrápous*? For *oi-dípous* the mystery is an apparent not a real one: *of course* the answer is himself [i.e., man]." But "Man," who crawls with four limbs in infancy, walks with two in life, then hobbles in age with the third leg of a cane, partly doesn't answer the Sphinx. *Oi-dípous* is the "knower" ("I know" or *Oîda*) of "feet" (*poús*); he is the person with swollen feet (*oîdos*) from birth, because his ankles were pinned when his biological parents sent him away from Thebes, when he should have been crawling on all fours. When threatened by a stranger bearing a double prong where the three roads meet, he kills his father; and, late in his life, he will get around only with Antigone's help, as it were on his two feet and hers. "Oedipus" is the answer to the Sphinx's riddle—we gather as much with the help of scholarly readings of Sophoclean word-play.

The Sphinx killed a number of Thebans who couldn't answer her riddle; "*I* came, know-nothing Oedipus, *I* stopped the Sphinx," Oedipus says with the first-person emphasis. For him, the answer to the riddle was a self-recognition. The disaster (tragedy) of such simple answers is Sophocles' interest in *Oedipus the King*.

There is natural embarrassment in discussing a book that has been read and re-read for millennia. All summaries cast peculiar angles of light on the play, most notably the Freudian perspective that "it can scarcely be owing to chance" that a canonical masterpiece deals with "the naked admission of an intention to commit parricide," once we look past all the ways in which an artist "softens" and "disguises" the intention (these are excerpts from Freud in 1928, discussing three powerhouse geniuses at once–Sophocles, Shakespeare in *Hamlet*, and Fyodor Dostoevsky in *The Brothers Karamazov*). Freud misrepresents Sophocles, since the one certainty in the play is that Oedipus never intended to live out the life that was prophesied for him. The only really naked admission in the play comes from Tiresias, who offers the following plot summary of *Oedipus the King* (from the Knox translation):

> Listen to me now. The man you are trying to find . . . the murderer of Laius, that man is here in Thebes. He is apparently an immigrant of foreign birth, but he will be revealed as a native-born Theban. He will take no pleasure in that revelation. Blind instead of seeing, beggar instead of rich, he will make his way to foreign soil, feeling his way with a stick. He will be revealed as brother and father of the children with whom he now lives, the son and husband of the woman who gave him birth, the murderer and marriage-partner of his father. Go think this out.

With utter simplicity (made even more intelligible by Knox, who intended his translation for the modern stage), Tiresias re-asks a riddle about the identity of Oedipus, but, this time around, Oedipus cannot answer immediately. Tiresias advises that Oedipus "think this out," which is as profound a general recommendation as I can imagine in any circumstance. Then Tiresias leaves the stage.

The prophet reveals what Oedipus doesn't know for the time being, like an insight-oriented psychiatrist who is too quick with what he understands as "psychological truth." The Sophoclean chorus responds with some charm despite its befuddlement, "I cannot agree with him, nor speak against him. I do not know what to say." Their reaction is what ours might be to Freudian insight about the Unconscious. If any person with any psychological training, psychoanalytic or otherwise, says that he or she knows what our problem is, then we are understandably curious about the truth-value in what we hear. But if Sophoclean (and Freudian) insight is correct, then we are the last people who can judge truth-value, since he speaks of intentions and motivations which are not conscious to us, or which belong to some part of our past that we no longer recall.

In *The Interpretation of Dreams* early in his psychoanalytic career, Freud goes on to say that we actively rather than passively forget important moments in our lives. Such active forgetting is defensive in nature—defensive, because there are aspects of our past that we need to forget or "get past," if only to get along somehow in life. The more we "repress," since forgetfulness (or repression) is the most powerful of our psychological defenses, the more self-fulfilling and prophetic psychoanalytic insight becomes. How do we avoid such conundrums of analysis? Simply, we don't, and, increasingly, people just don't go into psychoanalysis. But we can't dismiss Freud quite so easily, because one of his questions stubbornly will not die, unlike the Sphinx: in any psychology, including any theory of love, can we be sure of our own insight? If the answer is yes, because we believe in what we believe "now," then there's no perceived need for psychological theory, Freudian or otherwise. If we are not so sure, or if love and truth undergo what Freud plangently called "vicissitude," then we need to re-think, as Tiresias recommends.

Oedipus is in conflict with his past even if he thinks he remembers all its details. What he remembers turns out to be true, just not the truth as he understood it. As happens repeatedly in *Oedipus the King*, revelation of the past involves the obviousness of the present. He believes his parents were King Polybus and Queen Merope of Corinth, and indeed they raised him with great love, far away from Thebes. He flees Corinth because of a prophecy that he will kill his father and sleep with his mother. Late in the play, on the cusp of Oedipus's moment of full revelation, we have an "insight-oriented" exchange with an old Corinthian messenger. The messenger arrives with the news that King Polybus has died from natural causes, and—this is a nice touch—he asks, would Oedipus consider becoming the King of Corinth? But there is other news from that city:

MESSENGER
Polybus was not related to you in any way.
OEDIPUS
What do you mean? Was Polybus not my father?
MESSENGER
No more than I am—he was as much your father as I.

OEDIPUS
How can my father be on the same level as you who are nothing to me?
MESSENGER
Because he was no more your father than I am.

Even in the context of a relentless tragedy, the back-and-forth is funny: we can be absolutely certain that the old Corinthian messenger is not, was not, and couldn't have been father to Oedipus, King of Thebes. But all certainties become dubious as the messenger and the king discuss pertinent details:

MESSENGER
He [Polybus] had been childless, that was why he loved you.
OEDIPUS
You gave me to him? Did you . . . buy me? or find me somewhere?
MESSENGER
I found you in the shady valleys of Mount Cithaeron.
OEDIPUS
What were you doing there?
MESSENGER
Watching over my flocks on the mountainside.

"What were you doing there?" and the old man's deadpan response is as good as any Shakespearean exchange with a fool or gravedigger. Tragedy lies in what the messenger was in fact doing there:

OEDIPUS
A shepherd, were you? A wandering day laborer?
MESSENGER
Yes, but at that moment I was your savior.
OEDIPUS
When you picked me up, was I in pain?
MESSENGER
Your ankles would bear witness on that point.

That would be: the *pinned* ankles. Thus, Oedipus is the biological son of Laius the Theban. Jocasta, wife and mother, has witnessed all the above; soon, she will vanish into the palace, and we later learn of her suicide. Earlier in the play, Jocasta recommended that Oedipus simply look the other way—if he were to stop being so good an investigator, it would be to his benefit (less personal pain). Her premonition that knowledge gained would be dangerous was acute. In *Oedipus the King*, unequivocal truth is revealed; Jocasta hangs herself and Oedipus blinds himself because of it. If false certainty is hazardous, so too are the revelations of knowledge.

IV

If psychotherapy involves self-discovery, Oedipus endures severe psychotherapy. As a patient, he talks about what burdens him—namely, his responsibility as a king. His crisis doesn't abate as a result of his talk or investigation; nor can he ignore his situation, especially since he is the last person to overlook or ignore detail. His crisis intensifies. Part patient, but also a doctor, he attempts to cure himself and lessen his difficulty through the acquisition of knowledge, just as his daughter will heal herself by way of a bold action in *Antigone*. He says that he will end the plague that grips Thebes. As *Oedipus the King* begins, a "pollution" has already killed crops and animals and, mysteriously, has caused the women to become infertile. Thebes suffers a winter of discontent, as critic Francis Fergusson might claim (his *The Idea of a Theater* insists that tragedy participates in a rhythm of life—in the case of *Oedipus the King*, a "perennial quest" for well-being, beginning in the dead of winter).

When Oedipus confers with Tiresias, he hopes that the prophet will cure the sterile season. Oedipus would be one of grateful: "Save yourself and this city, save me, from all the infection," Oedipus pleads. But the prophet in Greek tragedy, as critic H. D. F. Kitto has nicely argued, is just a prophet, someone who works under the premise that events are not random and, therefore, can be predicted. Tiresias is vaguely scientific (with his love of prediction and so on), but he doesn't assume the role either of doctor, scientist, or savior for anyone, despite the fact that he exposes truth and points to cure when he speaks. So, Oedipus must assume a doctor's role; and, because treatment for Thebes also involves self-discovery for Oedipus, he becomes rather like his own therapist.

As Fergusson says, there's rhythm in the play, but it is not redemptive. A cycle of inquiry and disquiet leading to more inquiry happens with each visitor, like the Corinthian messenger, whose news, like all news in the play, is both good and bad (mainly bad).

"A *shepherd* were you? A *wandering* day-labourer?" Even single words are disconcerting. In what sense did he "shepherd"? "Wandering" at Mt. Cithaeron (where, incidentally, Sophocles was born) anticipates old Oedipus as a nomadic exile approaching Colonus. The Corinthian messenger plainly informs us that he wasn't idle in the least at Mt. Cithaeron; he was busy "saving" the baby Oedipus. To do well by the king–to provide him information or to save him–is no good news, but at least Oedipus was saved. Nothing is random; there is no wandering. Dr. Oedipus wanted to "save Thebes," but playing the doctor-king for Thebes started the whole catastrophe, from the moment he met the Sphinx. If *Oedipus the King* in any way recapitulates the process of discovery in a doctor-patient relationship, it is a fearful advertisement for psychotherapy.

⸎

Any effort, including Freud's, at making Oedipus into a modern psychological study runs into the issue of "the Greek mind," which the modern sensibility may not fully understand. Is *Oedipus the King* a psychological work? Some scholars have doubts. Here is Sir Maurice Bowra in his *Sophoclean Tragedy*: "just as in life a complex situation may force us to take sides and to pass judgements, so in Sophoclean tragedy the conflicts make the same demand. And when this happens, we are particularly likely to be led astray by modern notions. The Greeks had strong feelings, but these did not always work in the same way or the same field as our own." Next, G. M. Kirkwood in his *Study of Sophoclean Drama*; he quotes colleague Gilbert Murray (not to flatter Murray, but to bury him): "[in discussing Shakespeare and Aeschylus, Murray speaks of] 'stories and situations ... deeply implanted in the memory of the race, implanted, as it were, upon our physical organism ... We say that they are strange to us. Yet there is that within us which leaps at the sight of them, a cry of blood which tells us that we have known them always.'" Kirkwood responds that such a view, with its cries of blood and so forth, "appear as a deplorable leap in the dark." Did Freud (do we) leap in the dark by understanding Oedipus as a doctor and patient rolled into one? Most severely, because he's probably right, here is Vernant in his *Myth and Tragedy in Ancient Greece*: "Freud's interpretation of tragedy in general and *Oedipus Rex* in particular has had no influence on the work of Greek scholars." The implication is that the scholars have thought Freud too superficial to be taken seriously, and that Freud is no Greek scholar.

But Vernant himself, like many other classicists, observes *at minimum* a dual role in the person of Oedipus. He is a victim as hero and an exile as native and king. "Oedipus" has inherent multiple meanings, and to call him the incarnation of the patient-doctor relationship is just another way of saying that "Oedipus is 'double,'" as Vernant says. And he continues, "He is a 'savior' king who, at the beginning of the play, is the object of prayers of an entire people as if he were a god . . . but he is also an abominable defilement, a monster of impurity concentrating within himself all the evil and sacrilege of the world, who must be ejected as a *pharmakos*, a scapegoat, so that the city can become pure once again." Single-minded heroism is not in the spirit of Greek tragedy, if I read Vernant correctly. The Greek hero is more of a muddle, and Oedipus is an archetypal muddle. He is a *pharmakos*, which is a complicated word connoting "scapegoat," "recipe," "good drug," and "bad drug." A *pharmakos* in the family is like a doctor who really shouldn't treat relatives or himself.

Professional psychology might not offer much to the interpretation of *Oedipus the King*, but the converse is not true. Take the concept of *pharmakos*, which critic René Girard calls "the theme of the ambivalent drug." Girard sees the same theme—or "double structure"—in many literary places, as in Shakespeare's *Romeo and Juliet*, where Laurence as friar-pharmacist observes, "Within the infant rind of this small flower/Poison had residence and medicine power." A very early "discussion" of the *pharmakos* can be found in Plato's *Phaedrus*, which I described as a tacit source for Freud in chapter one. In the *Phaedrus*, Plato mentions *pharmakos* as an aside: *What should be a remedy need not be*, he says.

The precise context at the conclusion of the *Phaedrus* is a discussion about how we can weaken memory as we try to help it, but the tragedy of a remedy is my concern. Plato's observation has two implications. First: love is a medicine; but the *pharmakos* can never be simply beneficial. Second: the more powerful the emotional drug, the more "ambivalent" its effects.

In other words, *Oedipus the King* is important to psychology because after we read it, or re-read it with new sensibility, we begin to understand that, as Thomas Mann wrote, "all heightened healthiness must be achieved by the route of illness." Mann refers to what he understood as Freud's debt to Nietzsche, but, more probably, the insight about our "route" is purely Greek or Sophoclean. Cure by love is a problematic or tragic remedy for us, a rock-strewn path.

⊟

In search of any cure, I think people seek to understand whatever difficulty lies beneath appearances, with a thought that if a cause is known, a fix is possible. That is a rational approach. When Freud studied dreams or symptoms in the clinic, he adopted the same stance. What is the latent (not the obvious) content of a dream? What do psychological symptoms mean in terms of processes of which we are not aware (unconscious ones)? Both questions were revolutionary in the history of ideas. For our contemporary purpose, however, at a time when dream analysis on a couch is more a stereotype than a common practice, and when symptoms demand "real" treatment more than gratuitous interpretation, Freud's revolutionary questions seem to preoccupy intellectuals and no one else, and the Freudian revolution no longer drives therapeutics in psychiatry and psychology.

Yet: by far the greatest amount of psychotherapy conducted in the world never happens in a therapist's office or by way of medications. People have a tendency to work through problems at great lengths themselves, or they fall in and out of love, in the expectation that happiness in the emotional life will be its own curative reward. Can happiness be the remedy we envision it to be? When Freud writes, in the trickiest sentence of his masterwork *Die Traumdeutung*, that *the interpretation of dreams is the royal road to knowledge of unconscious activity*, he does not say that the deepest knowledge regarding our dreams or symptoms equals cure. We certainly hope that interpretation and knowledge will help us in our struggles; Freud hoped as much for his psychoanalysis, since he was a closeted optimist, even late into his career. To be clear, however, he offers potential remedy instead of nostrum; he describes the road, not the end of it.

V

A detailed reading of *The Interpretation of Dreams* is not my intention in this chapter or in this book, but precisely in *The Interpretation*, Freud inaugurates a method that will repeat itself in his career. A work of literature speaks to a problem that he wants to address; he might allude to the work, quote bits of it, or perhaps he will write at some length about the meaning of the work for him. These references are not incidental; Oedipus is a case in point, only partly because the Oedipus complex is so central to Freudian psychological theory. To read *Oedipus the King* and the Theban plays as books in parallel with Freud invites us to think about how the plays could have been helpful to him as more than corroboration of a theory. It is hardly possible to read about the Oedipus complex in Freud without thinking for oneself about relationships between children and parents. Regarding parental love and the love of children for their parents, Freud suggests that we consult Sophocles. When we do, it comes as a surprise that thinking about "a complex" becomes just the opposite of a reiteration of stock theory.

Compared to the 230-odd dreams described in sometimes oppressive detail in *The Interpretation*, I prefer a few sentences from his chapter V (in a discussion of "Typical Dreams") as a primer to Freud's "dream of interpretation," in critic Ken Frieden's useful turn of phrase:

> If anyone dreams, with any sign of pain, that his father or mother or brother or sister has died, I should never use the dream as evidence that he wishes that person's death *at the present time*. The theory of dreams does not require as much as that; it is satisfied with the inference that this death has been wished for at some time or other during the dreamer's childhood. I fear, however, that this reservation will not appease the objectors; they will deny the possibility of their *ever* having had such a thought with just as much energy as they insist that they harbour no such wishes now. I must therefore reconstruct a portion of the vanished mental life of children on the basis of the evidence of the present.

The reconstruction sounds like the investigative work Oedipus performs so fiercely in *Oedipus the King*, except that an interpretation in psychology differs from, say, the latest news from Corinth. We can doubt all interpretations; sometimes we reject them out of hand as unbelievable, like one of Freud's objectors. Oedipus has no such luxury; what the messenger says turns out to be absolutely true. What, then, is the truth-value of an interpretation in psychology, whether of a dream or anything else?

Much depends on what might be called the level of the interpretation. If someone says, "I had a dream in which my father died" or even if he says outright "I wish my father were dead," Freud's interpretation at its highest level offers that the hidden wish or the expressed wish is *nothing new*. At a very low level of interpretation, one could say "ah, yes, all of us hate our loved ones to the point that we want them dead on occasion." To take a different example of the same point, Freud tells the story about a child whose father *did* die. The boy told Freud, "I know my father's dead, but what I can't understand is why he doesn't come home for supper." One could say that the boy misconceives what a biological death is—and the misconception is very touching. But perhaps a better reading would have it that, for a long time, the idea of his father was the anticipation that he would come home for supper. The confusion that he experiences now, even in the face of what he knows as indisputable fact, has a no-less irrefutable history.

We are close to understanding the main implication of a statement offered in my last chapter, that love is always form of memory. It would be most unfortunate if, by that statement, one inferred that love involved some recollection in tranquility of all moments in which we felt love. The logic is circular, and the interpretation is not particularly helpful in articulating how complicated love is. Freud's best dream for what interpretation could accomplish involves "reconstruction," which really can't be completed, and could be doomed from the start (tragically), because of the fallibility of our memory. At so stratospheric a level of interpretation, does it help us to think about how love, as reconstruction, is probably how we love? Is Freud just trying to confuse us?

The tragic world-view of Oedipus comes to mind just at this moment: there are so few things that are certain in life; it's quite tragic that we are so certain about anything in life. Actually, we can't be absolutely certain that Oedipus loved Jocasta: she didn't raise him; when he married her, he had "won" her and the Theban throne like lottery prizes; and we have rather little information about how husband (son) and wife (mother) got along in their domestic life. I suspect that Oedipus truly loved Merope, his mother in Corinth, but I don't have data to prove it. Based on the Theban plays altogether, Oedipus was capable of vast love (and extreme rage), as his relationships with Antigone and his sons attest. He is as complicated as any of us, and his problem lay in certainties that inevitably bring him to hazard: what can we possibly conclude from so much grim experience?

No one wants "ambivalent" love. Spouses and children would object to the sophisticated, professorial sort who says, "I love you, provided that you understand that all love is ambivalent." As we know, psychological sophistication is simply not good for a rhetoric of love. So, in expedient fashion, we pronounce love as if our ambivalence didn't exist, despite vast evidence (Sophocles' Theban plays, personal history, Freud's writings) which suggests that the course of an affection is usually rocky, not a just-so story, nothing like a dream in midsummer. Tragedy lurks in the difference between what we know about emotional ambivalence and how we ignore it for compelling reasons.

Maybe it isn't necessary that our world view be tragic; love actually helps us believe that tragedy is not our fate, and we certainly would prefer to think so. But aren't we reentering a vicious cycle when we indulge that preference? Love as a nostrum is a fantasy, but no one in their right mind would refuse such a drug. Likewise: to say, "I love you without ambivalence," is a fantastical statement, but we want to hear precisely those words, and will go to desperate lengths to believe them when we hear them. Freud, via Sophocles, tries to tell us about this morbid, cyclical, and viciously tragic state of affairs. The Oedipus complex is an obsession with tragic recurrence, and Freud will visit tragedy again in his career.

The Oedipus story is just a prelude.

After *The Interpretation*, at a watershed in his career, Freud considers not tragedy, but a mythic transformation.

Three

Narcissus

CRITIC CHRISTOPHER LASCH once referred to the culture of narcissism in his contemporary America, in the late 1970s. By narcissism, he meant something different from egotism or arrogance. He spoke of a society that suffered a "void within;" it subscribed to the "world view of the resigned," and in the "banality of pseudo-self-awareness" that characterized so much of its self-congratulation, the culture (i.e., Americans, but really every Western man and woman) trivialized personal relations in the process of shattering faith in the regeneration of life. Lasch's *Culture of Narcissism* couldn't be recommended as reading for pleasure, unless one delighted in pain. Today, more than a quarter century since Lasch wrote, do we say that the culture of narcissism is ours to keep?

More recently, popular author Alain de Botton has offered a (stock) metaphor for narcissism, reminiscent of Lasch's inner void, in his *Status Anxiety*: "Our 'ego' or self-conception could be pictured as a leaking balloon, forever requiring the helium of external love to remain inflated, and ever vulnerable to the smallest pinpricks of neglect." Throughout his book, de Botton avoids the word "narcissism" (he refers to our "self conception") but, in truth, he can't stop talking about it. "Our" balloon, which is the bubble of a narcissistic culture, leaks a lot, he goes on to say, and a general anxiety about detumescence or the fatal pop can't be avoided. His status anxiety refers to an anxiety of the status quo, in which the only thing we have to fear is unmet need. The culture of narcissism doesn't change; each generation describes it anew.

It would help to understand what narcissism means and why self-image is so problematic. The experience of dealing with narcissists (we don't lack for it in daily life) needs to be part of our study. So, I would ask the reader to look to his or her experience in some detail. Talk to the nearby narcissist, and you eventually must wonder, if only to yourself: "is it possible for a person to be *that* narcissistic?" Obviously, I beg the matter of what a narcissist is, but, still, we can answer the question easily. Yes, a person can be that narcissistic, and—what's more—the narcissist doesn't appear to be much troubled. To the extent that narcissism doesn't feel all that bad for some members of the vast club, perhaps Lasch overstated his case and maybe status anxiety isn't so terrible an affliction. In a culture full of narcissists, some must be pretty content. The self-satisfaction should cause us despair (as de Botton suggests; Lasch was just disgusted). Perhaps so. But if we want to understand narcissism, we shouldn't begin with a prejudice about what it is.

To love oneself, as Oscar Wilde said, is the beginning of a life-long romance, but can any such project be rosy at all times, for a lifetime? An ardent narcissist doesn't necessarily experience a void and rather enjoys self-awareness. Such is the nature of the narcissist's favorite occupation, which is self-preoccupation. At the start of a famous essay Freud wrote in 1914, his "introduction" to narcissism as he called it, he observed that self-love can have the quality of a perversion. Perversions, we should note, involve perverse delight.

⊜

A hard thing to do in reading Freud is to look past the sexual material, though it often profits us to do so. One way to understand a perversion (but not the only way) is to think about sex: the narcissist, Freud says, echoing a sexually obsessed, pre-Freudian psychological literature dating to the turn of the twentieth century, "experiences sexual pleasure in gazing at, caressing and fondling his body, till complete gratification ensues upon these activities." But narcissism relates to masturbation about as convincingly as masturbation does to blindness. A key aspect of a perversion, like that of any habit, is how hard it is to renounce. I often wonder whether it would help us, just to keep things simple, to assume that whenever Freud talks about a sexual motivation, especially when it comes to the narcissistic life, he refers to something that we must do, though we can barely explain the necessity to ourselves. Does self-love amount to an instinct that we can't stop, even if we think, rationally, that we should renounce it?

The Narcissus myths—plural, because there have been so many versions over time—all have to do with the complexity of love, and they usually also have to do with false fulfillment and inexorable consequences. Even if Narcissus was fated to love himself, he couldn't be fulfilled in that love alone, and he dies. The story stands in contrast to sentimental versions of love to which we more naturally incline, but sentimental love—in which one is fulfilled in eternal relationships with others—relates to narcissistic love as one side of a coin to the other. Freud pursues a subversive line of questioning. He's not curious about whether we are narcissistic, but how we must be: when we talk about relationships with our loved ones, do we refer to narcissistic tendencies that we'd rather not admit to having? His "On Narcissism: An Introduction" of 1914 could just as easily have been entitled "The Genesis of Any Love," but it would help to unload some of narcissism's dour connotations, like the psychiatric notion of "pathological" narcissism (a disorder of personality) and the idea that whole societies can be disordered, as Lasch and de Botton both suggest.

It's striking to me that psychiatrists and some social critics are particularly bad in explaining what essentially is a literary concept in its nuances. Regarding (status) anxiety and inner emptiness, these have been around for a long time, and narcissism simply isn't always to blame. Nevertheless, Lasch and de Botton are onto something when they refer to the centrality of narcissism, even if it appears that neither read Sigmund Freud with particular affection. Narcissism doesn't result in inner emptiness or some existential concern about one's status in the world, and it doesn't exactly help to understand narcissism as a social problem.

A culture might be superficial or hopelessly self-satisfied, and we don't lack for evidence of superficiality and auto-aggrandizement in what we call our culture. To understand narcissism in the Freudian sense, however, is to acknowledge that self-love is inescapable. We discussed tragedy and necessity in our last chapter, but when it comes to narcissism, Freud leads us to a different source. A superficial and arrogant person is merely a one-dimensional creature, and perhaps a whole culture or society can seem one-dimensional just as people can be, but the idea that narcissism is a necessary (and primordial) aspect of an individual psychology is an insight that merits a link to a complex *myth*. In nominating Narcissus as a modern hero of love, Freud did not critique culture. He wanted only to psychologize in an original way. We tend to think that Love (the capitalization seems appropriate) means that we need to get beyond ourselves. Good luck, says Freud.

I

Intention.

I want to tear down the exceptional preeminence now generally awarded to the self, and I pledge to be spurred on by concrete certainty, and not the caprice of ideological ambush or a dazzling intellectual prank. I propose to prove that personality is a mirage maintained by conceit and custom, without metaphysical foundation or visceral reality. I want to apply to literature the consequences that issue from these premises, and erect upon them an aesthetic hostile to the psychologism inherited from the last century, sympathetic to the classics, yet encouraging to today's most unruly tendencies.

Course of action.

I have noticed that, in general, the acquiescence conceded by a man in the role of reader to a rigorous dialectical linkage is no more than a slothful inability to gauge the proofs the writer adduces and a vague trust in the latter's rectitude. But once the book has been closed and the reading has dispersed, little remains in memory except a more or less arbitrary synthesis of the whole reading. To avoid this evident disadvantage, I will, in the following paragraphs, cast aside all strict and logical schemas.

The above is a young (23 year-old), acerbic, and droll Jorge Luis Borges, from an essay entitled "The Nothingness of Personality." He starts us off appropriately in our discussion on narcissism: what we know about ourselves may consist in imperfect reflections and recollections, at best. He doesn't talk about a psychology (it would be a psychology in a hall of mirrors anyway); he refers instead to "an aesthetic hostile to an old psychologism." Translated: there's a vast mirage out there, and we could call it the understanding of personality. Borges suggests that we begin with the premise, absurd though it may sound, that personality doesn't exist at all. The belief that a self must exist is the worst of today's unruly tendencies that Borges would overthrow if he could. The older Borges didn't trust Freud, but the young Borges sounds Freudian: in fact, he nicely describes Freud's own intention and course of action at a turning point in Freudian theory.

By the time he wrote about narcissism in 1914, Freud had published *The Interpretation of Dreams*, *The Psychopathology of Everyday Life*, and *Three Essays on the Theory of Sexuality*. Considering those works alone, putting aside the case studies that also added to his controversial fame, he had already conducted a shocking series of self-analyses, broached the subject of unconscious motivation, and posited a theory that adult behavior could be traced to "points of fixation" early in life, from birth to approximately age five or six. The first inkling of narcissism as a central Freudian topic can be found in his case study (published in 1910) of Daniel Paul Schreber, a Prussian judge whose autobiography, *Memoirs of My Nervous Illness*, recounts his change from Herr Doktor to "Miss Schreber," a sexual metamorphosis still astonishing to read. If there is a foreground to Freud's discussion of self-love, it has to do with work that drew him ever closer to the realization that selfhood is a kind of mirage—a tenuous construct, a very changeable image, or, as the young Borges would say, better thought of as nothing than something it isn't.

The "nothingness of personality" is worth considering whenever, as often happens in dealing with narcissistic types in particular, one doesn't quite know how to respond to them, either intellectually or emotionally. We need a clinical example to work through, and I borrow one from a book I studied in training, *Essential Papers in Narcissism* (1986). Parenthetically, as time goes on, I have thought that there are only two essential papers: the story of Narcissus and Freud's use of it. But the introduction to *Essential Papers* provides a thumbnail summary that is helpful, mainly for the last line (this summary is not the clinical example, which I'll get to in a moment):

> A handsome young man, Narcissus, was much loved the nymphs, including Echo, who was rejected by him. The Gods vowed to punish him for his callousness by causing him to fall in love with his own image in [water] ... However, the mirror image fragmented each time that Narcissus reached out to embrace it, causing him to pine away in melancholy, and ultimately to die. In his place, the nymphs found a flowering plant growing where once his body had been. A *New Yorker* cartoon shows Echo standing behind the mythic hero, who is gazing wistfully into the water as she asks, "Is there someone else, Narcissus?"

According to the cartoon, jealous Echo worries about the fidelity of Narcissus, who would never have her in the first place. Her question about who he really loves couldn't be more astute: who he loves just isn't clear to her. All that we know from the myth (and the cartoon) is that Narcissus will not love Echo.

The clinical example recapitulates Echo's quandary: "A little girl comes home from school, eager to tell her mother about some great successes. But the mother, instead of listening with pride, deflects the conversation from the child to herself, begins to talk about her own successes which overshadow those of her little daughter." This vignette, we are told, was not an isolated event between mother and daughter, but a part of a "chronic ambience"—if you will, a characteristic of the perpetual hell in their relationship. The terms of the story can be changed at will (father for mother, son for daughter, any intimate relationship will do), but perhaps the emotional experience is the same. I imagine the daughter's quiet implosion, a kind of collapse of her inner dominos. Given that no success will be admired by mother unless mother's success gets discussed, what can the daughter possibly say to her? An outside observer has the luxury of merely disliking the mother; that observer might also feel the avenging need, as I rather do, to put the mother in her place. Living inside the relationship, however, is different altogether.

While possible to imagine the daughter's response (at any age) in dramatic ways, I wonder whether her only pragmatic response is silence. She could ask, "are you so absolutely full of yourself that you can't celebrate me?" But that would be profitless, as daughters in such cases might fully understand. As I suggested earlier, the answer to the question "can you be that narcissistic?" can take myriad forms, basically all variations of "yes."

Or do we misrepresent the mother, since the vignette's characterizations of both mother and daughter are so thin? We read that the mother intended to overshadow her daughter, but would the mother acknowledge that intent? I have wondered how mother would respond if asked, "did you want to make your daughter feel vanishingly insignificant?" The answer would be no—in mother's eyes, the very suggestion of any malicious intent "to overshadow" is not only wrong, but malicious in itself. Mother *loves* daughter. She would reject any contrary claim, and regarding any outsider's inquisitiveness into the nature of their love, mother is far more likely to explode in rage than to realize once and for all: "Ah, I finally understand: I am an insufferable narcissist." If mother had arrived at a revelation of that type at any time, there would be no chronicity and no ambience.

It's better to begin with no assumptions about mother's or daughter's personality at all—which was Borges' suggestion. We shouldn't assume that mother is so terribly narcissistic that she can't love her daughter, nor should we assume that the daughter is narcissism-free. The case of mom-daughter illustrates why Freud, rightly, took on narcissism as a "frontier" concept. The Narcissus myth, even in the bare form described several paragraphs before, is not about self-love so much as the labor of any kind of love. Sometimes you hope, like Echo, that you might ignite a lover's interest. Sometimes, you think that love is reciprocated in some way. And, at last, when love fails or doesn't quite fulfill expectations, you wonder what can be learned from an experience that is so painfully hard to forget. Regarding the Narcissus myths in their particulars, we will have more to say later, but we aren't quite done with the case at hand.

Whether the daughter is a little girl or very much bigger and (presumably) better able to defend herself, I wonder about her own narcissistic yearning, which adults-as-children can feel as acutely as a child. Maybe, in fact, more acutely: a vast number of patients and people have told me, in no uncertain terms, that they were unique and powerful in every other context except with their mother. Another group of people report in no less uncertain terms that they were unique and powerful in every other context except with their father. What do we conclude from such reports? Rather than one narcissism, we have two, but two equals some vanishing quantity in terms what is communicated between children and parents. Maybe the actual drama has to do with how people don't meet the needs of those closest to them, not out of narcissistic malice, but because of something fundamental in human personality.

The last sentence could be considered pessimistic, even objectionable when it comes to parents loving their children and children their parents, but Freud would say that some impressions of personality are driven by how we want life to be. I'm not sure what an unconditional love free of all narcissistic taint might be, because such a love strikes me as surreal, and certainly not the kind of love that I see either in clinical practice or in daily life. To be clear, there are endless testaments of unconditional love; there is love that moves one to the very soul; but a love free of narcissism Freud will not buy, maybe for compelling reasons that we should examine. In our example, daughter wanting to break through to mother (or break her in half) could well be her fantasy. That she fails, but persists in wanting to break through, is mythological material, like the eternally unrequited love of both Echo and Narcissus. Here's the kicker: the daughter loves her mother very much.

II

In London, towards the end of his life, Freud scribbled a meditation relevant to all work on narcissism that had occupied him for the preceding three decades:

August 3 [1938]. —The ultimate ground of all intellectual inhibitions and all inhibitions of work seems to be the inhibition of masturbation in childhood. But perhaps it goes deeper; perhaps it is not its inhibition by external influences but its unsatisfying nature in itself. There is always something lacking for complete discharge and satisfaction–*en attendant toujour quelquechose qui ne venait point* [always waiting for something which never came]—and this missing part, the reaction of orgasm, manifests itself in equivalents in other spheres, in *absences*, outbreaks of laughing, weeping . . . and perhaps other ways. —Once again infantile sexuality has fixed a model in this.

We shouldn't believe too literally that inhibition of a private pleasure in childhood results in some impediment to meaningful work in life; one worries that people will encourage their kids inappropriately. To "masturbate and, therefore, work better" is not Freud's prescription. His meditation goes much deeper indeed, and the real problem doesn't have to do with moral or social scruples about self-gratification. Rather: masturbation in the end doesn't satisfy like the real thing. For every action or pleasure (in love) there is reaction (ideally, a partner's reciprocation), and reaction is part of the magic of intimacy. Without it, sooner or later, there will be evidence (symptoms) of a void in pleasure. I don't think that Freud discusses what the psychologists of his era called "auto-eroticism" (masturbation being one instance of it) so much as he addresses a fundamental problem in narcissism. If narcissistic tendencies are so unfulfilling, why have them at all? In essay after essay from roughly 1910 to his death in 1939, he will seek his answers in the individual past.

To this day, the concept of sexuality at any time before puberty strikes the ear as odd, however much we believe that we have assimilated Freud into our sensibility. Regarding very early sexuality, Freud said in his *New Introductory Lectures* (1933), "enough can be seen in children if one knows how to look," but what do we really observe? Here are some random instances:

For no apparent reason at the dinner table, a six-year-old boy squeezes his mother's breast with the comment "it's a boob."

My wife and I wonder whether it is appropriate to have our naked five-year-old girl sit in the same bathtub with our naked six-year-old boy. At bath-time, that is.

An odd line picked up at school (first grade), with more rhyme than beauty: "There's a place in France/where the naked ladies dance. /The men don't care / if they see their underwear."

Or: Freud's still-astonishing association, from *Three Essays*, that the sated infant pulling away from the nipple looked like an adult's *après* consummation glow.

Freud's developmental organization of the "libido" (for which we should read "erotic drive") into phases of progressively complex interests—oral (ages 0-2), anal (ages 2-4), and genital (roughly age 5, all the ages being approximate)—was based on such observations, in part. But even the most informed among us might think that a child's sexual interest is very different from an adult's sexual wishes, and might contend that Freud missteps in equating the two. If anything, the sexual experience of childhood seems fragmentary—a boob, a bit of nakedness or underwear, a titillation with something they know not of. The question of when the fragments cohere into a real awareness of sexuality remains open. Freud thought such awareness happened very early, and said so to the consternation of his contemporaries, but then he ran into a different, conceptual problem.

Even if body parts are associated with their respective pleasures and are erotogenic in turn, these parts do not amount to a whole self. As Freud put it in the Narcissism essay of 1914 in a key passage, "we are bound to suppose that a *unity* comparable to the ego cannot exist in the individual from the start; the ego *has to be developed*." Richard Wollheim, one of Freud's best readers, has described how Freud rejected the thought that he was just another sex writer in a long line. Among others in Freud's time, Havelock Ellis in *Studies in the Psychology of Sex* and Richard von Krafft-Ebing in *Psychopathia Sexualis* (the latter being a jaw-droppingly pansexual document, readily available in a modern translation) had established sex as preternaturally interesting material, which, of course, it always is. But those who would read Freud as another Ellis or Krafft-Ebing simply misunderstand the psychoanalytic project, says Wollheim:

> It cannot . . . be too often insisted that, though Freud heavily emphasized the element of sexuality in human nature, he utterly rejected pansexualism, which he regarded as a travesty of his theory. . . . Indeed one of the most

significant reasons why Freud did lay such emphasis on sexuality—that is, its importance as a causal factor in neurosis—required him to postulate another group of instincts over and against sexuality. The explanatory value of the concept of sexuality in mental disorder depended on its not enjoying a monopoly in the domain of the instincts.

Yes, but if not sex, then what instinct could be anywhere near as interesting?

⊟

Freud responds with his dense opening to "On Narcissism: An Introduction." Unlike his student Otto Rank, whose discussion of the origin of personality (in his *Truth and Reality*) begins with a momentous and lucid epigraph from Leo Tolstoy—"The most important event in the life of a man is the moment when he becomes conscious of his own ego"—Freud gives us a cold dissertation, with too much in it:

The term narcissism is derived from clinical description and was chosen by Paul Näcke in 1899 to denote the attitude of a person who treats his own body in the same way in which the body of a sexual object is ordinarily treated–who looks at it, that is to say, strokes it and fondles it till he obtains complete satisfaction through those activities. Developed to this degree, narcissism has the significance of a perversion that has absorbed the whole of the subject's sexual life, and it will consequently exhibit the characteristics which we expect to meet with in the study of the perversions.

Psycho-analytic observers were subsequently struck by the fact that individual features of the narcissistic attitude are found in many people who suffer from other disorders . . . and finally it seemed probable that an allocation of the libido such as deserved to be described as narcissism might be present far more extensively, and that it might claim a place in the regular course of human sexual development. Difficulties in the psycho-analytic work upon neurotics led to the same presupposition, for it seemed as though this kind of narcissistic attitude in them constituted one of the limits to their susceptibility to influence. Narcissism in this sense would not be a perversion, but the libidinal complement to the egoism of the instinct of self-preservation, a measure of which may justifiably be attributed to every living creature.

In these lines, narcissism metamorphoses from a perversion to a madness (a neurosis not susceptible to influence or therapy) to an aspect of all life. Why does Freud introduce this Protean subject? And why is he so slippery in discussing it? An insightful Mark Edmundson, in his *Towards Reading Freud* (1990), says that Freud is uninterested in the likes of Paul Näcke and preoccupied only to emphasize his own psychoanalysis as the royal path to understanding the mind: "'Narcissism,' Freud is saying, was born in the year psychoanalysis was born, 1899, when Freud completed the manuscript of *The Interpretation of Dreams*," Edmundson writes, "For 'Paul Näcke,' one is tempted to read, 'not Ovid,' 'not Milton,' 'not any of the hundreds of writers who have made use of the Narcissus myth.'" If we take these comments to heart, everyone, maybe even the mythic Narcissus, seems to have gotten narcissism all wrong.

Knowing something about poor Paul Näcke helps me, however, in reading Freud from line to line. In 1899, Näcke published a study of 1,500 insane patients under his care (he was the superintendent of an asylum outside of Leipzig); he was curious to know how many of them demonstrated a "narcissistic attitude." By way of background, mainly to understand more about the attitude, we should turn to Havelock Ellis, who wrote about the "autoerotic" fascination that people have with their own bodies, first in a short paper in 1898 (which Näcke read), then at greater length in the first volume of his *Studies in the Psychology of Sex*. From *Studies*, consider the following description, which is neither Ellis's nor Näcke's (actually it was written in a letter by a Dr. C. H. Hughes to Ellis), but it captures the attitude in question: "men . . . absorbed in admiration of their own manly forms, and their sexual organs, and women, likewise, absorbed in admiration of their own mammæ and physical proportions, especially of the limbs." Is such self-admiration normal or insane?

To the best that Näcke could ascertain, only four men and one woman (of 1,500) were narcissistic in this way. In turn, Ellis wondered whether Näcke had happened upon a phenomenon more common among the sane, a sensibility (here is Hughes again, quoted by Ellis) "allied to that æsthetic sense which admires the nude in art." That aesthetic sense, I think, is remarkably common: I see it when people glance at themselves in mirrors admiringly—for whatever reason. Is there a self-regard that isn't absolutely sexual? Freud's first paragraph, especially the coy phrase "complete gratification," suggests that narcissism necessarily involves the stroking and fondling of organs. By the second paragraph, narcissism is clearly something different, a self-regard possibly related both to self-love and other love. Freud asks two related questions: has he seen narcissism among his neurotic patients and, as Havelock Ellis wondered, could it be normal?

Freud thought that some neuroses were inaccessible to psychoanalysis, beyond all "susceptibility to influence." He referred to them as paraphrenias (or "the narcissistic neuroses"). Today, we speak of the "psychoses," among them schizophrenia. When Freud refers to the narcissistic attitude in schizophrenia, he relies on commonplace observations in schizophrenia, not on Paul Näcke's more esoteric interests. As is familiar to any psychiatrist, the schizophrenic attitude is mortifying to see, and narcissism doesn't quite describe it: a very ill schizophrenic in an interview room barely acknowledges the room, never mind the interviewer, and if that is the extreme of narcissism, then it is a universe in which love of others—sexual or otherwise—is a logical and emotional impossibility.

If "narcissistic attitude" fails as a description, a worse failure is "the libidinal complement to the egoism of the instinct of self-preservation." I suggest that the reader re-read the second paragraph quoted above, only to gag at that phrase, which helps very little in characterizing any narcissism, despite the fact that it is often quoted as if its meaning is perfectly clear. (I think of Freud's own misgivings about his essay as a whole, expressed to a colleague, that "On Narcissism" was "a difficult birth, and it bears all the marks of it.") An instinct for self-preservation may be common to all living things, and Freud wants to say that narcissism is an instinct of that variety. He doesn't quite say it. Five or more years will pass before he does say it with conviction, in books like *Beyond the Pleasure Principle*, *The Ego and the Id*, and *The New Introductory Lectures*.

The highly packed phrase, "libidinal complement to the egoism of the instinct of self-preservation," can only be broken into its parts; the whole of it is simply too cumbersome. Narcissism is not Havelock Ellis's auto-erotism, but there is a sexual aspect to it. Narcissism is egocentric, just as self-preservation is, by definition. There is an instinct that has everything to with sex but precedes it in the life of the mind. The ego must come into existence, and the ego eventually must fall in love, but these are mutually exclusive propositions in some cases, as in schizophrenia. So: what is narcissism for the rest of us? If we think back to the mother responding to her daughter's news of success: she's a narcissist, but that is the nature of her love. Whatever is wrong in the mother-daughter relationship, the narcissist-mother thinks there is something wrong with her daughter if she can't return her love. We notice in broad terms, Freud would say, two instincts in mother: one directed at daughter (whom she loves) and the other directed back at herself—"the more one is employed, the more the other becomes depleted," though he acknowledges that some parents forgo the need for constant adoration (a "high phase" of maturity, he says). But, in tracing Freud step by step, we should observe that the ego couldn't have come into existence merely because we are loved by others or, for that matter, not loved by them.

Regarding what Borges called the self's preeminence, at some point, we must have been narcissistic ourselves to have an ego in the first place, but not so mammothly narcissistic as to become as ill, as in the pure tragedy of schizophrenia. Narcissism, ego, and love are as tightly knitted as the mother and daughter in our example. Yet in the end, my sample case only hints at the most interesting aspect in a narcissistic world. Consider the narcissists that you meet—say, a hateful boss, whose condescension is endured only because you realize he's a narcissist beyond all hope of change. Such a person may disturb your sensibility, but fortunately you have two options, the first more practical than the second. You could appease him while inwardly acknowledging that he is a troglodyte. Or, you could assert your own ego, resist any wound that he could inflict on you, and in so doing get fired. He says like a Freudian father, "I disown you," and you rejoice in no longer having to contend with his delusions of ownership. A condition of pleasure lasts for as long as saved money holds out, at which point you would reconsider all options, including groveling, *except* for a renunciation of narcissism. The last point is perhaps most central to Freud's analysis, and most difficult to grasp: narcissism does not diminish in the course of countless unfortunate jobs and other opportunities for a loss in self-esteem. In fact, one could argue that self-esteem is almost beside the point in Freud's conception of narcissism. You could go back to work for the same boss, returning yourself to the very hell you just left, and *still* be a narcissist in your own reinvented way. The troll won't defeat me, you mutter to yourself.

We can revise the above scenario to bring it closer to home. A parent says, "You are not my child. I disown you." Here I might apply an analysis by logician Herbert Fingarette (from an essay on self-deception in psycho-analysis): "Taken as a biological statement, the first sentence ["You are not my child"] is false. Taken as a disavowal of identification which the second sentence ["I disown you"] reveals it to be, *the first sentence can be lived up to or not*—but it is not false (my emphasis)." Unlike statements of truth or falsehood, narcissism operates at a different level. Fingarette suggests that we think of any number of analogous claims, like "I am an American" or "I am no longer a Democrat." They are statements of belief and self-definition. "You are not my child. I disown you," far more fiercely than "I am no longer a Democrat," is the angry voice of narcissism crying in a wilderness. The rage has to do with the wilderness not cooperating, and the disowned offspring not only doesn't matter; he or she no longer exists. Narcissism is the drive or instinct for self-definition in spite of the world, enacted repeatedly over a lifetime, regardless of reality or the real status of our relationships. Bosses, parents, and other people relentlessly do find a way into our heads, needless to say. How someone else's narcissism gets tangled in ours is so complicated a matter that we might as well make a mythology of it, except that the myth of Narcissus already exists.

III

Psychiatry no longer worries about the mythic or literary origin of its greater concepts—we address Narcissus in this chapter, but Eros (Love), Thanatos (Death), Ananke (Necessity), and Melancholia (Grief) are some others. Actually, modern psychiatric parlance doesn't have much to do with any extant myth, but that is a problem with the modern parlance, not the problem in Freud. Part of Freud's "charm" (it is not too strong a word) is the ease with which he invokes anecdote, story, and myth in defense of what he has to say. Some have found his strategy as suspicious as it is alluring, as in this off-the-cuff comment by philosopher Ludwig Wittgenstein:

> [Freud] is extraordinary. —Of course, he's full of fishy thinking & his charm & the charm of his subject is so great that you may be easily fooled. He always stresses what great forces in the mind, what strong prejudices work against the idea of psycho-analysis. But he never says what an enormous charm the idea has for people, just as it has for Freud himself. There may be strong prejudices against uncovering something nasty, but sometimes it is infinitely more *attractive* than repulsive. Unless you think *very* clearly, psycho-analysis is a dangerous & foul practice, & it's done no end of harm & comparatively little good.

The charge of foulness is very deep here; the attraction or revulsion of Freudian insight is less the crux of Wittgenstein's complaint than his insight (to paraphrase him) that a logical investigation or analysis is precisely not what psychoanalysis does. Freud wouldn't seem so fishy if his readers weren't so often swayed to the point of astonishing conviction by his formulations— hence, one speaks of his charm, as opposed to his logical force. Freud says that narcissism is something we observe in everyday life and in clinical practice. That is a true statement (we intuit it as true), but we could just as easily say that there are remarkably arrogant people in the world, that there might even be a form of arrogance that amounts to a self-destructive disease. But narcissism is not arrogance; the former is a more complicated concept, and unless we think very clearly, we can confuse it for the latter, which is uncomplicated.

Narcissism is like the concept of a perfect map as Lewis Carroll once described it—it is a map as large as what it depicts. Freud doesn't explain who the literary Narcissus was at the start of "On Narcissism," because it suffices to allude to a figure whose self-attitude can be gleaned only by reading the Narcissus story in all its suggestiveness.

Freud's strategy should be familiar to us, because of our examination of Oedipus. In sum: it must be that _____ is an aspect of all human psychology. Fill in the blank as you see fit: the Oedipus complex, narcissism, and, later in his career, Eros or the pleasure principle, and Thanatos or the death drive. Freud liked to think about what he called the indefiniteness of the greatest story telling, and when he refers to a character from fiction to "introduce" an idea about mental operation, he appropriates indefiniteness in his theory. This maneuver seems peculiar, and yet Freud rather liked and indulged it. When he talks about our "instincts" or "drives," as he does throughout his career, we intuit that they must exist–nothing could be *more true* than an urge to mate, for example. But just at such moments (when we think we're close to a tangible truth), Freud pulls us back, and redirects us to indefiniteness. "The theory of instincts is, so to say, our mythology," he famously stated in *The New Introductory Lectures*, "Instincts are mythical entities magnificent in their indefiniteness." The Narcissus myth is like a theory of instinct in that sense, and by "indefinite," he also means "irrefutable" or an instance of what Wittgenstein calls fishy thinking full of charm. Even without mentioning any aspect of the myth as it has been passed down over centuries, and to a far greater degree than Havelock Ellis, Paul Näcke, or Otto Rank, Freud steals a story for himself. Are we, then, attracted to Freud as theorist, to the truth of narcissism (the concept), or to the inherent charm of the understanding the psyche by way of stories told about it?

It would help us if we could turn to the Narcissus story as a single document like the text of *Oedipus the King*. Ovid's *Metamorphoses* is the most famous source, so we might consult its famous Narcissus (and Echo) passage in Book III, and begin to read it in search of relevance to Freud and psychology. We don't lack for abbreviated renditions of Ovid's narrative, as in the one cited earlier in this chapter. The pity is that the Narcissus myth can't be found in one place, as Otto Rank discussed in his "Contribution to Narcissism" of 1910 and *The Double* of 1915 (both of which Freud read) and as Havelock Ellis elaborated eloquently in "The Conception of Narcissism" written some years after "On Narcissism." However closely we read Ovid's or any other version, we come to realize that the Narcissus myth—adapted, co-opted, and rewritten over time—is larger than any given source, and therefore hard (but not impossible) to map.

The version by Ovid (in Latin, dating to roughly 8 BCE) is central, but we might consider two Greek variations next to Ovid. Peculiar to the *Metamorphoses* is the combination of several stories into one. Three principle figures are involved: the prophet Tiresias (whom we know from Sophocles), Echo, and Narcissus himself. Ovid says that the gods cursed Tiresias because he didn't answer the question "who enjoys sex more, men or women?" to their satisfaction. His answer ("women") angered the goddess Saturnalia (also known as Juno) in particular, and she summarily blinded him. Her husband Jove, who thought Tiresias was dead right, gave him the power of foresight to match his wife's curse. Blind but newly gifted, Tiresias's first prophecy, when a beautiful boy named Narcissus is born to Liriope the water nymph, was that the child will live to ripe age only if he does not know himself. Tiresias's prognostication is vague—Ovid speaks of his "empty words"—but after the death of Narcissus, Tiresias's fame spread widely. His power of prophecy becomes the stuff of legend, but his story is a sidebar in Ovid's version.

Echo, described as a nymph who talks too much, is fated by Juno to repeat only the last part of others' sentences. Previously, Echo would talk at such unsolicited length as to prevent Juno from checking on her philandering husband Jove. Whenever Echo spoke, Jove's various nymphs always had time to flee before Juno could catch them in clandestine acts. Juno takes her revenge on Echo. The endless talker is condemned to be an obligate listener; her curse is that she cannot speak until spoken to. Her verbal echoes are precisely what catch Narcissus's attention when the two of them finally meet. Narcissus is as beautiful as art to Echo, but Ovid depicts Narcissus, at least at the start, as impassive, almost inert, someone who returns no one's love.

Male nymphs, female nymphs, boys, girls, men, and women are nothing to him, because he shuns all company. He is sixteen years old. Ovid mentions his adolescent and vaguely condescending pride, but he seems more oblivious than vain.

The long-awaited encounter between Echo and Narcissus is a pure parody of communication. In my comments thus far, I have borrowed from critic Kenneth Knoespel's thoughtful discussion in his *Narcissus and The Development of Personal History*, and I borrow his screenplay-like version of Ovid as well:

NARCISSUS	Is anyone here?
ECHO	Here!
NARCISSUS	Come!
ECHO	Come!
NARCISSUS	Why do you run from me?
ECHO	Why do you run from me?

Echo sustains her paramour's interest only to the degree that she is misunderstood, as Knoespel has remarked. In the exchange between them, Ovid offers tacit commentary on love dialogue as good as any literary critic or psychologist: meaning operates at one level; what is said operates at another. Whenever one party is interested and the other is not, the levels could not be more separate, but, still, Echo tries to love Narcissus. He rejects her, and she undergoes a terrible anorexia. She becomes a skeleton of her former self, and vanishes in the woods, which seem to be all around in Ovid's descriptions.

The number of Narcissus's disaffected lovers turns out to be quite large. The goddess Nemesis, whom poet Ted Hughes nicely calls "the corrector," hears one male nymph's prayer. Retribution is in the air; just as Juno wrought havoc on Tiresias and Echo, Nemesis will punish Narcissus. I mention Hughes, because his *Tales from Ovid* nicely translates the nymph's prayer into a fierce lament with eye-for-eye requirements: "'Let Narcissus love and suffer /As he has made us suffer. /Let him, like us, love and know that it is hopeless. /And let him, like Echo, perish of anguish.'/Nemesis, the corrector, /Heard this prayer and granted it." The water-reflection scene follows, with Narcissus perfectly struck—"dumbstruck," I suppose, would be the colloquial form of Ovid's great Latin word *adstupet*—by a resplendently beautiful image as he takes a drink from a calm pool of water. "Not recognising himself /He wanted only himself," Hughes says.

One can't help notice an ensuing change in the language, regardless of the translation one uses. Ovid now writes as if he were noticing Narcissus for the first time—he tells of beauty like a statue carved from Parian marble; locks of hair worthy of divinity; an ivory neck, cool white skin, and subtlest hue of color to the cheek; a prone position that invites all variety of expectation. The description is beautiful, Latinate in every sense, and equivocal in one important aspect: Narcissus should recognize himself, but doesn't. Whether he is further along in self-knowledge at the end of the long scene (when he dies unfulfilled) is open to question. He dies before manhood, hardly lives to old age, and while true that after a good number of lines, he arrives at a realization ("Oh, I am he!"), nevertheless the insight seems too late and suspect, not the kind of self-knowing that we would call profound, and maybe not what Tiresias meant by "knowing oneself."

In Pausanias's *Descriptions of Greece*, which postdates Ovid by a roughly a century, we have the marvelously practical commentary that *no one in his right mind*, whether in myth or not, would fail to realize that he saw a reflection of his own face in water. Regarding the significance of a self-reflection, all readings of Narcissus from Ovid through to Freud scatter in different directions. Pausanias offers that Narcissus had a twin sister who died. In mourning, he sits next to the water, and "knowing that it was his reflection the he saw, but in spite of this knowledge" finds relief in the likeness. In this version, Narcissus lives, and, regarding the Ovidian metamorphosis of Narcissus into a flower, Pausanias simply asserts that the flower must have been there before. Not incidentally, a school of thought maintains that the Narcissus myth primarily explains the Narcissus flower, which grows in or near water, tends to droop over water, and is poisonous when ingested, with mind-altering effects. Regarding what myths or stories "explain" in our lives, we will have much more to say as this book proceeds; we would be justified for the moment to wonder what the Narcissus myth is trying to explain, precisely. Pausanias says that Ovid missed the Proustian point, as it were: the beautiful boy in love mourns, and love (in the largest sense) attempts to recover what is lost.

In a second Greek variation attributed to Conon, a contemporary of Ovid's, a man named Ameinias loves Narcissus, but Narcissus rejects him. Narcissus is beautiful, but "proud" towards Eros, the god of love. Narcissus's pride is the problem in this version; by contrast, Ameinias (not Narcissus) serves as an exemplar of what one does for love. When Narcissus, the rejector, sends Ameinias the gift of a sword, Ameinias kills himself with it, and dies for love. As he dies he curses Narcissus. Later, Narcissus sees himself in water, becomes "confused," and kills himself in the belief that to be loved by the unacceptable Ameinias was a kind of unjust torment. Narcissus finds his watery image pleasant, and he indeed he falls in love with himself, but only suicide will end his confusion and his curious pain. The descriptions of rapture and evanescence that we find in Ovid—the reaching for an image in water only to watch it ripple away, the Pygmalion adoration of an image—are absent in Conon. Narcissus "became in a strange way his own lover," the author remarks, unsympathetically. After his death, the Narcissus flower grows from Narcissus's spilled blood. Conon says that those who heard the story decided it was wise to honor and fear Eros in public ceremonies, and to make endless sacrifices to Eros in private.

Especially in light of the variations, it would be very hard to conclude that the myth of Narcissus for Freud meant something straightforward. Well into the Renaissance, the Narcissus theme had moral dimensions: self-love was folly as all illusion was folly; the tale of Narcissus warned us against our own easy tendency towards folly. By the nineteenth century, however, in the wake of Narcissus stories by Calderón de la Barca in Spain, John Milton and Edward Young in England, Jean-Jacques Rousseau in France, and a host of others, the Narcissus theme had become an ink-blot test for anyone studying the nature and origin of personality. Looking back at the ancient sources, if we merely describe what we read, the figure of Narcissus embodies all the themes that Freud thinks are germane to love. Narcissus seems an unwitting child in an adult's eternal game; he is straight, gay, bisexual, asexual, beautiful like a flower, poisonous like the same flower, alive, dead, innocent, guilty, or what have you. Freud's narcissism was multivalent in the same way: the character of Narcissus as handed down from ancient sources, as would have occurred to a man of wide learning like Freud, was as complex as the meaning of self-love for Freud.

IV

I should reintroduce a theoretical term to move my discussion beyond the trivial statement that "the Narcissus theme is complicated" (I suppose I've made no more of a point so far). The term is "ambivalence," which, in the domain of psychiatric thinking, means that contraries need not exclude one another, especially when it comes to the emotions. To love and hate at the same time is to be ambivalent; fulfillment and the lack of it are linked as well; sometimes, a person can be conflicted and ambivalent about whom to love at all. Narcissus, who rejects all love, also rejects the idea of conflicted emotions in love, though he receives an education on ambivalence literally to the death. The lesson of his own watery reflection, to put a Freudian point on it, is not that he can't have himself erotically or emotionally, but rather that erotic or emotional possession is more than the realization of desire. The narcissism of Narcissus, Echo, Ameinias, and maybe even the Juno and Jove has to do with a belief that desires can be realized, yet the consistent theme in the myths is the persistence of desire due to frustration of that belief. Freud wrestles with this fundamentally ambivalent question: do love and self-love occupy the same place in the emotional life? The central section of "Of Narcissism" (section II of III) builds a complicated case that the choices we make in love are narcissistic at their most selfless. "A strong egoism," he says, "is a protection against disease, but in the last resort we begin to love in order that we may not fall ill, and must fall ill if, in consequence of frustration, we cannot love." It's not clear what specific illness awaits us if we don't love, but we know from personal experience that a loveless life is very hard to endure. "Strong egoism" presumably means something similar to narcissism; if an egoism were strong enough, one wonders whether one could survive a life-long loneliness somehow.

If we examine human behavior, Freud continues, we observe two broad categories of love, what he calls "narcissistic" and "anaclitic" types. The narcissistic type is illustrated by the instance of the beautiful woman, about whom Freud sounds at once condescending and envious: "It is only themselves that such women love with an intensity comparable to that of the man's love for them. Nor does their need lie in the direction of loving, but of being loved; and the man who fulfills this condition is the one who finds favour with them. The importance of this type of woman for the erotic life of mankind is to be rated very high." Freud relies on us to recall people from our own experience who would meet such a high standard of vanity; beauty and gender barely seem important, since the peculiar intensity of their narcissism matters above all. Actually, we could rewrite Freud to read, "the importance of any narcissist, man or woman, for the erotic life is to be rated very high," since he assumes that love must always be narcissistic in some way. Regarding the so-called anaclitic variety, a better translation would be love "dependent on (literally, 'propped against') others," but anaclitic love seems an afterthought, just another type of love in the service of self:

A person may love:

(1) According to the narcissistic type: (a) What he is himself (actually himself); (b) What he once was; (c) What he would like to be; (d) Someone who was once part of himself.

(2) According to the anaclitic type: (a) The woman who tends; (b) The man who protects.

and those substitutes which succeed them one after another.

Who are the "substitutes" which succeed one after another in the erotic life? The answer is: Me, those who remind me of Me, some version Me in the future, those who look after and protect Me. Of two things we may be certain. First, Freud's is no Pauline love that "vaunteth not itself." But, second (and not unlike Paul to the Corinthians), Freud is interested in a "whole knowledge" of love. Thinking back to his August 3 meditation, which I quoted earlier, Freud said that infantile sexuality fixes a model for human dissatisfaction. It shouldn't surprise us that infantile narcissism also fixes the model for other emotion in our lives.

In the best of his many side observations in "On Narcissism," Freud says that it is very hard for a person to give up a satisfaction he or she has once known. He refers to the state of bliss that was "primary narcissism," which occurs at the birth of the ego. We know that the state once existed, because we can observe its vestiges or mnemonic clues in our lives, Freud says. I quote the following passage (from chapter II of "On Narcissism") at some length; it merits study right up to the point when we wonder whether Freud, like Socrates, should be condemned on grounds of being dangerous:

The primary narcissism of children which we have assumed and which forms one of the postulates of our theories of the libido, is less easy to grasp by direct observation than to confirm by inference from elsewhere. If we look at the attitude of affectionate parents towards their children, we have to recognize that it is a revival and reproduction of their own narcissism, which they have long since abandoned. . . . [T]hey are under a compulsion to ascribe every perfection to the child—which sober observation would find no occasion to do—and to conceal and forget all his shortcomings. (Incidentally, the denial of sexuality in children is connected with this.) Moreover, they are inclined to suspend in the child's favour the operation of all the cultural acquisitions which their own narcissism has been forced to respect, and to renew on his behalf the claims to privileges which were long ago given up by themselves. *The child shall have a better time than his parents; he shall not be subject to the necessities which they have recognized as paramount in life. Illness, death, renunciation of enjoyment, restrictions on his own will, shall not touch him; the laws of nature and of society shall be abrogated in his favour; he shall once more really be the centre and core of creation* —'His Majesty the Baby', *as we once fancied ourselves.* The child shall fulfill those wishful dreams of the parents which they never carried out—the boy shall become a great man and a hero in his father's place, and the girl shall marry a prince as a tardy compensation for her mother. At the most touchy point in the narcissistic system, the immortality of the ego, which is so hard pressed by reality, security is achieved by taking refuge in the child. Parental love, which is so moving and at bottom so childish, is nothing but the parents' narcissism born again, which, transformed into object-love, unmistakably reveals its former nature. [My emphasis]

The best evidence for narcissism as a central concept in psychology can be found in the love of another person that seems most Pauline and pure. We barely need to read any further in "On Narcissism," since what he has to say here, at the close of his section II, is so important for our purposes.

⁊

Shouldn't a person be ego-less at least with respect to his or her children? A parent says, with leonine fierceness, that she loves her child unconditionally—which is to say, not exactly as she loves her spouse, since spousal love is always more complicated, not a marriage of fairy-tale nature. She is relentless in her view: even if her love must yield to the contingencies of life (that she can't guarantee the future success of her children any more than she can guarantee their immortality), still, she won't desist in being aggressive on their behalf. Most importantly, her will has nothing to do with her own narcissism. On the contrary, what mother wouldn't gladly sacrifice her life, selfhood, and well-being for her child? Freud's observes that an unconditional and eternal love such as a parent feels cannot have arisen de novo, just as the ego could not have come from nothing.

The contrast with spousal love is illuminating. What countless subtractions from ideal love have been suffered in the course of an adult marriage, if it survives at all? Samuel Johnson, reflecting on how people believe that marriage is unhappy, thought to amend that dark view with another that seems even blacker at first: "marriage is not commonly unhappy, otherwise than as life is unhappy . . . most who complain of connubial miseries, have as much satisfaction as their nature would have admitted, or their conduct procured in any other condition." Johnson broaches what Freud calls the "touchy point" (a grand understatement) in any narcissistic system. A child might never be better off than his parents; a child necessarily becomes subject to life's necessities; illness, death, renunciation of enjoyment, and restrictions do touch him. Likewise in marriage, the concept of it differs from its actuality, unless one's concept is coldly realistic. Against the onslaught of reality, there is narcissism, narcissistic fantasy, and narcissistic love—all of which begins to look very attractive.

Freud could have said that we love our children as we were once loved by our parents, but he did not. He says that one's own narcissism doesn't pass like a phase. At the very point in human development when we recognize a child's innocence, the purity of the child's joys and sorrows, and the seeming infinitude of possibilities in his or her life, Freud asks, What do we conclude about ourselves, on the basis of our own experience long after infancy and childhood? We stick to narcissism as fiercely as we do—which is the same reason why we love our children as much as we do—because of the ego. A narcissistic ego is a redundancy (and, as a corollary, there is no ego that isn't narcissistic), because narcissism was present early, and to that earliness one returns instinctively, however fallen our current state.

Freud discusses that "return"—a type of memory—in many places. I choose one particularly eloquent expression, written about a year after "On Narcissism," in his "Thoughts for the Times on War and Death" (1915). Freud insists that people do not change, despite the flux of circumstance:

> the development of the mind shows a peculiarity which is present in no other developmental process. When a village grows into a town or a child into a man, the village and the child become lost in the town and the man. Memory alone can trace the old features in the new picture; and in fact the old materials or forms have been got rid of and replaced by new ones. It is otherwise with the development of the mind. Here one can describe a state of affairs, which has nothing to compare with it, only by saying that in this case every earlier stage of development persists alongside the later

stage which has arisen from it; here succession also involves co-existence, although it is to the same materials that the whole series of transformations has been applied. The earlier mental state may not have manifested itself for years, but none the less it is so far present that it may at any time again become the mode of expression of forces of the mind, and indeed the only one. . . . This extraordinary plasticity of mental developments is not unrestricted as regards direction; it may be described as a special capacity for involution—for regression—since it may well happen that a later and higher stage of development, once abandoned, cannot be reached again. But the primitive stages can always be re-established; the primitive mind, is, in the fullest meaning of the word, imperishable.

The core argument of *Three Essays on the Theory of Sexuality* and *Totem and Taboo* (Freud's extended study of the so-called primitive mind) could not be more succinctly expressed. "Memory alone can trace the old features in the new picture" is, for me, a very moving sentence, which clearly applies to primary narcissism, because we are always trying (so Freud says about love) to refind an early state. But the sentence imparts something more than what a theory can explain.

The development of the mind is unique in that it can "regress" to earliness. So, unlike the village that has transformed irrevocably into the town, all towns can become villages again in the life of the mind. The sentence about memory tracing old features in the new *is* an accurate statement about the mind's development, and it is possible to see the child in every adult. If every earlier stage persists alongside the later stage which has arisen from it, then what we call development is also history and recollection. The implication for any meditation on love is what touches me: to what degree we regress and remember and to what degree we move on in our lives can't be easily determined, and there is pathos in the fact that we can't parse the difference in degrees with any certainty.

≣

Freud oddly claimed that he invented psychoanalysis "because it had no literature." The statement is a particularly hard to fathom when we consider that Oedipus and Narcissus stare us in the face as we read Freud, with the names attached to his central theories, no less. If he meant that there was no *psychoanalytic* literature before him, since he was the first analyst, nevertheless the working relationship between his ideas and their sources was problematic, especially in the case of Narcissus. What was he trying to describe in "introducing" Narcissus to us once more? The cleverness of the term "narcissism" has to do with the fact that it refers us to Ovid and elsewhere. The sources don't amount to a psychology, and Freud fully realizes that they don't, so narcissism becomes his vehicle for describing the self-love that engenders "the I" or "ego" in his theory. (At a more basic level, "narcissism" is a catchy name which has endured, but the endurance and utility of the myth takes us well beyond "catchiness.")

In real life, the ego falls in love with its own productions (as we love our children), and, if the ego in question reads Freud's books, then it might consider how mature love recollects an earlier narcissism. The circularity in reasoning might bother us, as it disturbed Wittgenstein, were it not for the fact that just when we become a bit inarticulate in describing the meaning of Narcissus and narcissism, we begin to understand the utility of literary allusion for Freud.

A contemporary psychologist trained in logic (to be named later) asks a central question, which provides a follow-up to my obsession about what Freud accomplishes by his allusion to myth: "*What kind of formal system will be rich enough to provide the vehicle for internal representation?*" No question has been more troublesome for the psychological sciences to the present moment in history. "Formal system" could be a logic or a rational discourse of some type; it could also be a story, fiction, tragedy, or myth—something of magnificent indefiniteness, as Freud would say. "Internal representation," or the representation of what is inside (as when we try to describe our love), is the interest of any psychology, and its burden. Let me remind you, Freud seems to say, of Narcissus: a beauty that causes Echo her pain; a reflection in water; the painfully funny revelation "Oh! I am he!"; the strange metamorphosis Narcissus undergoes (the flower as a new life), and more: the sibling or familial aspect of love in Pausanias; the homoerotic motif in Conon. A psychological theory could try to gloss such developments in a story of love, but does it achieve evocativeness and depth of meaning? Perhaps no "formal system" is rich enough, but that does not mean that we stop looking for one.

V

Scholars say that Freud introduced narcissism to bridge the conceptual gap (a very troublesome one in the development of Freud's theory) between erotic drive directed at "objects" in the world, including lovers, and the so-called ego-directed instincts, particularly the drive for self-preservation. "On Narcissism" is a watershed moment in his general theory. After 1914, we see an evolution in his theoretical psychology from the "topography" of the mind to the "structure" of it, the latter being more complicated than a map, with sometimes violent give-and-take among its structural parts. In terms of love, what do we gain if we look deep into the eyes of the person whom we love, only to announce, "you are such a narcissist"? A great deal depends on how you read the Narcissus theme in literature. Richard Wollheim has rightly observed that the concept of narcissism fueled change in Freud as a theorist. The character of Narcissus, as fiction and theme, fueled change in Freud as a thinker about highly complex matters, love foremost among them. (As a practical matter, by the way, it would be wise not to say "you are such a narcissist" to your lover. You would be misunderstood and, probably, rejected. Or, if the lover were smart, he or she would return the compliment, because it is truth for all parties concerned.)

Freud based his theories in what he called his clinical experience, but the "clinical" included the "literary" for Freud, in direct and indirect ways. In 1916, in "Some Character-Types met with in Psychoanalytic Work," he writes about an "enormous magnification," in all of us, of a sentiment articulated by Shakespeare's physically deformed anti-hero, Richard III: "And therefore, since I cannot prove a lover, /To entertain these fair well-spoken days, I am determined to prove a villain, /And hate the idle pleasures of these days." We think, says Freud, that "we all have reason to reproach Nature and our destiny for congenital and infantile disadvantages; *we all demand reparation for early wounds to our narcissism.*" Narcissus himself, interestingly, is never quite wounded as we are (Narcissus drowns without wound, one might say). But, unlike his overt references to Sophocles in discussing Oedipus, Freud makes no reference to any specific aspect of the Narcissus myth in "On Narcissism" (he doesn't mention Ovid, for example). And, surprisingly for so great an interpreter, he says nothing about the Narcissus flower, the metamorphic endpoint in Ovid and other versions. The Narcissus theme is pure background in Freud's essay, a background, too, for the "demand for reparation" that he describes in 1916. I refer to Erich Auerbach's sense, discussed in the chapter before last, of a "strange" and haunting background with its "suggestive influence."

A psychologist with a background in literature is a well-read psychologist, perhaps nothing more. A psychologist who thinks about literature as it applies to life is "strange" in Auerbach's sense—his is an oddity with purpose, perhaps even a rational and logically compelling one. The undeniable truth is that a literary psychology—for lack of any better term—is an embarrassment in most all contemporary departments of psychology and neuroscience, as philosopher Jerry Fodor has observed in a different context. Referring to the tradition of speculative psychologists (Freud among them), he writes that they "had trouble deciding what department they were in and were an embarrassment to deans." I quoted Fodor several paragraphs ago on formal systems, richness, and internal representation, but hesitated to mention his name, because Fodor and Freud are about as an unlikely a pair as one can conceive. Nevertheless, they both worry about the problematic of richness, with which every psychological theory contends. (Some of us are still trying to find the right department.)

Critic and historian Owen Barfield offers that what we really want to achieve in getting our minds around such problems as the "richness" of systems is *strangeness of meaning*, which he discusses in various places. I borrow the following quotation in particular, because my best professor once asked me to think about it as my career progressed:

> [Strangeness] is not correlative with wonder; for wonder is our reaction to things which we are conscious of not quite understanding, or at any rate of understanding less than we had thought. The element of strangeness in beauty has the contrary effect. It arises from contact with a different kind of consciousness from our own, different, yet not so remote that we cannot partly share it, as indeed, in such a connection, the mere word "contact" implies. Strangeness, in fact, arouses wonder when we do not understand: aesthetic imagination when we do.

Barfield responds to "What kind of formal system will be rich enough?" with "aesthetic imagination," a lovely answer, vague in its loveliness.

Let me try to explain why I think my mentor invited me to think about "strangeness" and Barfield's aesthetic imagination, in a medical career. There are many doctors who are aesthetic and well-read, but such qualities do not necessitate that doctors understand how germane their well-heeled sensibility is to the practice of medicine. There are many who advocate for an "art," rather than a "science," of medicine, mainly because to say otherwise sounds boorish. Barfield is very far from such trite advocacy. The aesthetic imagination in his sense is a fundamental challenge to rational understanding—and my mentor asked me to contemplate that challenge for myself in my own career.

Science is full of "understanding less than we had thought." Strangeness involves a power of a different order that could lead to more powerful explanation. In terms of the Narcissus myths, a person can think that narcissism is a concept that can be delineated and understood, but the understanding doesn't exclude wonderment about how narcissism explains so much in our lives, as Christopher Lasch and Alain de Botton have tried to articulate in their respective books, with middling success. Freud wasn't interested in a concept that would have some currency among the social critics or even psychologists. He was interested in truths about the human psyche that were so difficult to express that allusion to myth became useful to the psychologist. Narcissism as a psychological concept has had great currency to date, and everyday experience confirms that some kind of narcissism could be the most reliable aspect of human beings when we deal with them. Freud's point, to state it one last time, doesn't lie in the unremarkable truth that people are vain. Rather, the concept of Narcissus is like the powerful influence of characterization on our view of others: once you have encountered Captain Ahab in a famous novel by Herman Melville, you tend to notice Ahabs. What does it mean to say that we see Narcissus in those we meet?

Whatever we say about narcissism, it is not just a theory of erotics; yet, even Freud's closest advocates worried, on reading "On Narcissism: An Introduction," that it wasn't consistent with his theory of erotics and erotic attachment (his theory of "libido"). Freud's 1914 essay, as he takes such care to stipulate, is only an introduction; it could only be an introduction—allusive, suggestive, pointing the way towards some other understanding, yet referring us back to knowledge that somehow we already have. In the last section (III) of his essay, having made such difficult progress in articulating his extraordinarily "strange" frontier concept, he leaves the Narcissus myths behind him. At that point (as if mythology weren't enough for his grander purpose) he re-enters the world of tragedy. It is not the Sophoclean universe that had possessed him in his earlier career.

Four

Cordelia

A T THE CONCLUSION of "On Narcissism," Freud describes the condition of being in love in a spectacularly unromantic way. To love is to allow erotic drive to flow over onto "the object." The lover idealizes this object; he thinks that it possesses an excellence that can't otherwise be attained:

> This is the cure by love, which [the lover] generally prefers to cure by analysis. Indeed, he cannot believe in any other mechanism of cure; he usually brings expectations of this sort with him to the treatment and directs them towards the person of the physician. . . . An unintended result is often met with when, by means of the treatment, he has been partially freed from his repressions: he withdraws from further treatment in order to choose a love-object, leaving his cure to be continued by a life with someone he loves. We might be satisfied with this result, if it did not bring with it all the dangers of a crippling dependence upon his helper in need.

Since I cannot read Freud without some story in mind, I think of someone in therapy (let's say because of an inability to love), who decides that it's time to fall in love at long last. He dates many people to find disappointment over and again, but then, like a revelation, he finds his "object." He is very happy. His therapist says that his new-found gratification is precarious. Why? Countless cures by love have been inspired by the thought that it is "better to have loved and lost than never to have loved at all" (Alfred Lord Tennyson probably had a male lover in mind when he wrote that line). Tennyson speaks of the gamble; Freud follows the emotional investment. He suggests that both the winners and losers in love need cure by more rigorous analysis, as if the feeling of love itself were no inherent measure of success.

I don't mean to be cynical and neither does Freud. There must be a standard by which we can determine whether we have cure versus an emotional placebo, but in love what can it be? Freud knows that cure by analysis can seem dubious to someone in love, because compared to love's richness, therapy has the mere sterile force of the transference, which simply lacks the romance we seek. Freud couldn't be more aware of the pluses and minuses of a situation that doesn't lend itself to any rational arithmetic. He would throw up his hands at love's mystery, except that the "pluses" and "minuses"—the dualism of plus and minus ("Our views have from the very start been dualistic, and to-day they are even more," he would write years later)—makes him think of other kinds of dualism, among them the interplay of the comic and tragic in the emotional life.

A cure by analysis cannot be better than love, for two reasons, both tragicomic. First, as Freud suggests, love is the type of experience that has a person either renounce therapy or perhaps declare it, prematurely, a success. Second, cure by love and cure by therapeutic insight are two different things, related to each other only because we hope they could be related. You can love without much insight at all, just as you can undergo countless hours of therapy to no particular end. Even by the time of his brooding late essay "Analysis Terminable and Interminable" (1937), I'm not sure that Freud himself knew what a cure by analysis was or whether it could last over time. We suspect that the best part about any such cure would be the end of analysis. Karl Kraus, editor of the intellectual magazine *Die Fackel*, or *The Torch*, in Freud's Vienna (whose motto was "it's not what we run; it's what we run over"), arrived at the same conclusion when he declared psychoanalysis to be the disease for which it purports to be the cure. I don't know that Freud ever responded to Kraus's indictment, but I suspect he would say that love, too, is a disease of the same ilk as psychoanalysis, a crippling dependency that would be so much better if it weren't so debilitating. At least, after an analysis we know how bad off we are.

But the comic element in Freudian psychoanalysis runs deeper than Kraus's commentary. We might imagine Freud saying that cure by love would be just fine, far better than relief by fluoxetine or venlafaxine or the next generation of pill (if we think in biochemical terms) or by any type of talking nostrum or treatment, including psychoanalysis and the modern psychotherapy inspired by it. He would never deny that love was therapeutic, and would agree with Tennyson that effort alone counts for something, regardless of outcome. Freud prefers only that we have some idea of what we are doing psychologically when we do fall in love. Mostly, we don't have the faintest idea, and where there is an ardent ignorance, there is always the opportunity for comedy.

The tragic element is not far from the comic. An aspect of love that repeatedly draws Freud's attention has to do with a quandary which we might call the problem of the imperfect paradise, what Friedrich Nietzsche called "the never to be perfected imperfect." How unfortunate—to the point of tragedy, Freud seems to say—that we think so often in terms of perfections. There are many such idealizations, repeated in the print media, Hollywood movies, and most of all in our minds. We measure ourselves by them, mercilessly. The concluding section III of "On Narcissism" refers to two such measurements against impossible standards.

He describes the "ideal ego" for the first time in his writings; this idealized ego or ego-ideal will eventually be called the super-ego, which is to the (narcissistic) ego as a strict parent is to a child. It operates in the mental life as conscience, guilt, or shame—it is an embodiment (an internalization) first of parental criticism and subsequently that of society, as Freud says. "The subject's narcissism makes its appearance [after infancy] displaced on to this new ideal ego, which, like the infantile ego, finds itself possessed of every perfection that is of value." We need to add one other aspect that Freud would express most clearly in *The Ego and the Id* (1923). The super-ego operates unconsciously, not overtly: "a great part of the sense of guilt must normally remain unconscious, because the origin of conscience is intimately connected with the Oedipus complex . . . *the normal man is not only far more immoral than he believes but also far more moral than he knows.*"

There is no better definition of the superego, both in terms of man's overt immorality and man's profound or even occult moral sense, which is a ghostly presence in human action (as Immanuel Kant maintained, don't we have an innate sense of what is right?). After "On Narcissism," Freud will say that the ego-ideal or super-ego is the heir to the Oedipus complex, but by that obscure formulation, he means that the ego's relationship to the super-ego is like a grown son who calls home in from time to time just to be reminded about things he'd prefer to forget. As my favorite psychoanalytic "supervisor" once put it to me, one must always realize—though it is very hard to realize, she said, taking a shockingly long drag from her Benson-and-Hedges-100-menthol cigarette—that there is a hanging judge in all of us. Reflect on her point for yourself, based on your own experience; you will find that she is disturbingly correct.

We not only incorporate idealizations into the psyche, but we also tend to idealize the people whom we choose to love in the long term. Perhaps no adult "love object" would ever meet the demands of a particularly severe ego-ideal, but, in erotic love, where there is imperfection, there is also the willing renunciation of imperfection, because we want to believe in a paradise of love. If read as a personal ad, Freud would sound odd but wise: you don't seek me; you seek a perfection quite beyond yourself, but I am here for you—or, in his own chilly words, "what possesses the excellence which the ego lacks for making it an ideal, *is loved*." It's surprising how readily we respond to mixed (and, finally, sad) personal advertisements. That we do at all speaks to a Freudian tragedy that we should understand in its many nuances and variations.

෫

We are in a position to move from "On Narcissism" towards much else in Freud. In fact, we are about to run through his writings with three major stops in his career—1913, 1920, and 1930—to examine twin motifs of Freud's psychology of love. Freud gave these themes or motifs mythological names: Eros (representing love, sex, and life) and Thanatos (death or necessity). Before we start, I would alert the reader to biographer Peter Gay's comment that the hard intellectual core of Freud's late career is forbidding in the extreme, and that, accordingly, Freudian scholarship reminded him of Queen Victoria's "unsmiling sobriety" (Gay studied her, too). Parenthetically, in German, there is a word for "formality" that translates as "stiff linen": the scholarly recapitulation of Freudian theory can be stiffer. But Freud's theory and tone belie a surprising suppleness, which a reader gleans through his use of literary sources.

One can read Freud for a long time only to achieve a grossly inflexible view of why he discussed Eros and Thanatos together. Death-in-love and love-in-death are dialectically related, as a philosopher would say; Freud's "dialectical" relation refers to the real drama that links hypothetical forces. Here are two very different authors pondering the interrelation or dialectic—the first is Jean Laplanche, a Freudian of the "French school" and, second, critic John Crowe Ransom, an American with a taste for tragedy:

> *Seductive and traumatic* as it was, the forced introduction of the death drive could only provoke on the part of Freud's heirs every conceivable variety of defense: a deliberate refusal on the part of some; a purely scholastic acceptance of the notion and of the dualism: Eros-Thanatos on the part of others; a qualified acceptance, cutting the notion off from its philosophical bases,

by an author like Melanie Klein; and, most frequently of all, a passing allusion to or a total forgetting of the notion.

$$\rightleftharpoons$$

To be a tragic ironist is to be aware sharply and grimly, but not too painfully, of the constant involvement of life with death. In that spirit Homer sang, and the makers of the ballads, and Shakespeare the maker of sonnets and plays—

To-morrow, and to-morrow, and to-morrow
Creeps in this petty pace from day to day,
To the last syllable of recorded time;
And all our yesterdays have lighted fools
The way to dusty death.

It would be preferable to dismiss the double notion of Eros-Thanatos—or qualify it out of existence like psychoanalyst Melanie Klein—rather than to discuss it as forced. An ambivalence doesn't "force" itself (a concept of ideal love, on the other hand, does). Freud thinks than an intellectual and emotional acceptance of Eros-Thanatos, like quoting lines of *Macbeth* to oneself, entails that we understand how death-in-life contains everything (tragedy, irony, sharpness, grimness, and even humor).

Laplanche (in the first quotation) is correct when he calls Eros-Thanatos "seductive." The drama of love and death was and always has been seductive, as writers have known for centuries; we need only think of the poetical commonplace of sexual consummation as a death. It is not much of leap to think of love, which is different from sex, as a larger death, perhaps. Ransom (the second author) chooses famous lines that help us in an unexpected way. Someone clever has said that Macbeth and Lady Macbeth could be the happiest couple in Shakespearean tragedy, because they truly speak the same emotional language to each other. Their love is all about death and nothing much else, save ambition, which is a form of death. Clearly, bliss is not the subject of the Macbeth's lines. Death in life is, but then we need to read Shakespeare in contrast to Freud to understand Freud's take on the ancient dualism of life and death.

The background of Macbeth's often-quoted lament is important. A man loses his wife to suicide after her mental demise; he (Macbeth) knows that Malcolm's army advances upon him. We know he will be slain by Macduff;

and we are not crazy to feel close to him, as we often do with heroes, heroines, and anti-heros in Shakespeare, despite the fact that we know Macbeth as a consummate murderer. In reading the end of *Macbeth*, I don't think about Eros-Thanatos so much as I think of a pure and unforgiving nihilism. Only a moment passes before Macbeth himself characterizes that negativeness, unforgettably, as "a tale/Told by an idiot, full of sound and fury, /Signifying nothing"—to which we might add, *absolutely* nothing. In Freud, love and death operate together more forgivingly. Every-day existence is not without its tomorrow-and-tomorrow difficulties, but perhaps, if we are lucky, it never achieves Macbeth's more perfect nihilism.

The dangerous aspect of reading even good Freud criticism is the same problem that can happen reading Freud himself, who hardly lacks for a stiff-linen feel, especially in English translation. It becomes too easy to miss what is tragicomic in him. Freud liked an anecdote (mentioned in *The Interpretation of Dreams*) about a spouse who says to his or her spouse, "*if one of us dies, I shall move to Paris.*" *That* is an example of Eros-Thanatos in Freud. We have Death, in the form of death-wish, and Love, both in marriage and in Paris. When Freud addresses absolute tragedy in love (his central choices being Shakespeare's *King Lear* and, in particular, Cordelia in that play, and *Hamlet*), in a way that differs from his use of *Oedipus the King*, he takes us beyond the intellectual acknowledgment of death, erotic drive, and their dialectical relation. He asks us to think about just a scene or some dialogue—a bit of human drama—that captures the dialectical psychology. Think of this exchange, for example, between a loving daughter and a father who is troubled because he is bound to a "wheel of fire":

> CORDELIA   Sir, do you know me?
> LEAR   You are a spirit, I know. Where did you die?

Dramas in life can be reduced to not many words. Can a psychologist be free of pen-envy in reading them?

I

Reflecting on Shakespeare's universal influence, critic Maynard Mack once could barely suppress his annoyance: look at your bookshelf, and what do you find? "*Brave New World, Glimpses of the Moon, Pale Fire, The Sound and the Fury, Tomorrow and Tomorrow and Tomorrow*—one blasted Shake-

spearean title after another," he wrote, "all of those reminding you that for
writers of this century his works have become not merely a Swiss bank account of golden allusions and opinions, but a sort of extended credit system
enabling one to imply a great deal without having to say it." To imply a great
deal without the need to explicate or expound would seem the opposite of
what Freud tried to do in his career. Psycho-analysis was not meant to be a
form of psycho-allusion. Years from now, perhaps the "couched" analytic
part of Freud's project will become quite secondary, but I suspect that we
will still be wondering about what he implied. When Freud used literature,
he appealed to its power to represent psychological workings. But psychology borrowing from literature seems at cross-purposes, because a story or a
phrase from Shakespeare shouldn't reveal psychology better than a psychologist can explain it.

Despite surface claims to the contrary, Freud acknowledges that the greatest literature reliably trumps analysis. He borrows on the vast, accumulated
credit of imaginative writing. His kind of debt doesn't exactly yield scientific
truth, but Freud always thought that his science had a great deal to learn
from art. In 1913, at the start of the curious essay "The Theme of the Three
Caskets," he writes: "Two scenes from Shakespeare, one from comedy and
the other from tragedy, have lately given me occasion for setting and solving
a little problem." The problem wasn't little, and it certainly wasn't solved
in 1913: what is the relationship between love as a unifying force and death
as a destructive one? For the moment, let's set aside the question whether a
psychologist as scientist should be asking such a question. Freud thought it
worth asking more than once. By 1920, he had one answer; by 1930, he had
a different one, but the theme of the caskets was present at each step.

In 1913, the instance of comedy that Freud selected, from *The Merchant
of Venice*, is one of the stranger choices that he could have made. There
is better comedy about love, usually about people not communicating with
each other, in many places in Shakespeare. Freud was interested to emphasize
a theme that he thought had wide application. How best to characterize *his*
theme is hard to say, based on the beginning of "Theme of the Three Caskets." It seems that the problem in question has partly has to do with tendentious opinion and truth. People in love become very deeply convinced in ways
that can't be refuted, but the test of the caskets in *The Merchant of Venice*
intends to separate truth from falsehood in love, as if that were possible. Not
long ago, I read about a movie in which two men and two women experiment emotionally and in other ways with each other until they finally decide

with whom they want to partner. A critic wrote insightfully, "the way that each one insists on what they call the truth tells us a good deal about them." We might expand the insight: maybe the real question is whether a lover can be honest; we suspect that in love, at best, we reveal something of ourselves (sometimes not even that–and never the whole), and truth eludes everyone.

In *The Merchant of Venice*, anyone who seeks the hand of the beautiful Portia must submit to a test. If a bachelor fails, he doesn't get Portia, and, what's more, he must forsake all love to anyone (forever). This last part is a nice Elizabethan touch; courtly love speaks in "forevers." But: only in Shakespeare could the terms of a silly premise and sillier game be accepted by someone as clever as Portia.

Is it so curious, if we stop to think about it, that love has all manner of premises and counsels of perfection built within it? We can search our own experience for examples–the spouse who stipulates that "if you love me, then _____," as if love were an if-then proposition as in hard logic; a parent who feels more and more in the right as time proceeds in child-rearing ("my way or the highway," the parent says); or, as Freud will explore in the case of *King Lear*, how a person chooses a terrible fate out of what he believes is paternal (albeit narcissistic) love. A test of love-worthiness is just as presumptuous and outrageous as a parent or spouse who argues that she or he is in the right (based on love). Either agree with the parent or spouse, or be cast aside, as if by fate.

There is a great deal of compromise in love, it is said; but often the compromise feels as Charlie Chaplin's character must have felt when taken up by the teeth and gears of a large machine. Or, put in a more intricate way, though still in existentially comic terms, think of the following recommendation by Franz Kafka regarding how to respond emotionally without yielding to self-deception:

> perhaps the best resource is to meet everything passively, to make yourself an inert mass, and if you feel that you are being carried away, not to let yourself be lured into taking a single unnecessary step, to stare at others with the eyes of an animal, to feel no compunction, in short, with your own hand to throttle down whatever ghostly life remains in you, that is, to enlarge the final peace of the graveyard and let nothing survive save that.
>
> A characteristic movement in such a condition is to run your little finger along your eyebrows.

That's grim, but not untrue. You might sample for yourself in what ways the little finger running along an eyebrow becomes one's most articulate response in dicey matters related to husbands, wives, sons, daughters, lovers, siblings, insufferable relations, or whoever has put you to some kind of ridiculous and basically impossible test. But to the essence of the three-casket theme for Freud: he argues that the choice among caskets relates to the choice of love from various options. The real question is: what are "the options"?

In order to win Portia's hand, her suitors must choose one of three caskets, made of either gold, silver, or lead. Each casket bears an inscription, but only one has a picture of Portia inside: "who chooseth me shall gain what many men desire" is the note on the golden casket; "who chooseth me shall get as much as he deserves" for the silver; and "who chooseth me must give and hazard all he hath," for the lead. Three suitors take their chances; each comes at the problem fresh, without knowledge of previous mistakes by others. A Moroccan prince chooses gold, opens the casket, and finds a death's head inside. The Prince of Arragon chooses silver to find a picture of a blinking fool inside. Bassanio, who is Portia's own favorite, chooses lead after a speech that Freud finds a bit forced, because it glorifies dull lead. He complains (how very peculiar to think of Freud responding to Bassanio), "if in psycho-analytic practice we were confronted with such a speech, we should suspect concealed motives behind the unsatisfying argument."

Surely, Freud jokes with us; we need only read a bit in *The Merchant of Venice* to know that he does. Bassanio maintains that appearances are never what they seem, as Freud does all the time in his writing. Bassanio is willing to base his love-decision solely on that fact.

> So may the outward shows be least themselves;
> The world is still deceived with ornament.

His argument on behalf of lead runs for many more lines, but he makes his point in the first two. He opens the lead casket to find Portia's picture, and he will win her hand, but we are only in act III, barely half way into the play. We must assume that Freud knew *The Merchant of Venice* well: elsewhere in his writing, he comments on Portia's delightful slip of the tongue to Bassanio ("One half of me is yours, the other half yours—Mine own, I would say") as a self-revelation that either she didn't intend or let pass with exceeding charm. To say that Freud doesn't otherwise address *The Merchant of Venice* in "Theme of the Three Caskets" is to miss the point of the casket story, which is a précis of the play.

The Merchant of Venice describes three marriages (Portia to Bassanio; Portia's woman-in-waiting Nerissa to Gratiano; and the profligate Christian Lorenzo to Shylock's daughter Jessica), various contracts made and broken, the letter of social law in contrast to the spirit of human law, and, last but not least, the paradox of Shylock the moneylender as W. H. Auden nicely described it: everybody hates him, but people still need him. The settings of the play, Venice and Belmont, are two societies that are ostensibly wealthy. "Ostensibly" deserves to be underlined once or twice; there is remarkable deception in ornament throughout. A lover needs some cash to impress a girl; he seeks money from a male friend, whom some modern readers have viewed as his quietly gay partner (an unfortunate reading, I think). The friend takes out an equity loan to help out, even though he could lose a pound of flesh in the process. *The Merchant of Venice* couldn't be more contemporary in the sense of man's dependency on all kinds of leverage. To study the society of *Merchant*, a person need only study some of its deficit-spending egos, Freud seems to say. The casket story is central to a play that patently has to with what people desire, get, and give in a complex economy.

Having mentioned the casket test, Freud then launches into a flight of ideas reminiscent of the piled-on examples of errors, gaffs, and misrepresentations in his *Jokes and Their Relation to the Unconscious*. The casket story wasn't original to Shakespeare, he says. The Bard's source was a similar story from *The Deeds of the Romans* of the fourteenth century, and the Roman story should put us in mind of folk epic (Estonian), in which a woman contemplates lovers representing the sun, moon, and the stars. She chooses the stars in what Freud calls the astral version of the casket theme. But in Shakespeare a man chooses between three caskets, a casket clearly symbolizing "the essential thing in woman." (Sandor Ferenczi, possibly the most psychologically disturbed of Freud's followers, once said that the unconscious sees a vagina or womb in every concave object and a penis in every convex one. To "see" in this way is the problem, not the glory, of Freudianism.) We began with Portia choosing a lover who could best love her; now, Freud says, "With one wave of the hand, such as usually only happens in fairy-tales . . . we see that the subject [the real theme of the three caskets] is an idea from human life, a man's choice between three women."

And look, says Freud, at the examples we can gather of man's choice among diverse triplets: Shakespeare's King Lear chooses among his three daughters, just as the Prince in "Cinderella" chooses the youngest of three sisters, just as Paris chooses Aphrodite from three goddesses, and, for good measure, Freud alludes to Psyche, yet another fairest third daughter, and her love affair with Amor. Among his free-wheeling associations, Freud also includes the three *Moirae* (or *Moerae*) of post-Homeric Greek mythology: Atropos (death), Lachesis (accident), Clotho (fate) together spin the thread of human destiny, which they also cut short at will. At the end of his allusive riff, Freud says, "And now it is time to return to the idea contained in the choice of the three sisters [or caskets or fates], which we are endeavoring to interpret." We have mentioned certain tendentious aspects of lovers and tests of love; Freud himself pounds away at an argument that isn't yet clear.

We should notice the rhetorical strategy, which is uniquely Freudian and generally unsuccessful in the hands of psychologists other than Freud. All evidence orients itself along lines of influence as if in his personal magnetic field. I don't even believe that his associations are necessarily associated with each other: maybe Estonian myth has to do with *The Merchant of Venice* as elemental lead relates to the stars, as Cinderella relates to Aphrodite, Cordelia, Portia, and Psyche, but maybe not. Nor does it help if I were to add, as we eventually learn, that the illusion of choice is his theme. There are absolutely no counterexamples in Freud, as philosopher Karl Popper once correctly observed.

(Popper went so far as to study how, for any given argument in Freud, sometimes even in the absence of one, all data can always be interpreted as supporting evidence. Freud's "rationalism" had a great deal to do with his stubborn illogic, which Popper illustrated by way of a parable. A man crosses a busy street; he jumps back to avoid being hit by a car only to be knocked down by a passing bicycle. Lesson: you will be hit. By comparison, Freud is always right and spot on, according to Freud.)

Late into "Theme of the Three Caskets," Freud at last announces his thesis, which feels at once accidental, illogical, and rational. Love, he says, is a fine act of the human imagination, as we have always known:

> We know that man makes use of his imaginative faculty (phantasy) to satisfy those wishes that reality does not satisfy. So his imagination rebelled against the recognition of the truth embodied in the myth of Moerae, and constructed instead the myth derived from it, in which the Goddess of Death was the Goddess of Love. . . . The third of the sisters is no longer Death, she is the fairest, best, most desirable and most lovable among women. Nor was this substitution in any way difficult. . . . Just where in reality he obeys

compulsion, he exercises choice; and that which he chooses is not a thing of horror, but the fairest and most desirable thing in life.

Contrary to the notion that we desire love and choose it, Freud says that the real story is more unlikely than even the fairest stories conceived in the mode of comedy. The imagination in love can't see what it chooses. Love isn't merely blind; it is aggressively delusional. He turns his attention next to Shakespeare's *King Lear*, after a passing comment that, to me, feels like a bomb blast: "choice stands in the place of necessity"—i.e., you can believe you choose, if you like.

"If you want something badly enough and you believe in it hard enough, you will eventually get it: though tragedy denies this possibility, comedy affirms it," wrote critic Jonathan Bate, reflecting on Shakespeare's powers of dramatic illusion. I would edit Bate: in Shakespearean tragedies of love, one often seeks and obtains precisely as one does in comedy, just with different outcomes. In a narcissistic universe, we always find that for which we seek, sometimes comically, usually tragically. The similarity between comedy and tragedy allowed Freud to move as if there were no logical discontinuity from a discussion of the caskets in *The Merchant of Venice* to his brief and disturbing treatment of the three daughters in *King Lear*. A choice among three is not the link among his various sources. Desire is under scrutiny, the urge on the part of an ego who is eager, at last, to enter into the world of other egos. His fate could be predetermined, says Freud.

There are those who would say that reading Shakespeare is admirable but irrelevant to modern psychology. I respectfully disagree, based on the precedent of Shakespeare reliably overwhelming the sensibilities of very smart people. (Poet J. W. von Goethe's said of the Bard's characters: "They're coming at me from all sides! If only they would give me room so that I could breathe and speak!"). Shakespearean beauty of language and his verisimilitude in representing human character surpasses psychology, rendering *it* irrelevant. An objection might be raised in light of scientific advances in our psychology, as in the chemical treatment of depression or schizophrenia, but we should never confuse psychological insight with therapeutic success or failure. To ask why *King Lear* is tragic, or why life can seem to be tragic, is a human, not a scientific question.

Freud weighs in with an opinion that has the virtue of clearing some ground for himself, and it is perfectly simple: Lear must choose death. The tragedy of Lear wouldn't make sense as psychological tragedy if that necessity did not operate plainly, as a pretext to all action in the play. (Could Lear have changed to avoid what happens in five acts? Of course not. Do the Lears in our lives change?) All options collapse into Lear's one mortal choice, which decidedly is not the choice between Goneril, Regan, and Cordelia. Freud says that of the three inevitable relationships in life—to the mother who carried us, to the female companion of our bed (if we are heterosexual men), and to the mother earth who receives us—there is only one choice that will be fulfilled in the end. I quote Goethe again with an amendment: I wish Freud would give me room to breathe.

In *King Lear*, "choice of death" ostensibly happens at a moment of the highest pathos at the play's end, when the King enters with Cordelia in his arms. In the striking last sentence to his essay, Freud writes, "it is in vain that the old man yearns after the love of woman as once he had it . . . [from his mother, Freud says, though he means from Cordelia, who is like a mother]; the third of the fates alone, the silent goddess of Death, will take him into her arms." In the most haunting reverse pietà in literature, Cordelia is dead in Lear's arms, but the mad king isn't sure whether she lives, and his doubt has everything to do with the play's deeply affecting fifth-act pathos. To follow Freud's line of thought, we might wonder at what point Lear deliberates Death/Cordelia. The answer must be: from the very start, in act I scene i, when she says little ("Nothing, my Lord") out the belief that she expresses her love most honestly that way, at which point her father rejects her utterly.

Bassanio deliberates dumb and dull lead in a dissertation on the seeming nature of things. Cordelia, who has rather few lines in a play that has so much to do with her, embodies silence, and all Lear's rationalizations—about her and the patronizing and foul Goneril and Regan—deceive him in the end. Unlike, say, George Orwell's pedantic comment that *King Lear* is all about renunciation (a person would have to be willfully blind not to see it as such, he said; think of Lear renouncing his throne yet expecting royal treatment, or Lear renouncing the love of the people who truly love him), Freud refers to how readily we misread both action and language in the play. Renunciation is no more the subject of *King Lear* than simple greed is the subject of *The Merchant of Venice*.

Lear's choices, like Bassanio's, are active—one might say, driven by compulsion—and they renounce nothing. Altogether too belatedly, Lear chooses his youngest daughter, but he is mad, and he barely realizes the choice. The father-daughter reunion stings as very few moments in literature do:

LEAR   I know you do not love me; for your sisters
          Have (as I do remember) done me wrong.
          You have some cause, they have not.
CORDELIA No cause, no cause.

One could respond by thinking: No, Cordelia is wronged, as so many in *King Lear* are wronged—including Gloucester, Edgar, Kent, Cordelia (she has cause), and perhaps even Lear himself, who, for all his bluster, is a victim of fate, just as Oedipus suffers the consequences of his destiny. Freud says, in stark rejoinder, that we should reexamine desire and its relation to fate. He precisely does so in his later career.

II

The German philosopher G. W. F. Hegel once said on his deathbed, reflecting on his work over a lifetime, that only one person ever understood him, but that person misunderstood him. Hegel scholars don't like that story, and they dismiss it as apocryphal, but Hegel's language, like Kant's or Heidegger's, is no open book. According to Bruno Bettelheim's *Freud and Man's Soul*, the appreciation of Freud's language suffers from the mistranslation of his German into an essentially unreadable English.

"I do not doubt," wrote Bettelheim, "that Freud's English translators wanted to present his writings to their audience as accurately as possible—in terms of the frame of reference within which they wished him to be understood. When Freud appears to be either more abstruse or more dogmatic in English translation than in the original German, to speak about abstract concepts rather than about the reader himself, and about man's mind rather than about his soul, the probable explanation isn't mischievousness or carelessness on the translators' part but a deliberate wish to perceive Freud strictly within the framework of medicine." Bettelheim's observations couldn't be clearer in the case of the death drive and Freud's often-cited formulation that "the aim of all life is death." Bettelheim reminds us that Freud in his own German language—as an essayist respected, perhaps envied, by German writers as diverse as Hermann Hesse, Thomas Mann, and Albert Einstein—was primarily a reader's writer, that his interest in the human soul was to reveal it with some wonder. Freud may never have belonged within the framework of medicine, but neither was he obsessed with death, even when he was sick with oral cancer.

⊟

I mention all of the above by way of introducing Freud's *Beyond the Pleasure Principle* (1920), which is his central treatment of desire and fate. So much has been written about it that one feels mortified to offer an irreverent opinion about it. To me, however, *Beyond the Pleasure Principle* is too difficult to read unless one realizes the quandary lurking within it. Life's pleasure and the search for it usually run aground for some reason, as all of us eventually learn. Whether sexual, intellectual, or spiritual, pleasure is a theoretical construct of the highest sort, never to be achieved to the degree that we can imagine it, although we think we experience pleasure all the time. It takes a Freud, I suppose, to intuit sadomasochism in every pleasure, just as there are sadomasochistic aspects in all sex, even in the absence of costumes and other paraphernalia.

To say that we seek a pleasure is to entertain an expectation of what that pleasure might be like. Disappointment of expectation can feel like a masochistic exercise, and, truth be known, we are often our own best sadists. Sometimes when we deal with other people intimately, or possibly only when we deal with them intimately, the strangest intricacies of pain emerge. I don't refer to abstractions, and I'm not foreclosing the possibility of "simple" pleasure in intimate relationships.

Once I met a couple who had been married for sixty years; a bit stunned at the thought of six decades of togetherness, I asked the wife whether she had ever considered divorce in that remarkable period of time. She didn't pause before she answered, "Divorce? Never. But I think about murder every single day." She wasn't unhappy; indeed one could say that she had moved so beyond pleasure as to be free. *Beyond the Pleasure Principle* is about the paradox of all pleasures, especially the ones that are fulfilled over time.

From the very beginning of his essay, Freud doesn't condescend to offer us a definition of the pleasure principle. The omission is intentional and clever beyond question:

> In the theory of psycho-analysis we have no hesitation in assuming that the course taken by mental events is automatically regulated by the pleasure principle. We believe, that is to say, that the course of those events is invariably set in motion by an unpleasurable tension, and that it takes a direction such that its final outcome coincides with a lowering of that tension–that is, with an avoidance of unpleasure or a production of pleasure.

"Automatically regulated" and "unpleasurable tension" seem vague terms to me, no less so than "the pleasure principle." But one can glean his meaning: borrowing from the spouse just mentioned, it's not that her marriage didn't have tension; she delightfully could minimize it. The pleasure of her marriage depended on a certain capacity for homicidal thoughts and masochistic endurance.

In a great deal of clinical work, however, "unpleasurable tension" seems like a disease of imperfection visited upon us. At the risk of falling into the trap that Bettelheim warns against, let me put Freud's sentences into a very medical context. A patient comes to you experiencing no pleasure in life; he says he is depressed. His sleep and appetite are altered. His concentration and memory are spotty; love seems remote, and thoughts of suicide surface from time to time, like a leviathan for air. We should have no hesitation in assuming that the course of mental events in the case of a depression is no longer regulated by a pleasure principle. What to do? Especially today, with so many medications at one's disposal, one treats the depression with them. But does the treatment mean that you answer the question of what pleasure means for that person? Or have you simply lifted the unpleasure of a depression?

One becomes confused about pleasure in trying to explain it, as psychologist Jerome Kagan has argued in his un-Freudian meditation entitled "The Pleasure Principle" (1998). He talks about modern laboratory studies in which a caged rat presses a lever, which causes electrical stimulation to its brain by way of implanted wires. Hit the right part of the brain, and the rat becomes a lever addict. This scientific model for pleasure is ambiguous, Kagan warns, because a jolt of electricity isn't pleasure. Granted, it's tempting to think that about a relation between gratification (thus pleasure) and brain stimulation, whether by wires or via drugs, but Kagan is correct when he says that "no biological state defines pleasure because it is, finally, a judgment." He is no less skeptical about psychoanalytic insight, since Freud notoriously misread pleasure for his own purposes. Again, Kagan is correct: in *Beyond the Pleasure Principle*, Freud is outrageous where Kagan is cautious, circumspect, and finally uninteresting. Human psychology is all about pleasure, Freud maintains; the pity is that we have no way of discussing it except by way of speculation. Close to a century later, after many advances in the biological sciences, we say that we have treatments for serious unhappiness, but biochemistry and electricity still aren't pleasure.

Beyond the Pleasure Principle is either one of the most thought-provoking or most irritating monographs that one can read on happiness and unhappiness. I incline to the former view, but not without a frustration informed both by clinical experience and spurred by Freud's language in the essay. "Beyond" the pleasure principle we find—what, exactly? One doesn't ask a depressed person why he can't be happy (he will look straight through you), nor can you quite treat depression away once and for all, despite the aggrandizing claims of modern pharmaceutical companies and some doctors. Scanning the dozens of contemporary options among anti-depressant, anti-anxiety, and anti-psychotic treatments, one tends to agree with writer-doctor Anton Chekhov that there are too many choices in therapy, all in the absence of a cure. Treat enough unhappiness, and you begin to wonder what lies beyond the relief that you try to provide: perhaps only a different kind of unhappiness.

The pleasures we seek and the unpleasures that we would avoid are bound together, as Freud illustrates by way of three lines of argument. First: we are creatures driven by pleasure, but we also delay our gratifications. Such postponement is a necessary concession to the world, which frankly couldn't care less about our pleasure. The "reality principle" is hard to avoid, Freud says. For an adult, the notion that all gratification can always be immediate—at the press of a lever or with the dropping of a pill—is absurd. Postponed pleasure is a take-home principle no less potent than our imagination of pleasure. Second: certain behaviors suggest that the postponement of satisfaction is itself a thrill. Freud's legendary example in *Beyond the Pleasure Principle* is his one-and-a-half year-old grandson's game of throwing away a toy (he says "*fort*" or "away") only to ask for it back ("*da*," "there") over and again. There has been no lack of commentary on the so-called repetition compulsion, but it escapes me why the *fort-da* game captures attention over and above adult versions in the arenas of work and love. Third: Freud examines the relationship between pleasure and instinctual gratification. When we get more or less what we desire, presumably to our delight, something is still missing—and we don't refer to the disparity between perfect pleasure (whatever that might be) and what we have. Freud surmises that we catch a glimpse of some different fate. Bettelheim is right: "Death instinct" is a terrible translation of what Freud had in mind.

Beyond the Pleasure Principle is standard reading at most all higher levels of education, except in medical school and post-graduate medical training (including psychiatry), curiously enough. Or, I should say, at no point in my medical education was the book ever suggested to me, maybe because it was assumed that we had encountered it somewhere along the way. As time has gone on, however, three major questions in the book stick in my head. We ask them so routinely in clinical and everyday life that the oversight in my medical curriculum seems premeditated, as if we didn't need to read what we were likely to learn from seeing patients. And Freud's answers are curious. First question: What are the gratifications of pleasure? Answer: see "reality principle." Second question: Why do behaviors recur as if there were pleasure in the repetition? Answer: pleasure + repetition = death. Third question: Is there a biology of contentment? Answer: Yes, but it has to do with death. Let's examine each of these bizarre answers in turn.

III

The Reality Principle. Freud states the reality principle with greater clarity than he ever describes the pleasure principle. It "does not abandon the intention of ultimately obtaining pleasure, but it nevertheless demands and carries into effect the postponement of satisfaction, the abandonment of a number of possibilities of gaining satisfaction and the temporary toleration of unpleasure as a step on the long indirect road to pleasure." Like a dull preparatory education, after which you get a job that is less than fulfilling, "reality" implies postponement of pleasure—a delayed gratification with emphasis on "delayed." Pleasure is not hedonism, and hedonists aren't depraved: the reality principle doesn't stipulate an ethical standard. It merely states that one aspect of pleasure is the comparatively unpleasant pursuit of it.

As always, one needs to come to terms with Freud's claims purely for oneself. When he says that under the influence of the ego's self-preservative instinct, the pleasure principle is *replaced* by the reality principle, and that the ego's road to pleasure is necessarily a grand detour (the long and winding indirect road), I acknowledge that he might be right, but I inwardly protest. If the reality principle demands a tiresome education of sorts before we graduate to pleasure, then I think of the brilliant rejoinder of Lady Augusta Bracknell from Oscar Wilde:

> I do not approve of anything that tampers with natural ignorance. Ignorance is like a delicate exotic fruit; touch it, and the bloom is gone. The whole theory of modern education is radically unsound. Fortunately in England, at any rate, education produces no effect whatsoever. If it did, it would prove a serious danger to the upper classes, and probably lead to acts of violence in Grosvenor Square.

Aunt Augusta is responsible for one of the finest similes ever, useful in countless contexts. In Freud, pleasure is like a delicate exotic fruit; touch it and the bloom is gone. The reality principle assures us that such is the case. "[S]trictly speaking," Freud says,

> it is incorrect to talk of the dominance of the pleasure principle over the course of mental processes. If such a dominance existed, the immense majority of our mental processes would have to be accompanied by pleasure or to lead to pleasure, whereas universal experience completely contradicts any such conclusion. The most that can be said, therefore, is that there exists in the mind a strong *tendency* towards the pleasure principle, but that that tendency is opposed by certain other forces or circumstances, so that the final outcome cannot always be in harmony with the tendency towards pleasure.

He contradicts what he wrote four paragraphs earlier in the first sentences of *Beyond the Pleasure Principle*. We recall that the theory of psychoanalysis had "no hesitation" in assuming that mental events were *automatically* regulated by the pleasure principle. Reality and the reality principle now force us to think otherwise.

I will dispense quickly with a minor point to concentrate on a major implication. Freud said that psychoanalysis had no hesitation in *assuming* that the pleasure principle operates automatically. One can assume anything and still not be held accountable for later contradiction, assuming one revises one's assumptions. A generous reader could say that Freud doesn't contradict himself so much as he explores a line of thought wherever it may lead. I am not so generous, because I think we can't appreciate *Beyond the Pleasure Principle* unless we emphasize the Gordian knot of his position. A pleasure intimately linked with a reality principle complicates the former: the fate of pleasure is the disappointment of desire. But, as we all have witnessed from time to time, the renunciation of pleasure can become an end in itself (and can even be confused for pleasure), as in certain work ethics. From the point of view of pure or "simple" pleasure, such a development seems radically unsound, as Aunt Augusta opined.

What, then, is true gratification? Philosopher Arthur Schopenhauer, to whom Freud is indebted for his bleakness on the subject of desire, said that whenever we get what we want, we are like beggars receiving alms: there is reprieve today so that our misery can continue tomorrow. Freud insists that this view, with which he sympathizes, is not bleak; it is reality.

⊟

Repetition Compulsion and Pleasure. By repetition, Freud does not refer to the tendency to recall experience in memory, but rather the need or the drive to relive memory in life. His examples are magnificent or notorious, depending on taste. Freud wrote *Beyond the Pleasure Principle*, we should recall, between March 1919 and July 1920; psychological fall-out from the "terrible war which has just ended" provides a large body data for him. His insight into the phenomena of post-traumatic stress—in particular, nightmares in which war experience is revisited—sounds contemporary to anyone who has dealt with such cases:

> Now dreams occurring in traumatic neuroses have the characteristic of re-peatedly bringing the patient back into the situation of his accident, a situ-ation from which he wakes up in another fright. This astonishes people far too little. . . . [T]he patient is, as one might say, fixated to his trauma . . . I am not aware, however, that patients suffering from traumatic neurosis are much occupied in their waking lives with memories of their accident. Per-haps they are more concerned with *not* thinking about it.

The indelible instance of post-traumatic stress in my experience is the story of a fireman who would wake from sleep with an imagined bright light shining in his eyes. His nightmare was just the light, and at first it was a rare event. Before long, though, it would appear every night, and as his sleep became more and more troubled in anticipation of the light, his waking life turned into its own form of psychological trauma, seemingly removed from the initial terrible memory (which involved a severe injury to his leg at work on a winter morning when the day was "so bright"), but in my mind clearly related to it. After a while, I wasn't sure whether he and I became fixated on his lack of sleep or his memory of the original trauma, not that there was much difference between the two forms of pain. Regarding such mysteri-ous masochism, Freud offers no explanation; he proceeds merely to a more astonishing association: post-war neuroses put him in mind of child's play. "[T]he unpleasurable nature of an experience does not always unsuit it for play," he explains.

Does repetition mean that a person seeks to master unpleasantness through recollection? That is an excellent rationale, the kind that psychia-trists use when they ask patients to recall old emotional wounds in therapy in the hope that mastery over the past might ensue. Perhaps there is a role for such work, but I agree with philosopher Paul Ricoeur that child's play, no less than the mystery of post-traumatic stress, are mere fragments of a picture for Freud, which lead him to no conclusions, either in terms of theory or method. Ricoeur nicely summarizes Freud's grandson's game:

> We are presented with the case of a little boy, age one and a half. He is a good boy who lets his parents sleep, obeys orders not to touch certain things, and above all never cries when his mother leaves him. He plays at making a wooden reel disappear and reappear, at the same time uttering an expressive "*fort . . . da*" ("gone . . . there"). What does this game mean? It is obviously related to the child's instinctual renunciation that led us to say he is a good boy; it is a repetition of the renunciation . . . the child is staging the disappearance and return of his mother under the symbolic figure of objects within his reach. Thus unpleasure itself is mastered by means of repetition in play, by staging the loss of the loved person.

> This episode, dear to some French psychoanalysts, is nevertheless inconclusive in Freud's eyes.

The phrase "under the symbolic figure" regrettably puts one in mind of the worst excesses of Freudian symbol-searching by all Freudians after Freud, though the French could be the worst offenders. "The child had a wooden reel with a piece of string tied round it," Freud says, without reference to the reel as mother or anything else, "What he did was to hold the reel by the string and very skillfully throw it over the edge of his curtained cot, so that it disappeared into it . . . He then pulled the reel out of the cot again by the string and hailed its reappearance." What does the game or reel symbolize—what symbolism, for that matter, applies to the post-traumatic case that I described? The symbolism is less relevant than the sterile repetitiveness.

There is displeasure in post-war neurosis, but there is pleasure in child's play. Freud senses that "the child turned his experience into a game for a reason." Freud's insistence on a reason hardly surprises us, since we know that as a thinker he always abides by the dictum that *everything has a meaning*. The meaning of repetition compulsion causes Freud no end of consternation, in part because it seems to have no salient purpose or meaning.

Beyond the Pleasure Principle has been called "as profoundly free and as audacious" as any production in Freud's "metapsychological, metaphysical, and metabiological fresco," according to J. Laplanche. Critic J. C. Ransom, whom I also quoted earlier, talks about how we should read about death as both Freud and Shakespeare do, with "tragic irony." I am a great admirer of Freud and tragedy, but his audacity in *Beyond the Pleasure Principle* is embattled, his fresco is cluttered, and if he is free and ironic in his speculations and associations, he also seems a bit adrift. In the next transition that he negotiates—from *fort-da* to a summary of "twenty-five years of intense work" that preceded *Beyond*—he asks us to contemplate an equation that only adds to the difficulty of understanding him: traumatic neurosis equals play equals the transference. While there is a brilliance in seeing the repetition compulsion as the common ground of those very different things, there is oddity as well. Pain equal to pleasure equal to therapeutic insight also could refer to an extraordinary confusion.

In the first chapter of this book, I addressed the transference in psychiatry, and we might recall Freud's description of it, from his *Outline of Psychoanalysis*: the patient sees in his therapist "the return, the reincarnation, of some important figure out of his childhood or past, and consequently transfers on to him feelings and reactions which applied to this prototype." We learn in *Beyond the Pleasure Principle* that it doesn't suffice that a person *recall* that figure from the past; he is obliged instead to *repeat* the emotional affair with that person (an adult version of the *fort-da* game if there ever was one):

> [The doctor] must get him [the patient] to re-experience some portion of his forgotten past, but must see to it, on the other hand, that the patient retains some degree of aloofness, which will enable him, in spite of everything, to recognize that what appears to be reality is in fact only a reflection of a forgotten past. If this can be successfully achieved, the patient's sense of conviction is won, together with the therapeutic success that is dependent on it.

Today, when a good number of psychiatrists would disavow their Freudianism in favor of here-and-now scientism, and when many people would disown any heavy-handed shrink who pushes a transference too far, it might be wise to rewrite this key passage, which applies only partly to the doctor-patient relationship: regarding the important people in our lives, we always re-experience a portion of our forgotten past transferred onto them; the secret is being aloof or objective enough to realize it.

Freud would contend that in all relationships involving desire, it's the repetition compulsion (and not desire) that we should notice. In terms of the people with whom we choose to become emotionally intimate (not necessarily sexually), for all the diverse reasons we invoke about why we chose as we did, we are obliged to re-examine our motivations. A good piece of general advice is never to psychoanalyze those closest to you, but certainly we can wonder to ourselves whether we have revisited our past in choosing them, as Freud suggests we do. We can resist that line of questioning and the psychoanalytic conclusion, if we like. Nevertheless, there is an eerie feeling that Freud comes close to a description of how emotions work in the world every single day:

> we have come across people all of whose human relationships have the same outcome: such as the benefactor who is abandoned in anger after a time by each of his *protégés* . . . ; or the man whose friendships all end in betrayal by his friend; or the man who time after time in the course of his life raises someone else into a position of great private or public authority and then, after a certain interval, himself upsets that authority and replaces him by a new one; or, again, the lover each of whose love affairs with a woman passes through the same phases and reaches the same conclusion. This 'perpetual recurrence of the same thing' causes us no astonishment when it relates to *active* behavior on the part of the person concerned and when we can discern in him an essential character-trait which always remains the same and which is compelled to find expression in a repetition of the same experiences. We are much more impressed by cases where the subject appears to have a *passive* experience, over which he has no influence, but in which he meets with a repetition of the same fatality.

Even a person wholly biased against Sigmund Freud would have to concede that we know such people. Maybe we are such people. *Repetition of the same fatality* is a haunting phrase; more haunting still, the repetitions can be observed in the pursuit of pleasure and fulfillment in our lives.

Summarizing our discussion thus far, the reality principle invites the temporary renunciation of pleasure. In neurosis and in play, the tendency to repeat speaks both to pleasure and unpleasure; and if we believe in the idea of transference, we tend to repeat the past in many of our emotional attachments, often without awareness of the fact. An instinct for death would seem a far cry from these points, unless one naturally thinks in tragic terms.

The Death Instinct. Beyond the Pleasure Principle can be roughly divided in half: the first three chapters address the pleasure-reality problem and repetition compulsion, as we have seen, and the next three discuss the death instinct, with his seventh chapter as an uneasy attempt to bring both halves together (there is no sin in limping to a conclusion, he says, alluding to an eleventh-century Arabic poem, in which we read "I change between two conditions, distress and ease; and I veer between two winds, the tempest and the breeze"). The second half is a personal but densely concentrated discussion that extends to biological matters. Over three chapters, Freud's death instinct amounts to a concept of contentment with respect to final outcomes—what he terms "a Nirvana principle." We should keep in mind that Freud is interested in what contradicts the pleasure principle, and, as he will eventually conclude, the only contradiction to pleasure is death. As so many of his critics and readers have asked, What justifies his insistent and morbid overstatement?

IV

Freud sounds very biological in the second half of *Beyond the Pleasure Principle*. An *instinct* for death suggests behavior predetermined by our biology; and it would be quite a revelation to learn that certain highly complex human behaviors, like repetition compulsion, are hard-wired in the manner of fish and bird migrations, as Freud suggests in his fourth chapter. Today, however, there is very little reason to read Sigmund Freud on biology; indeed there was no point in 1920 to read *Beyond the Pleasure Principle* as undiluted biology either.

In his sixty or so pages from start to finish (the book is remarkably short, but it reads long), he alludes to the metaphysics of Immanuel Kant (time and space as "necessary forms of thought"); he "unwittingly steer[s] our course into the harbour of Schopenhauer's philosophy" in examining how life *is* death; he offers a dose of Platonic myth, from the *Symposium*, in which we learn that once there were three types of human being—man, woman, and man-woman. (We are but tallies looking for our other half, said Plato.) In the literary domain, we get passing references to Aristotle on the mystery of why tragedy is enjoyable, Friedrich Schiller (hunger and love make the world go round, as the poet said), and Torquarto Tasso in *Gerusalemme Liberata* (about how Tancred kills his lover Clorinda by mistake), and to other writers not mentioned by name. These references shouldn't distract us from the theme that underlies them all: sooner or later, we need to "make friends with the necessity of dying," as he said in "Theme of the Three Caskets." In Freud's hands, what once was a motif of fiction and philosophy becomes a topic for biological consideration in 1920.

In a vehement, three-paragraph crescendo in chapter v, the crucial sentences imply that we never quite realize where we're headed instinctively in life. "The aim of life is death," but we certainly seem to partake of "the circuitous paths to death," paths which amount to a "picture of the phenomena of life;" but, these detours notwithstanding, "the organism shall follow its own path to death." Sex, we might think, makes good sense as a biological instinct, as does an instinct for self-preservation (which is a synonym for ego-instinct in Freud's vocabulary), but now the ego-instincts are subordinated to an individualized death instinct. Our compulsions, our postponements of pleasure even at play, and the "repetitions of fatality" in the transference were all hints of what was a biology of death all along.

So Freud contends. To digress for a moment, there have been modern reports to support the idea of a predetermined mortality. There are genes, we are told, that cause programmed death in cells and some organisms. Scientist W. R. Clark has recently suggested that some paths to death are really the ways and means of biological mandate: a genetic program for death "is not one of resistance to death, but one of active participation in the process," he says. But when Freud talks about the death instinct, despite whatever biological evidence he marshals for his argument, he refers to a problem in psychology for which biological death was an analogy. As I read *Beyond the Pleasure Principle*, death refers to a tragic force in life, and in referring to a biology of predetermined death, Freud refers to the necessity of tragedy, as if "biology" were simply another word for "tragic necessity."

Schopenhauer's pessimism is hard not to notice throughout the second half of *Beyond the Pleasure Principle*. Fortunately and unfortunately, the bleakness isn't all about death and necessity—for human beings, matters are even bleaker. If we can stand to hear to about it—it is a very difficult subject to address, and so we don't like to discuss it—there is the fundamental grief of dealing with people in the world. Even with the most therapeutic and humanistic of intentions, a few years in real clinical psychiatry can be a very humbling experience for those who seek to change or "help" one's fellow man. The following passage, beautiful yet Teutonically dark, comes from Schopenhauer's *Art of Controversy*, which Freud unmistakably assimilates into his thinking:

As a child, one has no conception of the inexorable character of the laws of nature, and of the stubborn way in which everything persists in remaining what it is. The child believes that even lifeless things are disposed to yield to it; perhaps because it feels itself one with nature, or, from mere unacquaintance with the world, believes that nature is disposed to be friendly. Thus it was that when I was a child, and had thrown my shoe into a large vessel full of milk, I was discovered entreating the shoe to jump out. . . . But not before we have gained mature experience do we recognize that human character is unalterable; that no entreaty, or representation, or example, or benefit, will bring a man to give up his ways; but that, on the contrary, every man is compelled to follow his own mode of acting and thinking, with the necessity of a law of nature; and that, however we take him, he always remains the same. It is only after we have obtained a clear and profound knowledge of this fact that we give up trying to persuade people, or to alter them and bring them round to our way of thinking. We try to accommodate ourselves to theirs instead, so far as they are indispensable to us, and to keep away from them so far as we cannot possibly agree.

We never develop a level of comfort with the stubborn way in which people persist in remaining who they are. The only respite from pessimism in the passage is Schopenhauer's version of the *fort-da* game, which is more amusing than Freud's. I enjoy the thought of little Arthur expecting that his shoe will rise up from his milk by pure will. His disappointments as an adult were preordained, it seems, from the time he was a toddler.

Beyond mere pessimism, the truly disturbing aspect of Schopenhauer's meditation has to do with what a person can expect from a great deal of work to achieve psychological insight. If it is true that mature people don't change much, that their psychologies and psychopathologies are cut from the cloth of early character formation (as Freud rather consistently maintains in his career), then a great deal of psychiatry must be an exercise in futility. The cloth was cut long ago, and character is the fixed pattern. Likewise, psychiatrist Wilhelm Reich referred—in his wiser writings before his descent into much oddness in his late career—to the "character armor" that people wear in their emotional lives. "Armor" is a metaphor that fits almost too well: character may dent, but it will not yield. Schopenhauer agrees: no entreaty, representation, example, benefit, or persuasion will force a person to change, so that, in the end, one studies psychology only to know how to accommodate other people begrudgingly or avoid them completely.

Freud borrows from Schopenhauer's pessimism in saying that death is the natural and inexorable "natural law" that contradicts pleasure. Death means something quite different from biological demise; it is sterile repetition, compulsion just to repeat, or repetition without insight, as occurs in human relationships all the time. In *Beyond the Pleasure Principle*, Freud's interest in the so-called Nirvana principle, which is so closely linked to the death instinct as to be indistinguishable from it, relates to the idea that people, if given a choice, will persist in a state of psychological inertia that is their pseudo-Nirvana.

One should remain unconvinced that a postponement of pleasure, the repetition compulsion, and all transference phenomena logically reveal a *biologically determined* death instinct. The force of Freud's argument lies elsewhere, perhaps in the tragic consideration that people don't change or, as he puts it, that they secretly aspire to a prior state of inertness. But if I indulge his brazen and somewhat illogical equation of psychological and biological principles, Freud absolutely surprises me with as much force as Schopenhauer depresses me.

⊟

In chapter VI of *Beyond the Pleasure Principle*, Freud discusses one-celled organisms. Commentators avoid talking about this chapter in any detail, preferring no doubt to dwell on the importance of death in larger organisms with complex brains. After many readings, however, I think of the sixth chapter with more fondness than any in the second half of the book. Freud's eye for association was formidable, and he should be read at face value. He thinks that the saga of microscopic infusoria (protozoans and other one-celled organisms) had bearing on the recalcitrant difficulties of his field. Let us imagine, he had said in chapter V, an organism in its most simplified form, as an undifferentiated vesicle filled with a substance susceptible to stimulation. It would be an organism without a psychology, one would think, but then we have his discussion in his chapter VI, which closes the discussion spanning the preceding two chapters.

In the late nineteenth century, scientists (particularly Germany's August Weismann) observed, with no small astonishment, that certain unicellular species seemed immortal. They didn't mate in the sexual sense; they divided in two, and investigators could follow one organism, generation upon generation, in its geometrical self-replication. By all appearances, parent and progeny (in a sense, they were one in the same) never died and didn't age. After many generations of splitting in half in their typical asexual fashion, they curiously did "mate" in a limited sense. Two organisms would come in contact with one another and seem to exchange protoplasm, although we should note that this was gender-less conjugation. (The species in question did not differentiate into males and females.) Contemporary investigators hardly understood why they conjugated at all.

In a series of lectures published in 1920, intended for biology students at Johns Hopkins University, an American professor involved in basic research on paramecia offered this very Freudian hypothesis: "*Suppose that there were no death in man; there would be no need for reproduction.*" If the unicellular organisms in question mated at all, perhaps the creatures were mortal in ways that science had not appreciated. Yet, the infusoria did not die even if they were prevented from conjugating, provided that the cells could replace, or otherwise "rejuvenate," their "immortal substance," what we would now call their genome, or genetic material. Weismann himself, writing in the nineteenth century, surmised that natural death was an adaptation for the survival of species: once reproduction or rejuvenation became a specialized function within cells, evolution favored the function, not the cell. The death of the cell was a natural consequence of a specialized reproductive function.

Freud states the relevance of these findings for psychology: "it is a matter of complete indifference to us whether natural death can be shown to occur in protozoa or not. The substance which is later recognized as being immortal has not yet become separated in them from the mortal one. The instinctual forces which seek to conduct life into death may also be operating in protozoa from the first, and yet their effects may be so completely concealed by the life-preserving forces that it may be very hard to find any direct evidence of their presence." The first sentence is laconic (why has he talked so long about protozoa? He's not even interested in protozoa). The last is emphatic but tricky. Life and death forces are easily confused for each other. A bit later, he says that we must assume that death forces are "associated from the very first with life instincts." Beyond all pleasure lies the contradiction that Eros, which is precisely the life instinct, always had to do with death, as it were, from the very start of the action.

A question for us, a rather pedestrian one when compared to the preservation of life, naturally arises: as psychologists, what do we say to the poor soul mentioned at the start of this chapter, the one who decides that it is time to fall in love, and into life, at long last? The best use of psychology is to al-low for both recollection and critical reflection; but in a real crisis, as Freud will say with supreme wisdom in "Analysis Terminable and Interminable," *analysis is useless. Beyond the Pleasure Principle* allows no other alternative than to admit that when the moment comes to choose love, at that crucial juncture which all of us must pass sooner or later, the question "what would my psychologist say?" is beautifully and fundamentally irrelevant. The doc-tor can talk about great forces at play, but he does not say that they can be controlled by any means, scientific or psychologic.

V

Some modern science writing, inspired by the same deep biological concerns that motivated August Weismann, seems to me no less vexed than Freud by the paradoxes inherent in love. Take, for example, this passage from the evolutionary psychologist Steven Pinker, who obviously prides himself as an observer of all things contemporary:

> the sneering, body-pierced, guitar-smashing rock musician is typically not singing about drugs, sex, or Satan. He is singing about love. He is courting a woman by calling attention to the irrationality, uncontrollability, and physi-ological costs of his desire. I want you so bad, it's driving me mad. Can't eat, can't sleep, Heart beats like a big bass drum, You're the only one, Don't know why I love you like I do.

Freud would say that Eros, like any other phenomenon in the mental life, must be examined, not necessarily for the sake of explaining it. *I want you so bad* generally means *I want you to want me so bad*; but the plea goes unre-quited, and thus begins many a mystery and puzzle of love. Pinker goes on to say, somewhat improbably, that arriving at some determination of evolution-ary fitness is the real issue in love: "Of course, one can well imagine a woman not being swept off her feet by [the sneering musician's] proclamations. (Or a man, if it is a woman doing the declaring.) They set off a warning light in the other component of courtship, *smart shopping*."

He refers to a kind of biological consumerism that puts one in mind of the search for the best buy at a mall: a love fit for evolutionary purposes seeks good looks, earning potential, and intelligence (criteria that might—or might not—be met by the next available musician). Deny it if you will, Pinker says, but we have evolutionary concerns in mind when we go about our romantic business. We can yield to his argument and still not understand love, but he usefully refers to "the contradiction of courtship" in which two parts of romantic love conflict: first, "setting a minimal standard for candidates in the mate market" and, second, "capriciously committing body and soul to one of them." The caprice of love (revealed in all its contradictions) seems on target. No amount of rationalism in choosing a mate will ever diminish the illogic of Eros. Drugs, sex, and Satanic cult almost seem like acts of high logic by comparison.

The death instinct should not be understood as our best explanation for the compulsion to repeat. Repetition, as Søren Kierkegaard believed, was analogous to memory, a recollection but in the forward direction: a child who wants to hear the same story or watch the same movie over and again, such that all details are ingrained, needn't be an incarnation of Thanatos at all, though he seeks something like the absolute death of novelty. Similarly, one can remain quite unconvinced that any theory, including the likes of Pinker's, explains why we choose certain sexual partners rather than others. As great a theoretician as he was, Freud persists in his awe at the dynamics of love, as if he were witness to pure forces of nature, Eros and Thanatos, that make one feel small.

⛁

After *Beyond the Pleasure Principle*, particularly in *Civilization and its Discontents* (1930), his explanatory power had quite left him, Freud claimed. More than once in *Civilization* (*Man's Discomfort with Civilization* was the English title that Freud preferred), we hear him talking about how obvious his statements are, how he wastes ink and the printer's time in stating aspects of the human experience well known to everyone and hardly in need of a depth psychologist's commentary. He feels that he can't explain much anyway: "What is called happiness in its narrowest sense comes from the satisfaction—most often instantaneous—of pent-up needs which have reached great intensity, and by its very nature can only be a transitory experience," he writes, "When any condition desired by the pleasure-principle is protracted, it results in a feeling only of mild comfort; we are so constituted that we can only intensely enjoy contrasts. . . . Our possibilities of happiness are thus limited from the start by our very constitution. It is much less difficult to be unhappy." And, reflecting on how some people choose happiness by seeking—forever seeking—pleasure for pleasure's sake, and others only by avoiding pain, Freud says that there is "no sovereign recipe in this matter which suits all; each one must find out for himself by which particular means he may achieve felicity." Just as there is no sovereign recipe for happiness, there is no denying that a person finds his or her unhappiness with sovereign ease.

These obvious points aren't altogether trivial. I hope it's not too odd for me to observe the humor in what he says: it's easy to achieve unhappiness, and, like a renewing natural resource, unhappiness sustains remarkably well over time. Unhappiness is a near-perfect emotion—it is durable, available, and reliable; it's just not what we exactly want. In *Civilization*, Freud no longer feels obliged to justify a biological instinct for unpleasure. The ardor of argument in *Beyond the Pleasure Principle* is gone, and what remains is a tragicomic world-view that had been present dating to 1913 in "On Narcissism."

Keeping in mind the title that Freud preferred, we should say that "civilization" is not the first subject of his meditation: discomfort is. He speaks of a need to unbutton a collar, so to speak, to loosen what constrains the human psyche, since real discomfort in everyday life is the insidious feeling of constraint. We barely want to talk about the subject: maybe we live in the wrong city, have the wrong job, persist in the wrong relationship, or even (alas) live in the wrong skin. *Civilization*, or shall we say *Discomfort*, formally completes a line of thought that began with the "cure by love" passage in "On Narcissism"; we recall that it wouldn't be so bad a solution, were it not for the lover's crippling dependency on outside help. But who isn't crippled or otherwise discomfited sooner or later?

⛉

On the back cover of my worn copy of *Civilization*, I read in a liner note that "[t]he renunciations that men make, on culture's behalf, of their sexual and aggressive instincts . . . are an intolerable burden, the source of man's neurotic symptoms and of the larger tensions which threaten to undo civilization itself." I know that the sentence corroborates the standard opinion about Freud's subject matter in the book, but I have always found such commentary quite beside the point, because it misses the rub, the genuine no-exit that Freud takes such pains to describe. If a lover renounces the cure by love, he could turn neurotic—at least, he suffers "the intolerable burden" of renouncing erotic urge. If the lover indulges the cure by love, thus crippling himself in a dependent relationship, or even if his love is relatively unneurotic, then there will be dread in the form of tension still, because all pleasure is fleeting. One wants to say: heads you get discomfort, tails you do, too. If such is Freud's lasting contribution to the analysis of love, then perhaps we can understand why so many people have been wanting him dead since the time he died biologically.

I will not do justice to *Civilization* as a whole book. Beginning with his indictment of religious sentiment and his quite stunning analogy of the human psyche as an archeology of eternal Rome in chapter I, to the critique of technological progress in chapter III, to the analysis of Christian love in chapter V, to the study of the super-ego's unrelenting severity in the last three chapters, Freud's scope in the book is beyond that of my more restricted interest, which is the fate of love. I enter a side-door of the book, and draw attention to a footnote, one of my favorite moments in it. (Freud is the great footnote writer of his own work; it was a talent cultivated by annotating most all his books for later editions and reprintings.)

In chapter V, in a discussion about why the love of one's enemies is problematic (because religious commandment places a premium not on love, but the suppression of hate), he adds this aside:

> A great poet may permit himself, at least in jest, to give utterance to psychological truths that are heavily censured. Thus Heine: "Mine is the most peaceable disposition. My wishes are a humble dwelling with a thatched roof, but a good bed, good food, milk and butter of the freshest, flowers at my windows, some fine tall trees before my door; and if the good God wants to make me completely happy, he will grant me the joy of seeing some six or seven of my enemies hanging from these trees. With my heart full of deep emotion I shall forgive them before they die all the wrong they did me in their lifetime—true, one must forgive one's enemies, but not until they are brought to execution."

The reference is to Heinrich Heine, whom Freud quotes liberally in all his works. If there is a common theme to Freud's citations of the famed nineteenth-century German writer-in-exile, born of Jewish parents, whose books were banned by the German Diet because of their revolutionary nature, it is the irony of his honesty, as the above passage attests. *At least in jest* is the throw-away phrase that gives me pause, and I will end this long chapter with a thought about the tragedy in the jest.

To love those closest to us, as Cordelia does her king, is the highest and best expression of the human mind, surpassing the best imaginative production by science or art. Freud's final comment about the power of Eros, at the close of *Civilization*, is his hope that its power can maintain itself "alongside" its "immortal adversary," which we might call Thanatos, though he means many things by that name, including hate, meaninglessness, aggression, and death. Thanatos is no less immortal than Eros. Love might not triumph, but the struggle will be engaged: such is the final wisdom of *Civilization*, which rightly has been understood as Freud's tragic vision of the human condition.

But we should return to the devious honesty of Heinrich Heine: the comedy in what he says, his sense of all things coming to a gratifying conclusion, *is* the tragedy. It would be very nice indeed to see our enemies hung by the neck—we need go only a bit further to understand Freud's insight regarding such desires. What happens when forgiveness happens too late, after death and after the wrongs have been done, even if our supposed enemies have been hung? We broach the theme of choosing love and death with the realization that we choose neither alone, but both together. Freud explored "choice" from 1913 onward to his death, precisely the double-choice that operates to our mortification and aesthetic awe in Shakespeare's *King Lear*.

With one character in mind—Cordelia—we can rehearse about thirty years in Freud's intellectual development. Recall her answer to her father so early in the play:

Nothing, my Lord.

It is a statement of her love and discontent and a presentiment of her death. As an insight—that she honestly has nothing to say—it seems more profound than all theory since Socrates.

Five

Hamlet

THE PROTAGONIST OF this chapter says he will "unpack the heart with words," yet, famously, he's hard to fathom at his most densely eloquent. Freud was more obsessed by him than he was by the youngest daughter of King Lear.

Cordelia, who says nothing, "is death," but Hamlet requires a more complex diagnosis or explanation, in Freud's opinion. Does Hamlet (or the reader of Shakespeare's *Hamlet*) need Freud? Why does Freud want so much to diagnose or explain him? The unpacking of hearts is the central issue: if a psychology doesn't accomplish it, what can?

I

Before we delve into Freud's long preoccupation with the Dane, let me offer an afterthought on Cordelia. Based on a letter Freud wrote in 1934, we know that he entertained an explanation of *King Lear* analogous to his theory about the supposedly unconscious Oedipalism in *Oedipus the King*. Freud remarked that in *King Lear* there is no Mrs. Lear, and he wondered about what her absence meant. Cordelia "still clings" to her father in a way that her elder sisters do not. Cordelia's love is a "holy secret," and no one contends erotically (Freud's thought) for Lear except her. Freud isn't coy about elaborating an incest theory to "explain" *Lear*. The absence of Mrs. Lear means that Cordelia takes her erotic place. Lear's erotic love for her was so unacceptable to the King, according to the letter, as to drive Lear mad.

The 1934 reading is an instance of Freud at his worst on Shakespeare, although his "explanatory" commentary on *Hamlet*, along with Dr. Ernest Jones's book-length elaboration of Freud in *Hamlet and Oedipus* (1949), rivals it in badness. The only other serious contender for egregiousness would be Freud's endorsement of John Thomas Looney's *Shakespeare Identified*

(1921), a book that argues that Shakespeare was actually a nobleman named Edward de Vere, the seventeenth Earl of Oxford. Looney argues, in part, that *Hamlet* is Shakespeare's "self-delineation." Study the life of the Earl, Looney said, and Hamlet can be no one else but him; Ophelia is Lady Oxford; Polonius is Oxford's father-in-law; Horatio is Horace (Horatio) de Vere (Oxford's cousin); and Elsinore is the Elizabethan Royal Court, with which the Earl of Oxford was intimately familiar. Biographer Peter Gay has said that Freud sided with Looney because at least they shared the view that *Hamlet* reveals the artist's mind. Freud discussing Looney, just to be clear, does not help us understand Freud's real preoccupation with *Hamlet*.

The question that Freud must address to diagnose the Prince is Hamlet's mind. Incest, patricide, and the Unconscious are hallmarks of Freudian theory, but for those aspects to apply meaningfully to Hamlet, we must assume that our knowledge of Hamlet deepens by a Freudian psychotherapy that never happened. *Hamlet* is Shakespeare's longest play, a finite assembly of 21,000 separate words, many more in total word count, and it depicts the mind of an only child, whose vocabulary to describe his state of mind and mood is gigantic. Why does Freud take on his "case"? The bell-clanging Freudian answer, that Freud can explain the "mystery" of *Hamlet*, flies in the face of a much more sensible reaction–that Freud doesn't do anything of the kind. In fact, he interprets the play to a thinking person's near-complete dissatisfaction; and, what's worse, he leaves us with the task of articulating, very much like Hamlet to all those who would diagnose him with a problem, how and why we are dissatisfied.

If the Oedipus complex (for which I would read: emotional ambivalence) is universal, and if Prince Hamlet illustrates the complex, then there is nothing unique about Prince Hamlet or *Hamlet* the play. Short of poet T. S. Eliot's commentary that *Hamlet* was an artistic failure, no statement about the play sounds more counterintuitive than to say that it is psychologically banal. Regarding the Oedipus complex, I continue to follow Sophoclean scholar J.-P. Vernant in wondering whether *Oedipus the King* reveals any unconscious material at all. Oedipus learns about himself in ways that he might have preferred not to know, but unconscious motivation playing itself out as dysfunction in life doesn't apply to King Oedipus. Likewise, we can't say that Hamlet is dysfunctional, although Elsinore almost certainly is.

Hamlet procrastinates in killing his uncle, who has allegedly killed King Hamlet and married Hamlet's mother, Gertrude. The delay, as Ernest Jones and Sir Laurence Olivier (in an old film version) maintain, is evidence of neurotic indecision, the so-called "problem of Hamlet." Freud is a bit subtler in *The Interpretation of Dreams*: "Hamlet is able to do anything—except take vengeance on the man who did away with his father and took that father's place with his mother, the man who shows him the repressed wishes of his own childhood realized. Thus the loathing which should drive him on to revenge is replaced in him by self-reproaches." But Hamlet, who is able to do *anything*, probably psychoanalyzed himself (as Freud psychoanalyzed himself, beginning in *The Interpretation of Dreams*), only to conclude that inaction was philosophic in nature. The murder of a man in prayer, no matter his crime, is mere vengeance—not, in other words, the finest possible articulation of Hamlet's state of mind as he contemplates revenge. He's no angry Laertes or bellicose Fortinbras; he's smarter than either and can't be judged by their standards of getting things done. We know that Hamlet *eventually* kills Claudius (after Claudius inadvertently poisons Gertrude), at which point the play is nearly done: by then, Hamlet has said what he wanted to say, and the remnant silence once he is gone has a resonance that exceeds simple revenge or retribution.

If Hamlet had killed Claudius in act I, Freud would need to change his argument only slightly. Would Hamlet be any less Oedipal in nature? In such a revised *Hamlet*, the plot would read like a British-Danish version of *Crime and Punishment* in which the crime comes first, as in Dostoevsky's novel. The ensuing drama would be all about mortification for the act, perhaps; there would be a second widowhood for Gertrude, and her new availability for her son, whose "nighted color" might involve the kind of unacceptable eroticism that supposedly drove Lear mad—see above, with respect to Cordelia as a new Mrs. Lear. *Hamlet*, like Shakespearean tragedy in general, is full of murder (often gratuitous), but Freud says that during the entire progress of the play we watch a psychopathological preoccupation over what Hamlet wants and doesn't want, but we supposedly all should know what he wants. The answer is: his mother.

Beyond the celebrated Freud-Jones interpretation, psychiatrist Bennett Simon has raised another Oedipal issue that is wickedly far-fetched and, therefore, interesting. If Claudius and Gertrude were such fierce lovers, it's possible that their relationship had been ongoing for some time, perhaps for a very long time. In the incestuous royal court of Elsinore, what if Claudius, in fact, *was* Hamlet's biological father? Then, the ghost of King Hamlet would have augmented reason to be perturbed, because he is a cuckold *and* he has been murdered *and* his son isn't his. When Hamlet pauses in killing

Claudius as the latter prays, maybe Hamlet, who is no fool, comes to realize that his own personal history has never been as it seemed either to him or to audiences for over 400 years. Extrapolating Simon, Hamlet "represses" the knowledge that Claudius is his father, and we might imagine a Darth-Vaderian moment in act v in which Claudius turns to Hamlet to report, "I am your father." This scenario is more "Oedipal" than Freud's own reading of *Hamlet*, and it is just as bad.

Freud leaves it to us to explain why his interpretation seems so "poor in thanks" to the play that inspired it. One could just dismiss him as unappreciative of Shakespeare's rich characterizations and pedantic when it comes to all matters psychological. But neither comment would be fair, since Freud expressed his own discontent with poor interpretation, as we know from his celebrated (if somewhat out-of-place) reference to *Hamlet* in "The Moses of Michelangelo" (1914). He expresses his plain awe before Shakespeare: "how many of these interpretations [of *Hamlet*] leave us cold—so cold that they do nothing to explain the effect of the play and rather incline us to the view that its magical appeal rests solely upon the impressive thoughts in it and the splendour of its language. And yet, do not those very endeavours speak for the fact that we feel the need of discovering in it some source of power beyond these alone?" "Magical appeal," "need of discovering," and "source of power" are all very strong phrases in deference to Shakespeare; it seems Freud wants to say that all interpretative endeavor lags behind the Bard's impressive thoughts and splendor of language. If *Hamlet* is so emotionally and conceptually straightforward (its mystery so solved, as Freud would have us believe), then we barely need to read the play.

II

Freud takes on Hamlet as a patient, because he thinks he understands him better than all the doctors in the play and far better than the countless doctors over time who have ever read *Hamlet*. For those who would say there are no doctors in the play (as compared to *Macbeth*, for example), consider that Polonius diagnoses him—indeed, provides a whole medical history (Hamlet "[f]ell into a sadness, then into a fast, /Thence to a lightness, and, by this declension, /Into the madness wherein he now raves"—all of it due to a mad love); Gertrude intuits her son's affliction as *the* problematic condition or disease in Elsinore ("I doubt that it is no other but the main/His father's death and our o'er hasty marriage"); Claudius's diagnosis is regally pragmatic and surgical (Hamlet is dangerous to himself and others; "Diseases desperate grown/By desperate appliance are relieved, /Or not at all;" so, Claudius will send Hamlet to England); and even the good Horatio, both friend and pseudo-physician, advises him to guard against both the ghost of King Hamlet and against the specter of psychosis most of all ("what if it tempt you . . . and draw you into madness? Think of it"). The wisest of the play's doctors could be Ophelia before her mental demise. She knows that whatever Hamlet's illness might be, the patient is atypical. She thinks that it's prudent just to describe what she sees, rather than diagnose him at all: "He seemed to find his way without his eyes, /For out o'doors he went without their helps/And to the last bended their light on me." The key players in *Hamlet* are all part-time psychiatrists, each slightly amateurish in their assumption that Hamlet is just a patient.

Of bad diagnosticians in the play, Rosencrantz and Guildenstern are exemplary in how they fail to understand the patient. They broadcast their incomprehension immediately, at their first appearance with Hamlet, in act II, scene ii:

HAMLET	What have you, my good friends, deserved at the hands of Fortune that she sends you to prison hither?
GUILDENSTERN	Prison, my lord?
HAMLET	Denmark's a prison.
ROSENCRANTZ	Then is the world one.
HAMLET	A goodly one; in which there are many confines, wards, and dungeons, Denmark being one o' th' worst.
ROSENCRANTZ	We think not so, my lord.
HAMLET	Why, then 'tis none to you, for there is nothing either good or bad but thinking makes it so. To me it is a prison.
ROSENCRANTZ	Why, then your ambition makes it one. 'Tis too narrow for your mind.
HAMLET	O God, I could be bounded in a nutshell and count myself king of infinite space, were it not that I have bad dreams.
GUILDENSTERN	Which dreams are indeed are ambition, for the very substance of the ambitious is merely the shadow of a dream.

I have honestly tried to like Rosencrantz and Guildenstern in the same way that I love Horatio, because once they, too, were Hamlet's friends, and because it is possible that they had every good intention to lift Hamlet from his doldrums (even if they were assigned to Hamlet's case by Claudius and Gertrude). Also, they are killed later on, and thus deserve some pity. Their banter with Hamlet, in the hands of a comedic director, could be staged as the antics of fools, but to me Rosencrantz and Guildenstern annoy in a way that a Shakespearean fool never would, because they don't have a clue who they are up against, and they add arrogance to their ignorance. Sometimes, a philosopher once said, you can attack truth directly, but more often you encircle it, in deference to the complexity of truth. Rosencrantz and Guildenstern take dead aim, miss entirely, and still think they are on target. Playwright Tom Stoppard tells us sardonically that "Rosencrantz and Guildenstern are dead," but they have never died: there is always someone ready to explain us to ourselves.

To their credit, Rosencrantz and Guildenstern don't call Hamlet mad with a method as Polonius does, but one senses a no-less patronizing tone in their comments, as if they assume his mental frailty. Their fundamental diagnosis is that he is ambitious, therefore ill. Hamlet merely wants to know why they are in Elsinore and who put them up to coming there. Actually, Hamlet already suspects Claudius and Gertrude as instigators, but he seeks confirmation. His passing mention of "prison" yields a debate about whether Denmark or the world is a prison. (The root meaning of prison has to do with "grasping," so partly we're interested in who "grasps" and who doesn't—who "gets" the current situation and who doesn't.) The ensuing exchange operates at such mismatched levels that one can refer only to a travesty of communication between the parties–by "mismatch," I don't mean that Rosencrantz and Guildenstern are stupid, but next to the Prince they are, and, certainly, they aren't as smart as they think.

They were once Hamlet's comrades ("My Lord, you once loved me," as Rosencrantz says later in act III); but whatever affection there once was now is suspect, and the parties can no longer speak as intimates in any way. Hamlet already perceives a loss of "love," whereas the duo doesn't yet notice any breach in affection—in fact, they are trying to use that affection to their own ends. When Rosencrantz suggests, with Guildenstern following suit immediately, that Hamlet is ambitious, the real diagnostic problem becomes all but obscured by talk about ambition, dreams, and shadows (topics mentioned in order of increasing vagueness). Hamlet's pivotal line, "there is nothing either good or bad but thinking makes it so. To me it is a prison" and his metaphor for the universe as a boundedness in a nutshell refer twice to imprisonment in a dual sense: Who can escape the problem in Elsinore? (Answer: no one); and, Who grasps the problem in Elsinore? (Answer: Hamlet, who is in prison). But Guildenstern ties loose ends into a ridiculous knot when he discusses dreams of ambition and the shadows of those dreams. The overreaching Rosencrantz and Guildenstern fail to grasp Hamlet *or* the prison in question.

Maybe the duo's fecklessness shouldn't bother me quite to the degree it does. But Freud himself understood Rosencrantz and Guildenstern as archetypes for a most unfortunate type of psychiatry—to call it what it should be called: a stupid psychiatry. I don't want to practice it, so I read act II scene ii with what Hamlet would call "a fighting in my heart." Freud quoted *Hamlet* often in his writings (critic Norman Holland once dutifully catalogued 34 instances); he discusses Rosencrantz and Guildenstern in one longish meditation from "On Psychotherapy," a lecture delivered to general medical practitioners in 1904:

> reports reach my ears that this or that colleague has arranged appointments with a patient in order to undertake a mental treatment of the case, though I am certain he knows nothing of the technique of any such therapy. His expectation must be therefore that the patient will make him a present of his secrets, or perhaps that he is looking for salvation in some sort of confession or confidence. I should not be surprised if a patient were injured rather than benefitted by being treated in such a fashion. For it is not so easy to play upon the instrument of the mind. I am reminded on such occasions of the words of a world-famous neurotic—though it is true that he was never treated by a physician but existed only in a poet's imagination—Hamlet, Prince of Denmark. The King has ordered two courtiers, Rosenkranz and Guildenstern, to follow him, question him and drag the secret of his depression out of him. He wards them off. Then some recorders are brought on the stage and Hamlet, taking one of them, begs one of the tormentors to play upon it, telling him that it is as easy as lying. The courtier excuses himself, for he knows no touch of the instrument, and when he cannot be persuaded to try it, Hamlet finally breaks out with these words: 'Why, look you now, how unworthy a thing you make of me! You would play upon me; . . . you would pluck out the heart of my mystery . . . [then in Freud's italics] *'Sblood, do you think I am easier to be played on than a pipe? Call me what instrument you will, though you can fret me, you cannot play upon me.*

The discussion reads like the defense of a profession: Freud is aware that the psychologist's reputation is like that of the sophist in ancient Greece, a talker whose talk is dubious, but he says that most people don't understand what a psychologist tries to accomplish with talk, which is an insight beyond sophistry. I couldn't agree more, but I wince at Freud's claim that Hamlet is a "world-famous neurotic," because the phrase is so out of place in its context. Hamlet in act III, scene ii (the scene Freud describes) is the quintessence of awareness. He knows precisely why Rosencrantz and Guildenstern have appeared; and, later, he will do away with them as they conspire to kill him. To the degree that Hamlet "knows," whereas the duo seems particularly clueless, Hamlet sounds entirely unneurotic, and the scene amounts to a comeuppance that completes a line of thought that began in act II, scene ii. To call Hamlet neurotic merely advertises how Freud wants us to diagnose him.

"Neurosis," just to be clear, is not a fuzzy term, but it has become one. In common parlance, it describes either nothing specific (a "reaction to stress" perhaps, but what isn't?) or some vaguely nervous condition of modern man or woman. In Freud's estimation, "neurosis" was very specific: a disease in which a symptom substitutes for an unresolved and "repressed" conflict from the past. But, in *Hamlet*, all conflicts (including the presumably unconscious ones) are dramatized. Between act II, scene ii and act III, scene ii, Hamlet sits in the audience watching his players perform *The Mousetrap*, otherwise known as *The Murder of Gonzago*. The play wherein Hamlet hopes to catch the conscience of the king should also disturb the conscience of the Prince, since it dramatizes patricide and usurpation of a queen's love, but Hamlet has directed the performance; he has contributed the important lines; and, thanks to him, the stage is like an open forum of Freud's Unconscious. Consider act III, scene iv as well: if you are in your mother's bedroom (on top of her, in some film versions), and your father's ghost appears, talking about the whetting and blunting of purpose, we in the audience could justifiably think that very little escapes Hamlet's consciousness. The Unconscious is just a bit actor in his production.

Hamlet the play withholds nothing; if Freud thinks Hamlet the character represses Oedipal wishes throughout the play and especially when Claudius kneels in his chamber, then Hamlet is neurotic only if we seriously avoid reading the play. Hamlet thinks and knows beyond all "repressions"—certainly he thinks beyond the capacities of all his tiresome diagnosticians. As we contemplate Hamlet's indictment of all meddling doctors in *'Sblood, do you think I am easier to be played on than a pipe?* we should consider that

Freud's 1904 commentary flirts with a gross self-contradiction: if, in fact, *it is not so easy to play upon the instrument of the mind*, why does Freud think that he, alone, plucks the heart of Hamlet's mystery?

III

Hamlet fails as art, T. S. Eliot said, because "Hamlet (the man) is dominated by an emotion which is inexpressible, because it is in excess of the facts as they appear . . . Hamlet is up against the difficulty that his disgust is occasioned by his mother, but that his mother is not an adequate equivalent for it; his disgust envelopes and exceeds her. It is thus a feeling which he cannot understand." I cannot agree that the core subject of *Hamlet* is a son's feelings towards a guilty mother (Hamlet expresses many other feelings; and, for her part, Gertrude feels badly for Hamlet starting in act I), but the point regarding *inexpressible* emotion is pertinent as we consider Hamlet's "mystery." Eliot thinks that maybe there is no mystery, that Hamlet commits the very flaw which he advises his own players to avoid. He "saws the air" too much, he out-Herods Herod.

We should pause at the comment that Hamlet "envelopes and exceeds": what strong emotion doesn't envelope and exceed its provocation? Psychology is reliably curious about emotion in relationship to cause, but it makes no assumptions about a proportional fit between the two. Say a person falls in love or into a rage: to ask whether the emotion is "proportional," with an "objective correlative" (Eliot's famous phrase), sounds like some cold mathematical equation, which doesn't exist in the psychology that I practice or that I live from day to day.

"Mystery" in *Hamlet* means that the Prince's descriptions leave us chasing after explanations, just as a psychologist tries to rationalize a mood. Eliot eschews mystery; he settles on the idea that Hamlet is a rank melodramatist. Freud eschews mystery, too, but he is reliably preoccupied by Hamlet's "impressive thoughts," which anticipate and bury all critical judgments of the play, including Freud's opinions. One such impressive thought—we read it between Hamlet's lines, over and again—is that emotional expression might actually be *constrained* on all sides. (According to psychoanalytic theory, we aren't conscious of our repressions; to repress is to be constrained without realizing it.) Hamlet is eminently aware of all "boundedness"; he anticipates Freudian repression—which is nothing but a constraint on our power to articulate, an inherent limitation of which we aren't aware. Hamlet essentially discusses his rather Freudian theory into the deaf ears of Rosencrantz and Guildenstern.

Constraint is not quite the opposite of excess: there is no contradiction in thinking that Shakespearean language addresses and expresses both at the same time. What a person feels can defy articulation despite more lines by one protagonist than can be found in any of Shakespeare's works. To unpack the heart with words (even to excess) can be futile, because one will be misunderstood anyway.

The most famous soliloquy in our language concludes that it is nobler in the mind to suffer slings and arrows *or* to take arms against a sea of trouble. To interpret Hamlet as deciding one way or the other is literalism, which is the very opposite of richness in meaning, but people will still think about "To be or not to be" as a straightforward contemplation of suicide. Over centuries, smart people have tried to plumb Hamlet's depth, but they achieve parodies of understanding (perhaps Hamlet would enjoy them, as he relished *The Mousetrap*). One extreme example is Jacques Lacan's argument, in "Desire and the Interpretation of Desire in Hamlet" (1977), that Hamlet was primordially afraid of being castrated. 'Twere to consider too curiously, to consider so, as Horatio would say.

The shock in any attempt to interpret *Hamlet* is that we return, centuries later, to reread a play and listen to a personality who, as William Hazlitt observed, has grown so familiar that we can no more interpret the play than "know how to describe our own faces." Lacan, from the same source just mentioned, might be wrong about castration fear, but he is dead right on one point: "everything hinges on the question of what's going on in [Hamlet's] mind. However superficial this characteristic may seem to you, it's still the thing that Shakespeare seized on for his *Hamlet*." Freud was all too wary of Hamlet's foreknowledge that no one articulates what is on Hamlet's mind except the Prince himself.

⏚

Freud had a way of rehearsing and reiterating what his patients told him until, as he once put it, the information started to "speak" to him. These were not pure moments of revelation. He returned repeatedly to his case material to pronounce, as in *Inhibitions, Symptoms, and Anxiety* (1926) relatively late in his career, that "it is almost humiliating that, after so much work, we should still be having difficulty in understanding the most fundamental facts." Freud's way of framing a psychological truth—not freeze-framing it—is the debt that he owes privately both to Hamlet and to Shakespeare. The approach, which was iterative often to the point of self-contradiction, was more interesting than the conclusions he would report at any particular point in his career.

Clinical experience was always Freud's starting point, so it seems fitting that we should look at the few book-length clinical studies that he saw fit to publish during his lifetime. (I'll not address the studies he conducted with Josef Breuer.) In summarizing them, we can say that, in general, Freud's acumen and psychoanalytic process are as much on the couch as his patients were. Freud, the Dr. Hamlet of Psychoanalysis, reliably scanned himself.

⊟

In the case of a five-year-old boy named Hans, Freud conducts an analysis via copious letters from the boy's father with responses from Freud—a treatment by correspondence, with Hans's father as a surrogate for Sigmund Freud.

The boy sees "widdlers" everywhere—if his father draws a picture of a giraffe, the boy insists that he also draw the animal's widdler (his father obliges him); he notes that his baby sister has a particularly small widdler; he undresses dolls looking for widdlers; in a story book, a monkey's tail is a curly widdler. A penis here, a penis there—they all add up, but to what? Hans develops a phobic fear of large animals, like horses and perhaps his father. Freud argues that the case corroborates his thesis that children entertain sexual thoughts and castration fears, as he argues in *Three Essays on the Theory of Sexuality* (1905). Yet, in a postscript to the case, Hans, grown up at age nineteen, visits Freud to confess that "when he read his own case history it was like reading about a stranger: he did not recognize himself, could not remember anything of what was related." He wasn't phobic any longer, but it was as if his "treatment" had never occurred. Hans at age five might have been destined to his phobia, Freud argues, but in an eloquent expression of the strangeness both of psychological disease and treatment, Hans as young adult mainly notes a void in his memory.

⊟

In the case of Dora, an eighteen-year-old woman with a history of unexplained medical problems dating to childhood (she had "grown accustomed to laugh at the efforts of doctors"), Freud offers the less-then-profound insight that she doesn't want psychotherapy. Manifestly, she doesn't, and, after three months, she terminates her sessions just as Freud prepares to deliver a coup de grâce of psychoanalytic insight, that Dora was in love.

Dora's parents, in the midst of a sexless and unhappy marriage, had moved to a health resort outside the town of B— for treatment of the father's tuberculosis. There they befriend Mr. and Mrs. K, a couple also in the throes of discord. Dora's relationships with her parents had soured over an indefinite period of time—"she was clearly satisfied neither with herself nor with her family." Mrs. K, previously a patient at the same health resort, spends much time with Dora's father. Dora's mother keeps her distance from her husband, his sickness, and his convalescence. (One wonders what she was doing.) Mrs. K and Dora get along quite well, and the two see a great deal of each other, exchanging "intimacies" in long conversations. Dora looks after the K children as if they were her own. Mr. K takes a liking to Dora.

Dora subsequently reports to her mother that Mr. K made a sexual advance during a walk together along a lake. Dora's father confronts Mr. K with the allegation, which he promptly denies. The father suspects that Dora fantasized Mr. K's advance, but, as her treatment with Freud begins—a treatment arranged by her father to "bring her to reason"—she describes a previous episode in which she visited Mr. K's place of business in B— with a plan to attend a town festival with him. Mr. K had sent away his employees, and Dora reports that he grabbed and kissed her, that she felt violent disgust, and fled.

Freud's ensuing analysis touches on at least five sensitive issues: 1. the indisputable fact that there had been a sexual liaison between Dora's father and Mrs. K; 2. Dora's suspicion that her father covertly negotiated an "exchange" (Mr. K loses Mrs. K but gains Dora in turn); 3. Dora's disgust with her father as a consequence; 4. Freud's thought that Dora in fact loved Mr. K; and, last but not least, 5. Dora's disgust with Freud because of this hypothesis. We have, as critic Steven Marcus has observed, all the makings of a Victorian novel in which everyone has a secret and everyone conspires in thinking there are no secrets. Other critics have wondered, with understandable amazement and curiosity, why Freud chose to publish Dora's case. Not only is there no highlighting of cure, but Freud indirectly admits that the value of this particular psychoanalysis wasn't Freud's insight so much as the remarkable character of Dora, who, it seems to me, simply trumps Freud by walking out on psychoanalysis. Despite all of her entrenched psychological problems, or perhaps because of them, she played a kind of Hamlet to Freud's Guildencrantz.

⊜

The case of Daniel Paul Schreber elaborates on the problem of non-cure in psychoanalysis. After reading Freud's *Psychoanalytic Remarks on an Auto-biographically Described Case of Paranoia* (the "Schreber case"), one senses that the genre of the case history, whose ostensible purpose is to corroborate theory (regarding infant sexuality, for example) or to demonstrate clinical efficacy in psychoanalysis, accomplishes neither. The theme in the Schreber case is emotional ambivalence—which is also Hamlet's theme, though we call it Oedipal out of habit. Freud never treated Schreber; his knowledge of the case derived entirely from Schreber's *Memoirs of a Nervous Illness*, published in 1903. Freud's own *Psychoanalytic Remarks* appeared in 1911, the year Schreber died.

Schreber had been a respected judge in the city of Dresden; he suffered two nervous breakdowns, both related to what he termed intellectual over-exertion. The first lasted from the Autumn of 1884 to the end of 1885, and was remarkable for "severe hypochondria." Under a Dr. Flechsig's care in Leipzig, he recovered, after which, Schreber says, he spent eight happy years with his wife (although he lamented their not being able to have children) and enjoyed much professional success. A second breakdown, far more elaborate in its description and protracted in duration, began with a "tortuous insomnia" in the Autumn of 1893. He consulted Dr. Flechsig once more, but was transferred to the Sonnenstein Asylum in June 1894 due to a precipitous deterioration. He had "hypochondriacal" concerns about brain softening, a rotting body, and the Plague, was extremely sensitive to light and sound, sat motionless for prolonged periods, and attempted suicide by drowning. Later, he reported visions of miracles and the sound of "holy music" in his ears.

At Sonnenstein, he came under the care of its director, Dr. Weber, whose medical reports highlight the disparity between a deferential, witty, and intelligent Schreber in social company and a compelling portrait of derangement in private sessions. From roughly 1900 onward, Schreber submitted numerous legal appeals to reverse a court order that kept him at Sonnenstein. Dr. Weber opposed those entreaties; Schreber announced an intention to write a tell-all memoir of his madness, but the core of his legal argument was that, over the years, he had become completely harmless. The court concurred. In the summer of 1902, it rescinded all orders for Schreber's hospitalization. From the summary judgment, Freud quotes a succinct statement of Schreber's clinical problem: "He takes himself to be called to redeem the world and to restore to it its lost bliss. But this he can only do if he has first transformed himself from a man into a woman."

At some point in the late Summer of 1893, before Sonnenstein, Schreber had a feeling while half asleep—not quite a dream—that it "must be really nice to be a woman undergoing intercourse." Freud builds an extraordinary case out of this confession and from Schreber's phantasmagoria of his feminine transformation, as described in his *Memoirs*. Schreber probably wanted Dr. Flechsig to treat his second severe illness, but Freud speculates, "[p]erhaps a tender affection for the doctor was left over from [the first] condition, which, for reasons unknown to us, was now heightened to the form of an erotic inclination." Freud concludes that Schreber had always been gay, but Schreber's sexual identity is never certain one way or the other, if we attend to Weber's careful reports and to Schreber's own descriptions. Nor is his sexuality the only ambiguity. His physical organs seem to rot or vanish and then reappear by divine largesse, and perhaps his early hypochondriasis in 1884 was the first manifestation of his core illness. The Dr. Flechsig who treated him so successfully the first time becomes an imaginary persecutor, but Flechsig's identity is fused with the God who will impregnate him (Schreber), presumably the same God who had made Schreber's immortality possible through repair of his organs by "rays." Schreber's childlessness in marriage becomes his female fertility in the late disease. All the while, his "harmless" insanity is a backdrop to his eminently sane legal arguments that set him free from hospitalization.

Freud tells us that Schreber, a florid paranoiac, illustrates homoerotic passion and a psychotic defense against it. But, as in the Rorschach inkblot test, there are inkblots and then there is interpretation and "projection." The inkblot says nothing, but the interpreter speaks volumes that reveal the self, in theory. Schreber was a Rorschach for Freud—and, true to the form he imparted to most of his raw clinical material, Freud reiterates sexual theory. The "key" to Schreber's madness—a homoerotic secret Freud thought he had unlocked—probably would have had no bearing on the case, even if Freud had treated him personally. Schreber belonged to the realm of "narcissistic" psychoses, for which there could be no treatment through transference or psychoanalysis.

The Schreber case clearly interested Freud because sexual issues so dominate Schreber's *Memoirs*, but one needs to read Freud on sex with a measure of Dora-like indifference. The words "libido," "castration," and "eroticism" in all the case studies which Freud saw fit to publish refer us eventually to terms like "Eros," "Death," and "Illusion" (respectively) in Freud's later works. The terms may differ, but Freud's obsession with how states of mind represent themselves over a lifetime was consistent. In the concluding chapter of the Schreber case, we read Freud's desexualized thoughts about why people become sick: "*What we take to be the production of the illness . . . is in reality the attempt at cure, the reconstruction.* This succeeds more or less well after the catastrophe, but never fully: a 'profound internal change', as Schreber has it, has befallen the world. But the individual has regained a relationship to the people and things of the world, often a very intensive one, even if what was once a relationship of expectant tenderness may now be one of hostility." I italicize the first sentence, because of its implications for all psychology, Freudian and non-Freudian alike: a psychological symptom is an *attempt at self-cure*. What could Freud have meant? In what sense does *Hamlet* anticipate this enigmatic formulation?

IV

We have two additional cases to consider—by convention they are called the histories of "Rat Man" and "Wolf Man." Freud said that in both instances, the relationship between him and his patient had salutary effect. In the Rat-Man narrative, we find a section entitled "The Father Complex," about which psychoanalyst Juliet Mitchell has written with particular authority. She argues that Oedipal ideas did not amount to the unconscious "Oedipus complex" per se until the case histories were written:

Only gradually did the term 'complex' come within psychoanalytic writings to indicate the totality of *repressed unconscious* ideas that surround an emotionally colored event. (Previously it was used without the all-important connotation of unconsciousness.) The Oedipus complex is the repressed ideas that appertain to the family drama of any primary constellation of figures within which the child must find its place. It is not the *actual* family situation or the conscious desire it evokes. In the case of the 'Rat Man' we can see Freud bringing the Oedipus complex (though here it is not actually named as such) under the sway of the unconscious.

What "totality of repressed unconscious ideas" there might be, we simply cannot say. We can, however, be certain that actual family situations and the conscious desires they evoke are bystanders to an obscure process, which remains obscure. The power behind the idea of the Unconscious is not that it can made conscious by psychoanalytic fiat: *something* "appertains" to what happens in conscious life, but it is ghostly. We are inherently constrained in articulating the Unconscious, and Freud wrestled this difficulty even as he claimed his therapeutic successes with the Rat and Wolf men.

The Rat Man was one Ernst Lanzer, about thirty years old, a lawyer who had experienced difficulties in getting through law school due to obsessive thoughts. He told Freud that he had suffered obsessions since childhood, but that, especially over the last four years, his *"fears"* that some harm might come to people he loved, his often violent *"impulses,"* and certain *"pro-hibitions"* on action had become so intense as to debilitate him. He had just passed his final law examinations, but not without exceeding difficulty involving all three primary symptoms. While studying for the bar, as he related to Freud early in the treatment, he entertained a thought that if he were commanded to take his exams at the earliest opportunity, he might also be commanded to slit his own throat. He "fetched his razor," but decided that "it's not so simple as that."

Lanzer was unmarried, but he had a girlfriend named Gisela (actually his cousin), whom he wanted to see as he studied for his bar, but she was not in town because she was visiting an ill grandmother. He thinks to himself that he must kill the grandmother so that he can see Gisela. In turn, he feels compelled to kill himself for these murderous thoughts. Then we read—here we must consult Freud's personal notes on the case, not the case report—that Lanzer or Freud (one can't tell who) asks, "Who was it who gave him this command?" Regarding the blameless Gisela, we learn that Lanzer had proposed marriage to her on at least a couple of occasions, but she had demurred. Lanzer says *he* worries a great deal about *her* safety, and the fear that some harm might come to her in particular, he says, was a fundamental reason for his seeking treatment.

Reading the Rat Man case can feel like torture because of its endless details, as the above vignette might suggest. The nature of an obsession is Freud's general subject matter, but obsession is never a single thought and certainly not just a single-mindedness—it is always an overwhelming plurality of thoughts for Lanzer, at least. The name "Rat Man" comes from a story he hears during his military service. "I think I will begin today with the experience that was the direct cause of seeking your advice," Lanzer says by way of introducing his "rat story," but the reasons he sought Freud's treatment have already been announced: he has fears, impulses, and prohibitions. Now, we have a rat tale to flesh out those abstractions.

There was an Asian torture in which a prisoner would be tied up (Freud's commentary: Lanzer expressed himself "so unclearly" that he couldn't guess how and in what position the prisoner was bound). A pot with rats in it was secured tightly over the prisoner's buttocks (Freud: "once again he [Lanzer] stood up [from Freud's couch, as Lanzer often did during his therapy], showing every sign of horror and resistance"). The rats *bored their way in* (Freud: "Into the anus, I added, helping him out"). Having described the ghoulishness with Freud's help, Lanzer adds, "At that moment the *idea* flashed through my mind that *this might happen to someone who was dear to me.*" In a footnote to the italicized word "idea," Freud adds: "I am unfortunately unable to reproduce the characteristic imprecision of all that he says."

The Rat Man case attempts a too-precise representation of Lanzer's imprecisions: Freud looks for rats (in German, *Ratten*) in almost everything Lanzer reports to him (including his conflicted plan to marry—in German, *hieraten*—his Gisela). But the discussion of rats, *Ratten*, *hieraten*, and so on in the Rat Man case seems like a very long verbal arpeggio, whereas we already sense a psychological disturbance beyond words. Freud's task is to characterize Lanzer's obsessive style for us, but it's not easy work. Perhaps an idea of being obsessively thorough or complete "commands" Lanzer, in the same way that any of us can feel the abstract need to "do a good job" or "to succeed" to some anal or compulsive degree. The drive for success invites all kinds of dissatisfaction for the person so driven, even if it leads to success.

Although Freud is interested in "real" determinants for Lanzer's behavior—viz., why he is so obsessive—all that we know is that Lanzer's obsessiveness plagues him with contraries (impulses engendering prohibitions; fears driving impulses). Why would he think that a command to act (i.e., take an exam) should lead to an order to end life and all action? Such is the nature of his obsessiveness: it's not a function of conscious volition; it already guides his actions, and Lanzer can't describe this obsessiveness otherwise, except to rehearse countless details as he lives them.

The psychological interest is not that he has an unconscious problem, but rather that he can't articulate the too-abstract idea of his obsessiveness except by reportage of minutiae. Freud obviously sought to find a precise language to describe Lanzer's deep motivations, but even Freud's rhetoric can't avoid some degree of incorrectness or inaccuracy. When Freud invokes the Unconscious (think of Juliet Mitchell's phrase, "the totality of repressed unconscious ideas"), we shouldn't be so mesmerized by the word "Unconscious" as to overlook the intractable problem Freud faces in describing it. Lanzer himself expresses "the totality" of his motivation just by being Lanzer. In attempting a description of his behavior, Freud says that Lanzer's words must mean more than what they say; his behavior must refer us elsewhere—namely, to the Unconscious.

Yes, but as Hamlet warns us, no one returns from the bourne—the limits—of an undiscovered country. Psychologist F. A. Hayek (as a young man, Hayek studied psychology, before he decided on economics as his life work) once suggested that the "Unconscious" had been terribly misidentified, since it is really "above" consciousness, a super-Consciousness, and at best the "*late* discovery of the mind reflecting on itself." By the time the Rat Man appeared in Freud's consulting room, arguably, Freud was a doctor with little insight offered too late.

The "curative" insight in Lanzer's case addressed two aspects: castration fear and emotional ambivalence. How did the cure happen? Even the astute critic Steven Marcus, whose sympathy for the Freudian case history couldn't be more sincere, simply cannot say: "Again and again, what is recurred to is [Lanzer's] unacceptable, repressed, and denied rage at his father, his lady [Gisela] (and his mother) . . . He has no story to speak of, apart from his covert rage." When Lanzer listens to Freud's allusive and slightly crazed explanation (rats carry disease, rats bite penises, rats burrow in holes like penises, etc., etc.), only then "[the Rat Man's] *delirium about rats* disappears. When and how this process actually occurred is not recorded . . . but there is no reason to doubt that it did take place," Marcus writes.

Unqualified shock and doubt at Freud's interpretations might have been Lanzer's true reaction, with incredulity stunning him into temporary sanity. But, more to the point, Freud did not allow Lanzer to wallow in narrative "delirium." Repeatedly, and by way of Lanzer's own free associations (even if Freud contorts like a gymnast to create fixed meaning out of loose associations), he returns his patient to thinking about his ambivalent emotional relationships with most everyone, especially Gisela. No doubt she had quite justified qualms about marrying the Rat Man, but Freud concentrates on Lanzer's equivocations, because he witnesses them first hand (by contrast, he doesn't know Gisela).

In concluding his discussion, Freud writes:

> *Doubt* corresponds to the internal perception of indecisiveness that seizes the patient in the face of every intended action, as a result of the inhibition of love by hatred. It is actually a doubting of love, which ought after all to be what is most certain in his own mind, diffused throughout everything else and displaced for preference on to the tiniest and most indifferent things. Whoever doubts his love might, nay, must doubt everything else, however small, as well.

To which one can only respond, "well, OK": if you hate someone, loving the same person is problematic and doubtful at every level of discussion, from theme to detail. The issue of emotional ambivalence lurks in Freud's commentary as it guides his treatment. What he says about doubt refers to human psychology in general rather than Lanzer's problem in particular.

In a footnote to the quoted passage, Freud cites *Hamlet*, from act II, scene ii: "Doubt thou the stars are fire;/Doubt that the sun doth move;/Doubt truth to be a liar;/But never doubt that I love." The reference, supposedly about what love really is, couldn't be more evasive. Hamlet's letter in verse professing his love to Ophelia is possibly his most transparent (antic) "disposition," and yet one is always left wondering about Hamlet's love, whether he proclaims or denies it outright. "Never doubt that I love" needs to read against two astonishing lines in act III, scene i:

HAMLET	I loved you not.
OPHELIA	I was the more deceived.

If Hamlet's four words are powerful, Ophelia's five words are more so, because she articulates the problem of love that Freud spends five full cases working through with fastidious care. Love is devastatingly articulate and inarticulate: Freud looks to childhood and the transference for evidence of its ambivalences, but the lesson that emerges from his clinical investigations must, alas, be read as harsh. The cure of love, from the perspective of what Freud called the reality principle, *fails*—such is the necessary therapeutic shortfall that we call the psychopathology of everyday and of clinical life. We have explored this tragic failure more than once in this book—what remains to be seen, as we will explore in the realms of creative work and transcendence (the next chapters on Leonardo and Moses), is whether the reality principle can ever yield its grip. But we must take pains to acknowledge that, like the Unconscious, love can never be quite what it seems.

What happened to Lanzer and Gisela? Freud wrote to Carl Jung on October 17, 1909 (before his own estrangement from Jung) that "Last week the newspapers carried the Rat Man's announcement of his engagement." Freud was proud that he had been helpful; Lanzer did marry. Subsequently, he was called to military service and died in World War i.

⊜

In the first hour of his treatment, the Wolf Man threatened anal intercourse with Freud, after which he thought he might crap on Freud's head. The Wolf Man returns us to the lowest and commonest data of emotion, what poet W. B. Yeats called "the mound of refuse" from which the mind grows. The data collected over an ensuing four years of psychoanalysis with the Wolf man amounts neither to truth nor fiction. We are naturally curious as to how the Wolf Man could possibly remember what he reports. As in the preceding cases, the reconstruction of memory and the process of psychoanalysis can't be disentangled.

The Wolf Man was born to a wealthy Russian family from Odessa; his name was Sergei Pankejeff. He had one sister, two years older than he. At eighteen months of age, he contracts malaria and convalesces in his parents' bedroom (we will return to Freud's thoughts about this event later). At some point between eighteen months and three years of age, he sees a deaf-mute servant, someone who delivers water to the family's home; he feels "pity" for him, and when the servant dies sometime later, Pankejeff searches the sky, thinking that the water-carrier must be in heaven. Pankejeff suffers some disturbance of his appetite roughly at this time. At age two-and-a-half, a woman named Gruscha, a nursery maid, cares for him; he recalls her kneeling on the ground washing the floor; he urinates next to her, and she might have gently scolded him. Later, a woman named Nanja—his "beloved" Nanja—becomes his nanny. His parents either spend time at other family estates, or his father, due to bouts of "moroseness," is absent for prolonged periods of time. An alcoholic English governess arrives at the family estate to help Nanja with child care; Pankejeff has fits of testiness and inconsolable rage. The English governess is discharged. Just after his third birthday, he is "seduced" by his "sensuous" and "intellectually gifted" sister. Actually a number of seductions are described, but the first might have been her suggestion, in a bathroom, that they show each other their buttocks. (The sister would develop a psychiatric illness in her late teens, and eventually would commit suicide. Father, soon to be institutionalized on a chronic basis, suffered from manic-depression, as did a paternal uncle.)

Pankejeff avoids his sister after the putative seduction, but, in nanny Nanja's company, he takes to "playing with his penis" in front of her. Nanja calls this behavior "naughty." Roughly at age four, Pankejeff has a dream of wolves on Christmas Eve (December 25 is his birthday, so he is on the eve of a double holiday). Freud writes regarding Pankejeff's dream memory: "He had always emphasized that two moments in the dream had made the most powerful impression on him, first, the utter calm of the wolves, their motionless stance, and, second, the tense attentiveness with which they all stared at him. The sense of reality as the dream came to an end, which persisted after he had woken up, also seemed noteworthy to him." Pankejeff recalls as well that his sister often tormented him with pictures of wolves, especially one from an illustrated book of fairy tales. In his adult life, Pankejeff would "never tire" searching antiquarian bookshops for a copy of that same book.

The plot, already dizzy-making, becomes more so. Pankejeff, now about four years old, begins playing with insects, pulling wings off flies, chopping up caterpillars; he imagines beating and abusing large animals, like horses. He has problems falling asleep; he fears recurrence of his wolf dream. He describes another fear of a "lovely big butterfly with yellow stripes": at the moment that it lands on a flower, spreading its large wings, he runs away screaming. At age four-and-a-half, his mother decides that, given her son's ongoing anxiety, she would introduce him to Bible stories "in the hope of distracting and uplifting him." They begin by reading about the Passion of Jesus. From age four-and-a-half to ten, Pankejeff is described as obsessive-compulsive (one wonders: what has he been up until now?) with a distinct religious component to his behaviors. Each night, in a ritual, he kisses each of the holy pictures that he has collected in his bedroom; he crosses himself compulsively before he can go to sleep; he feels compelled to think on the Holy Trinity when he happens to see three piles of dung in the street; he thinks the word "GOD [*Gott*]" in strict relation to certain other words, such as "CRUD [*Kot*]"; and, in what Freud takes to be evidence of his preoccupation with the Holy Spirit, Pankejeff deliberately exhales his breath at the sight of people who evoke pity, including his own father, whom he visits in sanatorium (when Pankejeff was about age five).

At age ten, a teacher comes to the household to teach Pankejeff German.

Freud says little about the teacher, except that under his influence, Pankejeff's various religious compulsions, insect tortures, and phobias abate as he starts to take an interest in the military life, military uniforms, and Freud roundly calls "the German element." From age ten to Freud's first encounter with Pankejeff about a decade later, Pankejeff attended school "without undue interruption," but one cannot say that he is normal. He suffers from constipation so severe that weeks go by without a bowel movement. He begins to require enemas on a regular basis. At age eighteen, he becomes "compulsively infatuated" by a girl named Matrona: "He was walking through the village attached to [his family's] estate, when he saw a peasant girl kneeling at the edge of a pond, washing dirty linen in the water. He fell violently and irresistibly in love with the girl in an instant, although he could not even see her face." He contracts gonorrhea after their affair, and, within several years, he is committed to a sanatorium as a manic-depressive (his father's diagnosis). At the sanatorium, Pankejeff is "incapable of autonomous existence."

According to Freud, at age eighteen months, Pankejeff watched his parents copulating (three delights in an afternoon, no less) "in the manner of beasts." The infantile erotic imagination could know no greater provocation for illness, and indeed poor Pankejeff becomes an erotic basket-case: wolves in dreams (and in illustrated books) stare at him just as he stared at his parents; he falls in hopeless love with Grusha and Nanja and perhaps tries to demonstrate his love in front of them; Matrona is a late version of those two women; her position "on her knees," the only sexually stimulating posture imaginable for Pankejeff, causes a swoon; his "anal" obsessiveness, like his chronic constipation, relates to the fantasy that anal sex happened on the afternoon of the parental "primal scene," and anal sex is the very act he suggests to Freud in their first therapeutic hour. For Freud, the whole story, coheres as an anal tale.

An Austrian journalist named Karin Obholzer went to considerable lengths to locate Pankejeff in Vienna in the 1970s. In interviews published as *The Wolf-Man Sixty Years Later* (1982), Pankejeff said that Freud's reconstruction of the primal scene struck him as "terribly farfetched." Psychoanalysis, Pankejeff concluded, had not helped him. Regarding the experiments in recollection that Freud conducted with his patients, Pankejeff intuited that Freud was capable of massive failures in interpretation.

In reading Freud's history, one stops regularly to think, "No, Nanja didn't threaten him with castration"; "No, what the sister did wasn't exactly seduction"; and, above all, "Say again: he *remembered* the afternoon at eighteen months of age when he lay in his crib watching his parents?" The ways in which Freud could be wrong are more interesting than the slim chance that he's right. If Pankejeff, Lanzer, or Dora offered "free" associations, in accord with the first rule of psychoanalysis (to report what one is thinking, no matter what it might be), then we are the fools for assuming that associations can be so free.

Let's try our own reconstruction—we might think about "the first thing we remember" from our own lives. Let's say that at an early age, something happens—we recall the event dimly, but certain aspects of the memory are inexplicably vivid. We wonder about the significance of that recollection, but we hardly think it explains who we are. Then someone comes along to say, as Freud does in the first pages of the Wolf Man case, that a person "capable of screening out his acquired convictions" finds that "there are more things in heaven and earth than are dreamt of our philosophy" (the allusion to *Hamlet*, act I, scene v was one of Freud's favorites). The capacity to screen out convictions and to brood on "more things in heaven and earth" is to think as critically as possible about "our philosophy."

I cannot conceive, off the bat, of a new theory about how memory determines individual psychology, but I suspect memory does have to do with who we are. One can assault Freud's clinical approach on diverse fronts (speciousness, amorality, impracticality, falsehood, etc.), but it makes for interesting and convoluted narrative.

Take a simpler instance, less complicated than a case history: someone says, at a dull meeting, that he needs to step out to catch a "breast of flesh air." Whatever story we can conceive about him or the meeting may never be as good as the one line. What we should notice is that Freudian interpretation infects narrative and vice versa. Do they (interpretation and story) infect each other to such a degree as to invalidate both?

Our answer must be circumspect. So much depends on the interpreter—which is to say, his or her wisdom. In the intellectual wake of Freud, to believe truly that there are "more things . . . than are dreamt of in your philosophy" requires some acknowledgment about how interpretations fail. Someone once quipped that perhaps Hamlet really meant: search forever, but you won't find philosophy as truth anywhere—not on earth and not in heaven. But Hamlet's line is more transcendentally skeptical than mysterian. If an interpretation or philosophy must fail, as Freud seems to say along with Hamlet, in spirit, let it do so. People interpret themselves long before they ever show up at a doctor's door; memories that supposedly make up identities are self-interpretations, which are subject to vast misreading by patients and doctors alike. Hamlet anticipates all misinterpretations, because he already thinks that unpacking the heart with words invites gross misinterpretation, always. He knows, as a corollary, that all insight involves error. Freud is no less skeptical than Hamlet, but he is so wildly tendentious in his case histories that we tend to overlook the Hamlet in him.

We only need to think for a moment that all his cases offer perspectives both on insight and its failures. Hans forgets; Dora leaves; Schreber was never a patient; Lanzer dies (I bet the marriage would not have worked); and Pankejeff wasn't helped. One could throw out psychoanalysis for batting at best one-and-a-half out of five, but the five case histories would sustain no interest if they were not "rich," like the richness we seek in a characterization in random fiction.

One must add a cautionary note, however. When it comes to clinical psychopathology, Freud is usually neck deep in a "richness of characterization." In fact, his is an embarrassment of riches just as patients' stories can be too rich for anyone's good, either the patient's or treating doctor's. A good criterion for the usefulness of a psychological theory is whether we get any closer to "framing" the richness of individual history by way of the theory. "To frame" is not to explain: one might add that a good theory always anticipates that it can do no more than temporarily contain the problem of interest. "It is part of our idea of the natural order," writes philosopher Thomas Nagel in "Freud's Permanent Revolution," "that people's behavior is influenced by their mental condition; that the influence *should be larger and more various than we originally thought* should not surprise us." The italics are mine: a skeptical thought that there must be more in heaven and earth than can be conceived in *a psychology* is just the revolutionary aspect that Nagel aptly credits Freud.

Just one line after Hamlet's "there are more things . . . ," we read the Prince as he contemplates a great change. He tells Horatio and Marcellus:

> But come:
> Here as before, never, so help you mercy,
> How strange or odd some'er I bear myself . . .
> That you, at such times seeing me, never shall,
> With arms encumb'red thus, or this head-shake,
> Or by pronouncing of some doubtful phrase
> As "Well, well, we know,' or 'We could, an if we would,'

Or 'If we list to speak,' or 'There be, an if they might,'
Or such ambiguous giving out, to note
That you know aught of me—this do swear . . .

Arms folded thus, a shake of the head, a "well, well, we know": I have behaved in those precise ways with patients, full of a belief that I know about
them. Hamlet's lines suggest an antidote for such error: one can swear to side
with Hamlet. In terms of modern clinical work, that would mean giving up
a few knowing head shakes, taking nothing at face value, and thinking—and
it is very difficult to think this way—that unpacking the heart with words
might never reveal a psychology. In light of *Hamlet*, Freudian theory points
us in the direction of the shortcoming of psychological theory generally. That
would be *any* theory, Freudian or otherwise.

⮻

At my medical school, a students' club gathers to read Shakespeare. Sometimes,
they invite specialists to join them. On one occasion, a Shakespeare scholar
showed up, and he chided the students for how little they knew about
Elizabethan literature and for the superficiality of their readings. A student
asked the scholar, "What's your point?" The scholar found the question
offensive.

But, for me, it was a fine moment, because the scholar had no idea about
why the club gathers at all. A medical student reads a play like *Hamlet* out
of some need, which is not served elsewhere—certainly not by what we, on
the medical faculty, teach about human interaction. If asked by someone a bit
older, the student's question might be phrased differently: not "what is *your*
point?" but rather "what is *the* point—i.e., the meaning in all our work after
all?" Not without an urgent need to answer the latter question, as I describe
in the next two chapters, Freud points us to the appreciation of beauty and
the spirit as an antidote to all bad psychology and all condescending profes-
sors of any discipline.

Six

Leonardo

T<small>HE PERSON WHOM</small> critic Kenneth Clark called the Hamlet of art history was Freud's subject for a biography, written between the fall of 1909 and the spring of 1910, whose title has been translated as *Leonardo da Vinci and a Memory of His Childhood* or *Leonardo da Vinci: A Study in Psychosexuality*. The latter comes from Dr. A. A. Brill's translation, which was my first exposure to the book at some point in college. Reading Brill's introduction at that time, I ran across the following psychoanalytic "dictum," which has been hard to forget over time: *"no neurosis is possible in a normal sexual life."* The italics are Brill's, as is the presupposition that we all know what a normal sexual life is. After much clinical work, I can say that *living up* to the idea of a normal sexual life probably does contribute to what psychoanalyst Karen Horney has called the neurotic personality of our time.

Brill thinks he summarizes much of Freud by his dictum, but I have learned enough to be absolutely confused by it. When we realize that the relationship between sex and mental health defies simple formulation, perhaps *only* when we do, then Freud sounds like a sage and the Brills of this world sound tiresome or weird. "[W]e prefer to speak of *psychosexuality*," Freud wrote in an essay entitled "Wild Psychoanalysis" in 1910 (a better translation of "wild" might be "unhinged"—Freud argues that psychoanalysis in the wrong hands is craziness), "thus laying stress on the point that the mental factor in sexual life should not be overlooked or underestimated. We use the word 'sexuality' in the same comprehensive sense as that in which the German language uses the word *lieben* ['to love']." He finds it curious, as surely we all do, that lack of satisfaction happens when there is no lack of sex *and* when there is lack of sex. Freud adds that all therapists know of unsatisfied "sexual trends" that simply aren't gratified by sexual acts. I suppose he means that sex doesn't necessarily gratify over time (in modern terms, more sustained sex via medical enhancement does not change that truth); yet, there's nothing like sex as a model and metaphor for the pleasure we seek in life, as we know too well from modern media.

To understand Freud's intentions in *Leonardo da Vinci*, we have to broaden the concept of sexuality so much as to distort the meaning of the word. "Psychosexuality" really means the history of all love (maybe hate as well) that we have known, and maybe we can't be normal without coming to terms with that history and memory. That sounds like a good plan in theory, but as we try to survive any given day, the contemplation of all love that we have known gets shoved to one side for the sake of expediencies, such as paying bills, making a living, and getting the kids to school. Perhaps we have arrived at a stage in modern psychiatry where questions of the "tell-me-about-your-mother" variety are passé, but psychosexuality in Freud's broad sense remains a powerful conception, because he refers to one's capacity for love as a function of the past. The determinants of that ability are laid down early, as we have learned from his case histories, and, for that reason, the examination of personal history is worth the trouble, especially if we have problems in what we roundly call the "love life."

Freud once famously responded to a reporter's question about what it meant to be normal. His definition was operational, pragmatic, and not glib: to be normal is to be able to work and to love, he said. As wise as his answer sounds, practical success is hard to achieve (and maybe there are fewer "normal" people than we believe): as a footnote for a whole generation of us, Freud did not mean that it suffices to love one's work. His curiosity about work and love motivated him to write a brief biography about a man of extraordinary intellectual gifts and complex sexuality who finds his art, seems to lose it for a time as he pursues other interests, and then finds his art again in mid-life. The loss and the rediscovery make sense to Freud because of an early memory recorded much later in the artist's life. Freud's own title for his book in German, *Eine Kindheitserinnerung des Leonardo da Vinci*, puts childhood (*Kindheit*) and memory (*erinnerung*) up front, I think mainly because *Leonardo da Vinci* is an investigation of memory (far more than sex) as it relates to love and to the shadow-world between what we assume is normal and what we recognize as being sadly pathologic. Both early and late in Freud's career, he believed that people can suffer from their memories as they can from disease. In *Leonardo da Vinci*, we learn a bit about what it means to suffer from a memory, though I'm not sure that "suffering" is the right word, since health (and love) come from remembrance too, as we also learn from his book.

To anticipate Freud's argument, but also to preview my own comments about *Leonardo da Vinci*, I would suggest keeping a quotation (in two parts) in mind. The source is novelist Virginia Woolf, writing about the genre of psychological narrative with mixed respectfulness:

> A patient who has never heard a canary sing without falling down in a fit can now walk through an avenue of cages without a twinge of emotion since he has faced the fact that his mother kissed him in the cradle. The triumphs of science are beautifully positive.

Her essay, entitled "Freudian fiction," was a review of a novel entitled *An Imperfect Mother* by one J. D. Beresford. Reading Woolf, could a person desire to read it?

> we do not wish to debar Mr Beresford from making use of any key that seems to him to fit the human mind. Our complaint is rather that in *An Imperfect Mother* the new key is a patent key that opens every door. It simplifies rather than complicates, detracts rather than enriches. The door opens briskly enough, but the apartment to which we are admitted is a bare little room with no outlook whatever. . . . in the ardours of discovery Mr Beresford has unduly stinted his people of flesh and blood. In becoming cases they have ceased to be individuals.

Can the same be said of Freud on Leonardo or any psychologist with any patient? The first citation, especially the phrase "beautifully positive," is a wonderfully acidic comment that burns through all stock Freudianisms and all stock readings of Freud. The second delivers a verdict that applies to psychology in general, not just psychoanalysis: simplify rather than complicate, and you are guilty of writing like Beresford. Incidentally, Freud does argue that Leonardo's mother kissed him in the cradle in such a way as to explain much in the artist's life, but if we think of Leonardo as fodder for over-hungry psychological interpretation, then we overlook how Freud retreats from any heavy-handed triumph of positive science. His retreat is also part of his argument—the more important part.

If the gist from my last chapter has come across in any way (that the only thing more dangerous than a psychiatrist who explains Hamlet is the psychiatrist who tries too hard to explain all of us), the reader might understand my quibble with most post-Freudian "studies in psychosexuality." The word "psychosexual" is all wrong at worst, redundant at best. Redundant, because if human love and sexuality aren't psychological, I don't know what is. All wrong, because Freud's great contribution was not only that he thought about sex in life, but also that he could generate so *unusual* a study in psychosexuality as *Leonardo da Vinci*.

The curious aspect of his small, beautiful biography—he called it the only pretty thing he ever wrote—is that it builds a case for what he calls the "sublimation" of sexuality. No other term in the psychoanalytic lexicon is more problematic. Some, like philosopher Paul Ricoeur, have suggested that it be forgotten and never used again. Sublimation refers to that which is beyond sexuality—this "beyond," we think, should be the domain of love, since love is greater than sex, but all kinds of problems await us when we try to explain a sublimation. A narrative of it, in lieu of an outline as to how to achieve it, is what Freud's book attempts. One might feel cheated out of a secret mechanism for happiness (i.e., the patent key to sublimation), but it's not as if Freud withheld it maliciously.

Freud never stopped thinking that the inner psychological life amounts to what J. H. van den Berg called our haunted house, where ghosts of the past (including the sexual past) are everywhere. In *Leonardo da Vinci*, Freud concludes that escape from the haunted house is possible—perhaps. The equivocation is the interest. Among countless good and bad studies of Leonardo's genius, Freud's was unique in conceiving human brilliance as the possibility of taking leave of our demons while still being haunted by them. Paradoxical as the last sentence sounds, our best Freudian critics have noted the same conundrum, as in this passage from Malcolm Bowie, to whom I'll return in this chapter: "Freud's exemplary creative individual inhabits a time that is always simultaneously past-haunted and future-haunted." "Past-haunted" is understandable enough (think of one's history of personal failures); "future-haunted" is a contradiction in terms unless the future and past vaguely resemble one another, as Freud suggests they often do, both for geniuses and non-geniuses.

In writing about Leonardo, Freud becomes his own best critical ghost: he was too smart not to notice that an equation like "normalcy = normal sex" was meaningless, because it reduces to a tautology that leaves normalcy undefined. Normalcy, like disease, has a history, and normal people live in haunted houses no less than troubled people do. Freud thought to describe the demons so well that we might recognize them as if they were newly strange to us, though they are neither new nor strange. His psychobiography of Leonardo becomes something more than a Freudian fiction (in Woolf's derogatory sense) if we think about Bowie's paradox, which plays out subtly in *Leonardo da Vinci*: every person's past is his or her own chronic disease; but, if there is something in our minds capable of liberating us from that past, memory plays a role our self-treatment.

⊟

Once upon a time in the training of psychiatrists, we were required to write an "anamnesis" of any new patient assigned to us. *Leonardo da Vinci* is an example of what that type of biography tries to accomplish. "Anamnesis" translates roughly as "reminiscence"—that is, the patient's memories rendered in the form of a narrative, but not in the manner of a medical case history. The latter is essentially a story of symptoms; the anamnesis is more of a personal novel, as close to an autobiography as possible while still remaining an interpretive biography. The anamnesis has become a dying art today, because we tend to think that the here-and-now matters most—and for good reason, since current symptoms benefit most from what we offer in the clinical present, especially in terms of psychiatric drugs. By contrast, Freud was interested in the earliest past as we rediscover it in stories from everyday life. Psychoanalyst Donald Spence refers to the "narrative truth" in these clinical recollections, but two questions come immediately to mind in thinking about Spence's useful but problematic term.

First, are we able to write a good anamnesis if our views are already tainted by a theory of whatever variety? The answer is no: narrative in the service of theory bothered Virginia Woolf, because she thought (probably most of us should, too) that stories and theories deserved to be kept separate. Second, what does Spence mean by "truth"? A "narrative truth" is not one that we can prove, but rather an insight gleaned by hearing a story told. If I could teach insight (and the truth as well?) to my students, I would be doing them a real service, but I cannot—for reasons that clinical work has taught me in time. Here is what I have learned: when it comes to an understanding between people, which is a rare thing, I am often at a loss for words to explain how I arrived at my interpersonal knowledge. I find this knowledge believable, like some discovery. Yet, insofar as I can't explain the process of discovery, it is dubious at the same time. I find myself recounting stories in the hope that I can communicate *something* that sounds rational. My arche-type is Freud, who points us repeatedly in the direction of stories with the most complex of truths built into them, as in the enigma of a Leonardo. Why does he direct us so calmly at these complexities, unless they contain a quality close to veracity, but different from an empirically derived truth—a different truth perhaps, which we are quite unable to articulate logically except in story form?

I

"It is doubtful whether Leonardo ever embraced a woman in passion; nor is it known that he ever had any intimate mental relationship with a woman," Freud writes in his first pages. Without debating the claim, one naturally be-gins to wonder—we can't help but, if we read most any book on Leonardo—about his homosexuality. But even if he had been gay, he seems to have been unfulfilled. Referring to the so-called Jacopo Saltarelli affair when Leonardo was about twenty-four years old, Freud continues:

> While he was still an apprentice, living in the house of his master, a charge of forbidden homosexual practices was brought against him, along with some other young people, which ended in his acquittal . . . When he had become a Master, he surrounded himself with handsome boys and youths whom he took as pupils . . . [It is highly probable that] Leonardo's affection-ate relations with the young men who–as was custom with pupils at that time—shared his existence did not extend to sexual activity. Moreover a high degree of sexual activity is not to be attributed to him.

A biographer, Freud believed, should never be afraid to broach his subject's sexuality, whatever it might be, but the curiosity in Leonardo's story seems to be the sex he *didn't* have, regardless of his sexual bias. Alluding to a contem-porary description (probably from the anonymous source called Anonimo Gaddiano), Freud reminds us that Leonardo was a lovely human specimen, with an air of Narcissus about him: "he was tall and well-proportioned; his features were of consummate beauty and his physical strength unusual; he was charming in his manner, supremely eloquent . . . He loved beauty in the things that surrounded him; he was fond of magnificent clothing and valued every refinement of living." Leonardo as Renaissance persona was all beauty, intelligence, and untouchability.

Few biographical details about him are certain. He was an illegitimate son born, in 1452, to Ser Pietro da Vinci, a lawyer and notary, and a peasant woman then in her early twenties named Caterina. In that same year, Ser Pietro married, not Caterina, but one Albiera Amadori, who was sixteen at the time. It would be the first of Ser Pietro's three or four marriages to very young women; the first two of the marriages were childless. Perhaps also in 1452, but no later than 1454, Caterina married a local lime burner nicknamed Accattabriga or "the Quarreler," by whom she had at least three children, possibly as many as five. Leonardo's birthplace was about a full day's travel outside the city of Florence, probably in the village of Vinci, though some scholars refer to Anchiano, very close to Vinci. Caterina lived with her new husband and growing family in Campo Zeppi, less than an hour's walk from Vinci.

Ser Pietro and Albiera traveled often to Florence, where he conducted much of his legal and financial business, and after a time the couple essentially lived there. Back in Vinci, care for the infant Leonardo fell to Ser Pietro's bachelor brother Francesco, to godparents recorded in birth records (no less than ten of them), and to the paternal grandparents, who took legal and apparently quite loving possession of their only grandchild, according to Serge Bramly's immensely readable biography *Leonardo: The Artist and the Man* (1994). Leonardo didn't lack for attention, but psychoanalytic readings have notoriously wondered about who served the real role of mother. Dr. K. R. Eissler, in his *Leonardo da Vinci: Psychoanalytic Notes on The Enigma* (1961), says that, as an infant, Leonardo must have lived with Caterina in the Accattabriga household. Freud thought that Leonardo lived with Ser Pietro and Albiera only after the psychologically formative years (age 0-3) with Caterina. No one really knows.

All sources agree, however, that the boy's talents were apparent early. Ser Pietro consulted his Florentine business acquaintances, particularly artist Andrea di Cione (known as "true eye" or "Verrocchio"), for advice as to how to cultivate his son's gifts and, perhaps mainly, how to get him employed. Leonardo's first extant drawings date to 1473, sometime after his move to Florence, but what early evidence there might have been for unusual skill, including sculptures of children's heads and smiling women ("heads of women who laugh," according to Vasari's *Lives of the Artists*), clearly impressed Verrocchio. By 1469, Leonardo, now about seventeen years old, planned to live and work in the master's bottega on the Via de Agnolo in Florence. Verrocchio's commissions to the powerful de Medici family of that city made him a celebrity; his workshop, filled with young artisans, produced sculpture, jewelry, larger cast-metal work (church bells, for example), and, of course, paintings.

Right around the time Leonardo moved to Florence, his family life in Vinci changed fundamentally. His uncle Francesco, the bachelor who was like a father to him, married. His step-mother Albiera died, and Ser Pietro promptly remarried. His grandfather died, as did his grandmother Lucia a year later. According to what facts we can safely surmise, Leonardo had at least three possible mothers: Caterina, Albiera, and Lucia. Two of them were dead, with his biological mother absent, by the time he was eighteen. Regarding the return of Caterina (an event that Freud will reconstruct for us), we must wait about twenty years, during which time Leonardo grew into his genius, not altogether comfortably.

⊟

I have not forgotten that I am writing about Freud *on* Leonardo, but the background is necessary to read Freud properly. The notion that early life experience determines later development is our intellectual inheritance from Freud; it is a premise in his book, which was a first attempt at what came to known as psychohistory, or the application of depth analysis to history writing. Bias against psychohistory has been very strong, because people think—with justification—that there's only one thing worse than psychological determinism, and that is any psychiatrist trying to write history. In his *Clio and the Doctors*, historian Jacques Barzun spoke for many when he said that the virgin muse of history did not require (and she didn't seek) artificial insemination by any shrink. Regarding the discovery of "underlying" human motivations by psychohistorians, Barzun was deeply skeptical: "The thought-cliché natural to an age of physical science," he wrote, "is that what is most fundamental, most *underlying*, is automatically most enlightening. This is an unexamined impression." He argued that some reductionisms have nothing to do with human history in its complexity.

Much of the psychohistory that came after Freud, Barzun continued, amounted to really bad Freudian fiction, which had little to do with its subject matter (whether a historical figure or a social phenomenon), despite its purportedly scientific insights. I'm not sure the same judgment applies to Freud himself, especially if we re-read *Leonardo da Vinci* with fresh eyes. I view this "fresh" exercise as an antidote to any school of thought (Freudian thought included) which maintains that a code to decrypt da Vinci actually exists. Freud doesn't solve or explicate Leonardo's mystery so much as he relies on it, despite his tone and manner of argument through much of his book.

How best to describe that tone? His is a heavy hand, especially with respect to Leonardo's supposed celibacy. Yet Freud acknowledges that the truly interesting aspect of Leonardo's sexuality, like so much about him, was an enigmatic quality that we revisit every time we think about or see the Mona Lisa. Leonardo's presumed sexual abstinence adds to the mystery of his persona and, indirectly, to the fascination of his work. We tend to hear Freud saying that Leonardo rejected all sex, including interest in it. But the biographical details, which have been reworked many times since Freud wrote, contribute only to our continuing uncertainty about the private Leonardo.

⊟

Before 1476, the year of the Saltarelli affair, Leonardo's artistic production was sparse, limited to an angel in Verrocchio's *Baptism of Christ*, a tempera on wood entitled the *Annunciation* (in the Uffizi), which many believed wasn't Leonardo's work until Victorian John Ruskin defiantly attributed it to him (he wrote, "the scholars who have questioned this are—well, never mind what they are"), and a marriage portrait of one Ginevra de' Benci. Regarding how Leonardo otherwise occupied himself, we have commentary like the following, from art historian Kenneth Clark:

> Assuming that the "Ginevra" was painted in 1474, how did Leonardo spend the next four years? There are no documents bearing on his work till 1478, no drawings and only one picture which seems to belong to the period. At twenty-five years of age, he cannot have been obscurely devilling for Verrocchio, although we know that he lived with Verrocchio till 1476; and he had not yet begun the scientific studies which, in his later life, account for intervals in the sequence of his painting. Presumably Leonardo, like other young men with great gifts, spent a large part of his youth in what is known as doing nothing.

In the category of nothing, Clark includes dressing up, talking, taming horses, and learning the lute and flute. Freud emphatically says that sex was not among his diversions. He quotes Leonardo on his own supposed frigidity:

"The act of procreation and everything connected with it is so disgusting that mankind would soon die out if it were not an old-established custom, and if there were not pretty faces and sensuous natures."

The sentence can be found in so-called Manuscript A, and we might pause over it to reconsider what Freud calls Leonardo's "cool repudiation of sexuality." Bramly cites the same passage (which he translates differently) in a discussion of Leonardo's various commentaries, diagrams, asides, and surprisingly good jokes on the matter of sex: "The act of coupling and the members engaged in it are so ugly that if it were not for the faces and adornments of the actors, and the impulses sustained, the human race would die out." "Disgusting" versus "ugly" is like the difference between moral commentary and mere observation. One wonders whether Leonardo had real faces, ugly members, specific adornments, and graphic ideas (memories?) in mind. Bramly notes that, as a result of his training under Verrocchio, Leonardo could dissect anything, including carnal "ugliness," into its particular and usually myriad components, usually after much observation.

Sex was not exempt from his obsessiveness. Even more to the point about Leonardo's "pedantic exactness" (Freud's characterization), we have his sexual humor. Freud says that Leonardo's writings were not entirely available to him in translation, but he knew about Leonardo's *belle facezie* or "witticisms." He dismisses them as unworthy of a great mind, but consider the following selection, which I happily steal from Bramly:

In general, woman's desire is the opposite of man's. She wishes the size of the man's member to be as large as possible, while the man desires the opposite for the woman's genital parts, so that neither ever attains what is desired . . . . Compared to the size of the womb, woman has larger genital organs than any other species of animal. . . .

a woman crossing a treacherous and muddy place, who lifts up her dress both before and behind; therefore, as she touches both anus and vagina, she tells the truth three times when she says 'This is a difficult passage.'

[The testicles are] witnesses to coition.

Whether one is awake or asleep, it does what it pleases; often the man is asleep and it is awake; often the man is awake and it is asleep; or the man would like it to be in action but it refuses; often it desires action and the man forbids it. That is why it seems that this creature often has a life and intelligence separate from that of the man, and it seems that man is wrong to be ashamed of giving it a name or showing it; that which he seeks to cover and hide he ought to expose solemnly like a priest at mass.

Dr. K. R. Eissler cited the last of the passages as a "key to an understanding" of Leonardo's "relation to male genitality," whatever Eissler meant by that phrase. Man's relation to sexuality, male or female, is captured best, I think, in the first of the quotations, when Leonardo shrewdly observes that no one ever attains what one desires, presumably not only in sex. Even if Freud was correct that Leonardo had no inclination for actual sex, it seems nevertheless that the man could write (and draw) about it with gusto. Like the Ovidian and Shakespearean fascination with "the beast with two backs," the sexual act startled, disturbed, and mesmerized Leonardo. One need only consider, say, Isaac Newton (another famously abstinent genius) to realize that Leonardo's sexlessness had something unusually and unequivocally passionate about it, compared to an essentially banal Sir Isaac.

"Testicles as witnesses to coition" is no prudish observation; just so, the horse-taming, lute-playing, physically pretty, and resplendently dressed Leonardo was no prude, no small wit, and hardly sexless. Bramly says that all the clues in Leonardo's life eventually add up: he was at very least gay, at least curious about all kinds of sexual acts, and he preferred to have handsome young men around him for whatever reason. A boy nicknamed Salai lived with Leonardo from a young age; one Francesco Melzi, a *bellissimo fanciullo* (a very pretty boy) from an esteemed Lombard family, joined the master at age fifteen, later serving Leonardo as a secretary, studio artist, and finally his literary executor. And, as Freud mentions at the start of his book, Leonardo was anonymously charged (along with a scion of the de Medici family) with sodomy in 1476—a crime punishable by death, despite its prevalence in Florence at the time. The alleged victim was Jacopo Saltarelli, a goldsmith's apprentice, perhaps a male model for artists, and a male prostitute by wide reputation. Whether Leonardo had sex with any of the above is immaterial: his sexual mystery is at the heart of Freud's reconstruction.

II

Leonardo's sexuality, mysterious or blatant, would be of no interest if it didn't relate to his mature work and his mature way of working. Freud assumes it does; he suggests—in a blind leap in argument—that Leonardo had a fiercely intimate relationship with the woman who cared for him as an infant (Caterina rather than Albiera, Freud believed) that biased his life and work. The basis for this belief is a single childhood remembrance that "interested no one" for generations, according to art historian Meyer Schapiro. We find it at the start of Freud's second chapter:

> I recall as one of my very earliest memories that while I was in my cradle a vulture came down to me, and opened my mouth with its tail, and struck me many times with its tail against my lips.

To the consternation of scholars, especially Eric Maclagan (who first noted Freud's misunderstanding based on a mistranslation: the vulture is actually a bird called a kite [*nibio*, in Italian]), Freud proceeds to equate vultures with women in his next few pages, based on associations from antiquity. In Egyptian hieroglyphics, as described by the Greek writer Horapollo, "vulture" equals "mother," and representations of the vulture-headed goddess *Mut* were often hermaphroditic, depicted with both breasts and penises, "since only a combination of male and female elements can give a worthy representation of divine perfection," as Freud explains. Centuries later, according to Christian Church fathers, vultures were thought to exist only as females (no males in this species, the story goes), and to procreate, the female was inseminated by the wind. In terms of so immaculate a power to conceive, the vulture symbolized the Virgin Mary. Christianized or Egyptian, *Mut* the vulture was Leonardo's *mutter* (mother), according to chapter two, and presumably something very intimate (in terms of Leonardo's fantastical reconstruction in memory) happened in the crib. But here's the issue: a vulture is not a kite. In the eyes of his critics, Freud's bird error vitiated his discussion of the vulture-*Mut*-mother-Mary matrix. His argument was urbane but moot, if one can tolerate the pun.

In one of the less brilliant comebacks of all time, defenders of psychoanalytic orthodoxy maintained that, in any event, Freud and Leonardo were obviously both interested *in birds*, never mind which bird. The argument isn't exactly wrong: the supporting facts matter less than the type of history that Freud tries to write—a biography of Leonardo's imagination, perhaps. Biographer Charles Nicholl, in his *Leonardo da Vinci: Flights of the Mind* (2004), discusses kites (*nibio*), other kites (*aquilone* or "eagles"), Leonardo's interest in flight dating to 1505, his plans for a "big-bird" flying machine, and a certain fascination with swans as just so many variations on an imaginative theme that culminates in Leonardo's *Leda and the Swan*:

> The painting is lost, but can be partly reconstructed from preliminary sketches by Leonardo and from full-size copies by his pupils or followers. The earliest known sketches are dated to 1504-1505, precisely contemporary with the note about the kite. The theme is from classical mythology. Jupiter or Zeus, in love with the Spartan princess Leda, transforms himself into a swan and impregnates her, and from their union are born—or, in the paintings, quite literally hatched–two pairs of twins: Castor and Pollux and Helen and Clytemnestra. This—the bird, the mother, the half-bird children hatching strangely from their shells in the foreground—seems to revisit once more the ambit of the kite fantasy. Like that fantasy, the painting is clearly connected with Leonardo's preoccupation with flight at this time. '*Cecero*'—as in Monte Ceceri, from which Leonardo planned to launch his 'big bird' or flying machine in c. 1505—means 'swan' in Florentine dialect.

⊜

Freud never responded to his critics regarding the kite-vulture controversy, I suspect on obstinate principle. The vulture fantasy was his creative reconstruction, useful because it helped advance a theory of sexuality that we should not misread today. Plainly stated, the theory says: the study of the human psyche conceives meaning in life, a meaning inextricably linked to human love. The "conception" of meaning—its creation by powerful interpretation, rather than the mere discovery of meaning—is a process replete with what critic Malcolm Bowie astutely calls "surprise":

> For Freud in one of his theoretical moods, the surest sign of the unconscious at work was to be found exactly in the unforeseeable grinding of one structural order against another. In the continuous fabric of experience, a sudden snag appeared. The reasonable-seeming individual, equipped with comprehensible motives and credible goals, gave evidence . . . of other desires that were not reasonable at all. He or she seemed suddenly to be speaking or behaving from an alien region. And although that region could be expected in due course to reveal its continuities and regularities, its first emergence upon the scene was a scandal. One of Freud's extraordinary achievements as a writer was to preserve this sense of outrage in defiance of his own proficiency as a psychoanalytic explainer: rather than allow an all-purpose discourse of otherness and unknowability to inform his accounts of mind in action, he constantly rediscovered otherness in his own surprise, and wrote of it surprisingly.

The "grinding" of id on ego to produce "snags" in the fabric of our self-awareness is one overall way to view the Freudian project, but I think Bowie's insight is greatest when he indicts (as he believes Freud chastises) any "all-purpose discourse of otherness." "Surprise" is a characteristic rather hard to find in psychiatric writing these days, probably because it takes a rare, strong writer to make a good argument out of awe.

To read *Leonardo da Vinci* well, the first step is not to see Freud's interpretation of the cradle fantasy as some unlocking key. We are perfectly within our rights as readers if we think that Leonardo's memory is a weird recollection, a bird-obsessed Hitchcockian moment as recollected by a foremost mind of the late fifteenth and early sixteenth centuries. There are those who have argued that the idea of a *nibio* rapping at the mouth of baby Leonardo—like the way bees were said to land on the lips of the infant Plato, in anticipation of his sweet philosophic words—was just a metaphorical way of talking about how some kids seem destined to be extraordinary. Maybe in fact Leonardo was trying to mythologize himself as a genius; Freud's creation of meaning through Leonardo's story is a different order of curiosity. Adding personal audacity to the strangeness of Leonardo's report, Freud maintains that the origin of male homosexuality is the mother [*Mut*]-son relationship. He is quite matter-of-fact on the matter, but we should repeat, as a mantra, Bowie's important sentence, that Freud "constantly rediscovered otherness in his own surprise." He didn't write about Leonardo because he understood him (his arguments notwithstanding); he wrote about Leonardo to rediscover otherness with appropriate awe. Leonardo wasn't just gay and not just asexual: his strangeness had to do with his not being either. Leonardo's bird(s) is/are hardly less odd.

Leonardo's childhood memory leads us, as if in a strong current, to Freud's theory of homoeroticism. It is really a general erotic theory, not exclusive to gay choice. Based on other sources in Freud's writings, it can be distilled to four central theses. He says (his first point, borrowed from Plato) that bisexuality antedates whatever sexuality we happen to adopt later in life. Bisexuality isn't indecision or a polymorphous perversity, but an early state of affairs to which one can always regress, as if it is always a part of us. Among sexual curiosities, Freud believed (his second point) that we need to explain why it's as hard to convert straight to gay as gay to straight in terms of whom we choose as erotic partners. He thought that the resolute nature of such choice must have a cause that can be located at some point in the past. Third, as Freud says in the context of discussing lesbianism ("The Psychogenesis of a Case of Homosexuality in a Woman" [1920]), psychoanalysis *shouldn't* explain homosexuality; it *only* retraces ground: "It is not for psychoanalysis to solve the problem of homosexuality. It must rest content with disclosing the psychical mechanisms that resulted in determining the object-choice, and with tracing back the paths from them to instinctual dispositions. There its work ends." Sexual orientation, he goes on to say in the same essay, could be a biological (or, as we tend to wonder today, a genetic) issue, but the individual history of love is different from the determinisms of biology. To write the former is psychology's goal; the latter has little to do with psychology, on Freud's view.

In other words, a nature-nurture debate did not interest him. He maintains that only a person with Leonardo's childhood experience—and, as a result of that experience, only a person of his enigmatic eroticism—could have produced the work of Leonardo. His great retrospective non-statement (aren't we all products of our respective pasts and biological natures?) needs to be read against one last (fourth) claim, which, again, relates more to sexuality in general than to homoeroticism:

> I cannot neglect this opportunity of expressing for once my astonishment that human beings can go through such great and important moments of their erotic life without noticing them, sometimes even, indeed, without having the faintest suspicion of their existence, or else, having become aware of those moments, deceive themselves so thoroughly in their judgement of them. This happens not only under neurotic conditions, where we are familiar with the phenomenon, but seems also to be common enough in ordinary life.

The one reliable aspect of our own sexuality is that we can misrepresent or overlook what determines it. If, in recalling our erotic history, we can evade or flatly misrepresent the "important moments," then, we might conclude, what we call personal memory is a bit of a smokescreen. People conceal themselves even by their most vivid memories, just as occurs in the dream-work that converts latent content into manifest dream. If we protest that, in the absence of reliable memory, there is no personal past to discuss, Freud would calmly respond that the otherness of others isn't revealed by how obvious they can be.

We tend to think that the Freudian approach always has to do with a sexual story that we have "repressed," such as a reconstruction (like the bird fantasy) that refers "in fact" to our supposed foundations in infant-parent relations, what Freud wistfully called "the family romance." But if we read Freud on the similarity between the neurotic and the normal, or between genius and non-genius, some revision of what we mean by the "erotic," "sexual," or "libidinal" seems inevitable. Leonardo's aesthetic works—what follows is Freud's hypothesis, not mine—become truly meaningful if we understand them as primordial memories even more than the ineluctable reappearance of repressed sexual material. The Freudian point is that there is a relationship between history and psychology. It is not a causal relationship; all that we really know is that their relatedness is subject to the vicissitudes of memory. (That our memories contribute to our personality to such a degree that the reconstruction of memory *becomes* personality could be one of the more profound intuitions he ever had.)

Yielding to the spirit of Freud's argument, let's say that Caterina kissed her child frequently in the cradle, that she often smiled at him, and that their essentially exclusive relationship (sans father) had bearing on all that would follow. Freud discusses the recurrence of the maternal smile in Leonardo's later work, borrowing from the Victorian critic Walter Pater, who made the same thematic observation in Leonardo's works. Freud adds to Pater in suggesting that memory works backwards and forwards in a lifetime, as if there were no arrow of time. The cradle memory of love, fast-forwarded, becomes work of a kind that we have never seen since.

The oxymoronic concept of "forwards memory" invites the question of what it was that truly drove Leonardo to his art and study—that is, we wonder what a sublimation could be. In a recent book-length study, Volney Gay speaks of the "mystery of transformation" in sublimation, an almost religious transubstantiation of erotic drive into productivity. But I don't think it helps to make sublimation *more* transcendental, like a conversion of flesh to spirit. Freud uses the word "substitution" at various points in *Leonardo da Vinci*, perhaps most problematically in his concluding chapter:

> We no longer think that health and illness, normal and neurotic people, are to be sharply distinguished from each other, and that neurotic traits must necessarily be taken as proof of a general inferiority. To-day we know that neurotic symptoms are structures which are substitutes for certain achievements of repression that we have to carry out in the course of our development from a child to a civilized human being.

His horridly complicated second sentence—*a symptom is a structure which is a substitute for an achievement which we all have to accomplish in the course of development*—makes more sense if we read it backwards: in the course of development, we all accomplish and achieve many things, but these goals are substitutes, or constructions, that could be understood as symptoms of pathology in the severest instances, though they might also be indicative of a normal life or, in the unusual case, of genius. Inquiries into sexuality, memories, dreams, *belle facezie*, and the like (these are all constructions or "structures") are not opportunities to foreclose our understanding. To open the wormy can of "substitution" is to broach the differences between what is normal and what isn't—the two being separated by unclear demarcations. Freud believed, as the above over-packed quotation corroborates, that in many ways we are all Leonardos—not because we rival his genius; rather, because our own genius is just as possible as our pathology or our normalcy, because memory afflicts us (at least we are memory's grip) in normal and abnormal states.

Malcolm Bowie has said with a touch of drama that Leonardo, as an exemplary creative figure, "suffers from memories and from cataclysmic visions of the future. His ecstasy comes not from an escape from this tension, but a defiant manipulation of it." I don't know to what cataclysms he refers (maybe the painting and drawings of Leonardo's late career that suggested an interest in the Apocalypse), but I would agree that the strangest and most beautiful aspect of Leonardo—his enigmatic sublimity—has to do with a double business: looking ahead in his career was much like looking backward in time, at least to Freud's searching eye.

Norman O. Brown, a classics scholar who turned to psychoanalysis late in his career in search of some form of release from being a scholar, complained in the 1950s that the concept of sublimation pointed to no specific means *for* sublimation. Vexed but intrigued by Freud as if by a mind-altering drug, Brown also observed that we can't throw the concept of sublimation away, because then psychology in general (not just psychoanalysis) has not much to say about what so compels a person to his or her highest intellectual activity. Fifty or sixty years after Brown, we still like to believe that a link exists between human drives and noble stuff, like art and science, since perhaps a part of us believes that instincts for higher modes of intellection really do exist for the species Homo sapiens. But we are no closer to understanding mechanism in sublimation, the *how* of substituting love for work and vice versa, in Freud's pluripotent sense of substitution—i.e., how a substitution can variously lead to neurosis, health, or genius. We need to return to Leonardo's story to get more of a sense of sublimation as an activity or process, what Freud calls a mechanism of "defense." So far, the most that can be said about sublimation is that if you are able to find a way to transform erotic drive into an art, then good for you. But what threat demands the magnificent defense?

III

Prior to his move from Florence to Milan at the age of thirty, Leonardo painted the *Benois Madonna* and two great unfinished works, *The Adoration of the Magi* and *St. Jerome*. (The names for Leonardo's paintings were not his; he declined to provide titles to any of his works.) Lack of completion, or what Walter Pater called the way to perfection through a series of disgusts, would characterize his mature production in Milan from roughly 1482 to 1513 and in Rome under Pope Leo X from 1513 to 1516. The only thing more reliable than his leaving works and their sponsors in a lurch was his excruciating slowness, a "dilatory form of procrastination" (as biographer Sherwin Nuland described it) that caused some to maintain, according to Vasari in *Lives of the Artists*, that he never intended to finish a thing he started.

In *The Last Supper*, Leonardo took years to fill in the face of Judas or Christ, depending on which art historian one reads. The *Virgin and Child with St. Anne and a Lamb*, which drew crowds "as if at festival" (Vasari) when first displayed, has an incomplete landscape and unfinished robes. The *Mona Lisa*, famously, was never delivered as a finished commission. And if Leonardo did finish it after carrying it around with him for years, as some believe, there is the matter of its surprising physical smallness in life. Scholars tell us that over the centuries the *Mona Lisa* has been cropped terribly in the hands of derelict restorers, but the size we have today emphasizes the variance between what a work is and what one expects it to be (one can only walk up to it in the Louvre, and judge for oneself how small it is, compared to one's imagination of it). For Leonardo as well, incompleteness could well have been the gap between an idea and its execution, so that there was always a quiet contempt in the act of completing.

Regarding projects of vaster physical scale, *The Battle of Anghiari*, whose initial cartoon was drawn in Milan, was a fresco intended for a large interior wall of the Palazzo Vecchio in Florence (Leonardo traveled often to and from Florence during his tenure in Milan). The project occupied him from 1503 to 1506 before he abandoned it. In the 1490s, he conceived and modeled a massive statue of a rearing horse with rider for the Sforzas, his Milanese patrons. Scholar Martin Kemp describes it as being of such enormity that it would have rivaled the wonders of the ancient world. Vasari called it an insoluble problem in bronze casting; it was never cast, prompting a young Michelangelo to mock Leonardo when the two of them ran into each other in the Piazza Santa Trinità in Florence ("And the stupid people of Milan had faith in you?" Michelangelo said with high malice).

Late into his Milanese period, on learning of the death of his benefactor Ludovico Sforza in a French prison, Leonardo wrote, "The duke lost his dukedom and his property and his liberty, and none of the works that he undertook was completed." Seizing on the relevance to Leonardo's own career, Freud remarks that he raises "the same reproach at his patron which posterity was to bring against himself. It is as if he wanted to make someone from the class of his fathers [a class that included Ser Pietro, Verrocchio, two de Medicis (Lorenzo the Great and Leo X, who was Lorenzo's son), and Ludovico in Milan] responsible for the fact that he himself left his works unfinished." Even in the scientific and engineering studies of the Milanese period—this work, too, seems like so many fragments—the completion of tasks (on the one hand) and sublimation of erotic instinct into work (on the other) seemed incompatible.

Art historian Meyer Schapiro bristled at Freud's next line of argument, which he restated and denounced for the record:

> To explain why his art is so uneven and why he cannot finish his work, Freud points to relations with his father. Since Leonardo identified with him at a certain age, he had to treat his own children—his paintings and sculptures—as his father treated him, by abandoning his work. This analogy will convince few readers. However, Freud observes too that in identifying with his father, the young Leonardo strove to copy and excel him; he passed then through a period of intense creativeness which was renewed later when he enjoyed the support of a substitute father, his patron Sforza, the Duke of Milan. His great works were produced in those two periods of fatherly attachment. But since his sublimation to art, the argument continues, was unaccompanied by real sexual activity . . . Leonardo could not sustain his work for long.

The passage is from "Leonardo and Freud: An Art-Historical Study" (1956), a now-classic essay which anticipated all annoyance with Freud that has continued to the present, at least when it comes to aesthetic criticism. Freud might be forgiven his confusion over certain facts (think of the kite-as-vulture gaff), but can't be forgiven the shortcoming, as Schapiro saw it, that he says nothing artistic about Leonardo's art. That is, Freud could spin a tale about why Leonardo painted smiling women (he was recalling his mother), and he could gloss the incompletion problem (he was recalling his father's absence), but Freud doesn't touch on, and hardly explains, Leonardo's originality as artist—how, for example, his manner of grouping figures together, as in *The Last Supper*, "mark[s] an epoch and become[s] canonical, like an architectural order or a poetic form." Like other of his religious paintings, *The Last Supper* was "in spirit more dramatic than liturgical and theological": his achievement of bringing human symbolic action to static ecclesiastical art would influence the Mannerists of the mid-sixteenth century and arguably the history of art thereafter. Freud annoys Schapiro, because he offers embarrassingly little on such points.

But Schapiro really grumbles that Leonardo's works were *not* his children and that he grew up to be an artist far more than he suffered from some family romance. Does Freud abuse Leonardo's art? In his *Treatise on Painting*, Leonardo wrote about *sfumato* or the "smoke-like" effect he wanted to achieve in representing light: "In the streets when night is falling, in bad weather, note what delicacy and grace appear in the faces of men and women." How, indeed, does psychology gloss the subtlety of such ambition? Schapiro says psychology does not. Regarding Leonardo's allegedly unconscious preoccupation with his father, biographers have well documented that Leonardo's career was a progression of attachments to powerful men, all benefactors of his artistic enterprise. His working relationships with these men were rarely straightforward—in fact, they were sources of consternation for both parties; what more needs to be said? Schapiro's line, *"This analogy will convince few readers,"* is worth direct comment, since he calls into question one's conviction about psychological explanation in general when it comes to art appreciation. One recalls Jacques Barzun's complaint: an interest in what "underlies" a Leonardo says nothing about why we still gaze upon his works.

I quote Schapiro because he illustrates for me how a person can recapitulate Freud's argument and still not capture why we should bother to read Freud on art today. When he says that Leonardo abandoned his work because he became like his father, or that he painted his best work recalling his mother, he invites us to think about an uncanny aspect of memory. One way to understand the uncanniness is to compare Freud's conception to an idea of an absolute memory in which everything is stored somewhere. Consider theorist Steven Rose's comments about perfect, artificial memory (I quote him mainly for his first few words):

> *whereas all living species have a past, only humans have a history.* Although the biological mechanisms of each human's individual memory may be the same as those of our fellow vertebrates, artificial memory is profoundly liberatory, transforming what we need to and what we are able to remember. The multimedia of modern memory devices free us of the necessity to remember vast areas of facts and processes, liberating, presumably, great numbers of neurons and synapses to other purposes.

The Nietzschean observation "only humans have a history" (perhaps Rose intended the allusion to Nietzsche's *Use and Abuse of History*, but if he did, he misses its point) means that humans remember in such a way that their past becomes something more than bytes in an artificial memory. Computer memory does not select on the basis of any salience; it records indiscriminately. One supposes that there is liberation of a kind, if profitless memory finds its way into limitless storage (not in our brains), but human memory is unique and strange in that so many nerve cells and their connections can serve to revisit *certain* old issues. And we can't necessarily retrieve memory by simple acts of will. Often, in the search of lost time, memory involuntarily floods us with detail that we barely recall having placed in brain-storage at all.

The influence of the past is a provocative concept if understood appropriately—which is to say, if it is not diluted into the trivial assertion that we are products of our own histories. Leonardo overidentifying with his father(s) and being overloved by his mother(s) could amount to a Leonardo syndrome, but we should be very lucky to be afflicted by it, if we were to achieve his genius and artistic mastery. Virginia Woolf and Meyer Schapiro would say that a syndrome is one thing, the phenomenon of da Vinci quite another, and we should be interested in the latter, not the former. They are correct, except that Woolf, in chastising Freudian fiction, recoiled against a bad psychological novel by J. D. Beresford (not Freud); and Schapiro rather misses what motivated Freud's love of art. Freud's view on memory is Woolfian, with its atemporal movement forward and backward through our private rooms. Memory as an aesthetic, symbolic, or figurative recreation of the past—a *proper use* of history, as Nietzsche would say—invites us to rethink what memory and art try to accomplish in the course of a life. Freud asks what the art historian simply can't ask: he is curious as to why Leonardo bothered with art at all, though his (unanswerable) question is even larger than that: why do any of us do what we do?

It would be helpful, at last, to examine a working definition of sublimation. After looking at a number of plainly worded choices (including psychoanalyst Jacques Lacan's outrageous definition that whenever he gave a lecture, in the very act of speaking, he was not fornicating, and *that* was sublimation), I would opt for a tamer statement, from *A Layman's Guide to Psychiatry and Psychoanalysis*, written by Dr. Eric Berne, a popularizer of psychological theory who wrote in the 1960s. I quote from a chapter called "What People Are Trying to Do" in a subsection entitled "How do human beings express their urges?"

> Some of the most interesting and socially useful displacements of libido [erotic drive] occur when both the aim and the object are partial substitutes for the real aim and object. This occurs in what is called sublimation, that is, an activity which helps bring other people as well as its creator closer to the sublime or "higher" things of life. Many mental functions are organized to bring such refined forms of pleasure to people. A good example is painting. Here the artist substitutes as object the model for a love partner (and this model need not be a person, but may be some inanimate object, such as a landscape or a bowl of fruit), and as aim the thrill of artistic creation for the thrill of love-making.

This stock definition of sublimation (the substitution of a "refined" object for a "real" erotic one) introduces a central problem more than it resolves it. When Berne wrote, at a time when psychoanalysis enjoyed far more authority than it has today, one might have thought that sublimation would be a goal of all therapy, to have our primal drives serve socially-sanctioned, ennobling purposes. But his phrase "partial substitutes" is problematic. How partial?

Sublimation requires us to think against the erotic grain: art (or, for that matter, a lecture) is not the surrogate thrill of love-making; in over-hearing my own lectures, sometimes there is no thrill at all. Off-the-shelf psychology would have us believe a complete substitution for "real" aims is possible, but a sublimation, like a repression, isn't conscious. An artist merely paints his bowl of fruit. Problems emerge when sublimation is imperfect: the artist wonders why anyone bothers to paint any bowl of fruit; he becomes overtly symptomatic (perhaps unable to do his art), though arguably he was always symptomatic, even when he was happy at his art. Illness, as Freud once claimed, quoting poet Heinrich Heine, is a reason or logic for creative instinct, though the logic and rationality aren't necessarily apparent to the artist. The matter of sublimation in the case of Leonardo was Freud's opportunity to weigh into the insuperable difficulty of understanding human motivation. Lacan, quoted just a moment ago, says that "the function of the drive has for me no other purpose than to put into question what is meant by satisfaction." I think he is precise: the function of psychological study is not only to understand our discontents as a function, say, of the inhibitions of our drives, but also to understand our satisfactions, which, Freud argues, are problematic in their impermanence and inexplicability.

Anna Freud, in her *Ego and the Mechanisms of Defense*, articulated many years after her father—and better than he did—how the transformations of emotion and memory are defensive in the sense that we all seek mastery over life's circumstances and over our past, but we can't achieve it, and therefore we are always in a mode of retreat:

> Love, longing, jealousy, mortification, pain and mourning accompany sexual wishes; hatred, anger, and rage accompany the impulses of aggression; if the instinctual demands with which they are associated are to be warded off, these affects must submit to all the various measures to which the ego resorts in its efforts to master them, i.e., they must undergo a metamorphosis. Whenever transformation of an affect occurs, whether in analysis or outside of it, the ego has been at work.

We can take Anna Freud one step further to say that the transformations of affect are never complete. Instinctual demands are insistent but often unclear; the work of the embattled ego never ends. The "mechanisms of defense" don't become automatically self-evident in the endless process. In Freud's time, one required psychoanalysis to glean that one defended at all; today, despite the fact that we spot our defenses as if we had already psychoanalyzed (some people, without training, know passive-aggressiveness when they see it, for example), do we always understand what we defend against? At least in the concept and definition of sublimation offered between the lines of *Leonardo da Vinci*, we have a plausible idea about what is transforming into what—not Eros into art (that's too vague), but rather one memory into another beautiful representation of it—memory being the only way we have to contend with (and retrieve) the personal past. To repeat, I *infer* Freud's definition of sublimation as defense, but it nevertheless seems compelling to me, because it helps me to understand what so transfixed him in studying certain works of art. (We recall how he would contemplate these works, "spend[ing] a long time before them trying to apprehend them in my own way, i.e., to explain to myself what their effect is due to.")

Sublimation is a special kind of memory, as unique as one's genius, whatever it might be. Genius is love "in the comprehensive sense," not (necessarily) in retreat from erotic frustration and not (necessarily) as a result of latent sexual issues. The model for this complex love is memory. One simply doesn't capture Freud's most provocative argument about sublimation by having Leonardo say, "it was through an erotic relation with my mother that I became a homosexual" (the often-quoted conclusion to Freud's third chapter). Instead, if we have Leonardo say that "it is through memory that I achieve my art," I think we make a far more sophisticated Freudian claim. The contemplation of memory *and* art was one in the same for Freud, certainly when it came to studying da Vinci; and we shouldn't neglect a powerfully anti-theoretical aspect to his obvious (and finally anti-psychoanalytic) wonderment before the art of memory. If we want to learn how the psyche works, then understanding a theory—any theory—is relatively pointless; the point of theory is to look at the psyche as one would be transfixed by art (for Freud, these *three* modes—memory, art, and wonderment were one in the same, a "comprehensive" love).

IV

Roughly a decade after the Leonardo moved to Milan, in the summer of 1493, a woman named Caterina moved into his household. She fell ill, was treated by doctors, and died. He recorded this:

Expenses after Caterina's death for her funeral	27	florins
2 pounds of wax	18	"
For transporting and erecting the cross	12	"
Catafalque [a decorated frame to support coffin]	4	"
Pall-bearers	8	"
For 4 priests and 4 clerks	20	"

Bell-ringing	2	"
For the grave diggers	16	"
For the license–to the officials	1	"
Total	108	florins
Previous expenses		
For the doctor	4	florins
For sugar and candles	12	"
	16	florins
Grand Total	124	florins

Freud asks us to heed distortion in the literal accounting of the event: whatever is being expressed, it's not the actual expenses; nor is the preoccupation with numbers merely obsessional. Leonardo didn't record his expenses routinely; his diary, which "like the diaries of other mortals, often dismisses the most important moments of the day in a few words or else passes them over in complete silence," reveal the diarist's thoughts obliquely. Biographers have never been able to confirm who this Caterina was. Scholars like F. Bérence and E. Solmi have suggested, with fastidious justification, that she was a servant whom Leonardo hired because her name was Caterina, *not* Leonardo's mother.

Freud believes that she *must have been* Leonardo's mother, who would have been in her sixties at the time. As corroboration, he cites a work of historical fiction entitled *The Romance of Leonardo da Vinci* by Dmitri Merezhkovsky: "The novelist Merezhkovsky alone is able to tell us who this Caterina was . . . he concludes that Leonardo's mother, the poor peasant woman of Vinci, came to Milan in 1493, to visit her son, who was then 41. . . . This interpretation by the psychological novelist cannot be put to the proof, but it can claim so much inner probability, and is so much in harmony with all that we otherwise know of Leonardo's emotional activity, that I cannot refrain from accepting it as correct." But we don't know how Leonardo felt about the Caterina of 1493, whether or not she was his mother. On the occasion of her death and funeral, feelings about his actual mother that had been suppressed for years now emerge, Freud says, in the account of costs. An expense record should have no poignancy, but it does in this instance, because Freud believes that "what we have before us" is a memorializing statement of deepest mourning. When Leonardo recorded certain events in his life (his father's death on July 9, 1503, with the specific hour repeated twice in the same sentence, or Caterina's arrival to Milan "on July 16, 1493" without other comment), Freud says, we cannot assume that such documentation was unemotional. Based on what Freud calls inner probability, he thinks that we are witness to a sentiment revealed by an inhibition of its complete utterance. There are always residua of all transformations of affect, as Anna Freud would say.

Studies in science and engineering mark Leonardo's mid-career in Milan; Freud believes that such investigations are analogous to the accounting of 1493 and other such "subjections" of affect. In response to this line of argument, I think of a tough critic's comment (T. S. Eliot's, speaking of novelist Henry James) that a psychological narrative is "as disconcerting as a quicksand." I'm unsure whether to be convinced or disconcerted by Freud, but it's interesting, yet again, that a memory of Caterina fuels the psychological rumination. If we step back to look at Leonardo during his Milanese period, to address what Freud calls his subjection of feeling "to the yoke of research," we observe an exuberance at least partly intellectual, but surely emotional as well, in the sense of a fulfillment through work. Biographer Bramly says that, in Milan, Leonardo worked as if he were visited by divinity:

> At this period, Leonardo . . . was filled with that enthusiasm which Pasteur called "the inner god which leads to everything." It seemed that nothing was impossible for him, that he could attempt anything—and *understand* anything. He composed treatise after treatise; with supreme self-confidence, he sought to penetrate the secrets of art, water, air, mankind, the world (he was now interested in geology, in fossils, and in mountain formation); he investigated the origins of milk, colic, tears, drunkenness, madness, and dreams; as if it came under the senses, he talked of "writing what the soul is"; he dreamed of flying like an eagle or a kite and began to draw plans of "flying machines." Alongside a drawing of a bird in a cage, he wrote: "the thoughts turn to hope."

"Penetrating the secrets" was a sublimation of erotic drive and perhaps aggression, Freud says, but either one believes in the transubstantiation (Volney Gay's term) into such intellectual activity, or one abides by the metaphor that it's *as if* he were erotically or aggressively driven. (I think once again about Henry James's comment, mentioned early in this book, but with amendment now, that sex is what we think about when we have nothing *better* to think about.)

What Bramly describes as the driving force is different, yet he offers a very Freudian insight. The "inner God" (Pasteur's, Leonardo's, maybe Freud's as well) puts me in mind of an ancient conception from Genesis of a god who neither conceals nor reveals, but rather *alludes to knowledge*: "In the notes that show Leonardo engrossed in fathoming the great riddles of nature there is no lack of passages where he expresses his admiration for the Creator, the ultimate cause of all these noble secrets; but there is nothing which indicates that he wished to maintain a personal relation with this divine power," says Freud; to which we might add that Leonardo seemed obsessed by allusive "noble secrets" that inspired him to even more investigation. The iterative process was also Freud's inner god, a very demanding one.

Bramly says that Leonardo felt he could attempt anything, thought he could understand everything, but the supreme self-confidence didn't arrogate to certainty in what he knew, because, in his enthusiasm, he enjoyed *mysteries*—of water, air, and so on. Martin Kemp has discussed how Leonardo saw analogy everywhere and applied it always, as in his studies of hydrodynamics (especially of flowing and falling water), of clothing draping from a limb, and of the percussion-like fall of light on shadow, all of which he saw as one kind of study that was germane and essential to painting the *Mona Lisa*. Freud would say, in turn, that analogical power doesn't explain the emotional effect of Leonardo's greatest works. Unfortunately, neither does Freud explain Leonardo's genius by speaking abstractly of "ideal sublimation." How explicit should our understanding of Leonardo's artistic process be? For Freud and for us, an understanding can't be explicit, because we rely on an allusive and not definitive way of knowing, with Leonardo as our model. Why, then, does Freud sound so routinely dogmatic and imperious in what he says?

Richard Wollheim, in touch with Freud's intentions in psychological explanation far more than most, once asked, "How explicit is to be our understanding of what is revealed to us? . . . even in the most deeply psychological dramas [*Oedipus Rex, Hamlet*], generations of spectators have found it difficult to say what is was they understood." Wollheim refers to the imaginative literature that Freud read and loved, about which (indeed) it is routinely difficult to articulate what one understands of them, but he also refers to Freud's interpretive perspective on patients, art, and especially the work of Leonardo da Vinci. The Freud who finds it difficult to articulate what he understands—a Freud that we tend not to notice—can be rediscovered if we follow his discussion to its subtle last sentences.

The concluding sixth chapter of *Leonardo da Vinci* offers a warning about psychology which is directed, one must assume, not to the layperson, but to the faithful. We can substitute "psychiatry" or "psychology" for Freud's cumbersome word "pathography" and lose nothing of his meaning: "*It would be futile to blind ourselves to the fact that readers to-day find all pathography unpalatable.*" It would be futile, that is, to blind ourselves to how people mistrust the basic idea of psychological study. The mistrust is well founded on philosophical grounds, since thinkers have wrestled with the "problem of other minds" more or less since Plato. By pathography, I take Freud to mean "writing about individuals as instances of disease or pathology," a delving into the emotional life to reveal some deviation from whatever is held up as mental normalcy. Today, I think people still find pathography unpalatable, but at least psychiatrists have spent a lot of time in the century since Freud thinking about practical treatment for conditions like depression and madness, two of our greatest afflictions. Undoubtedly, treatment in such cases is a good thing—but, whatever the modern fix for illness, whether pharmaceutical, spiritual, psychotherapeutic, or exhortatory (think of the quasitherapists who tell us to stop the bullshit in our lives, as if that were possible by simple fiat), Freud admits that people have an honest problem with psychological thinking, which reeks of the very stuff that the quasitherapists ask us to give up.

He adds that one effect of a good pathography, especially when it comes to subjects like Leonardo, is that we come to recognize those subjects as being "distantly related" to ourselves. A two-part question arises: do we buy that a childhood memory represented the key psychological issue for Leonardo da Vinci; are we convinced that "memory" (in Freud's rather twisting sense of what constitutes a recollection of Caterina) and psychological understanding have to do with each other? I think the answer to the second question must be yes, because memories *are* important—which inclines me to think that the answer to the first part should also be yes, except that Freud is less than perfectly convincing as he summarizes his book's argument.

His précis runs as follows. As an infant, Leonardo enjoyed an unusual bond with his mother; he was "kissed by her into precocious sexual maturity." Throughout his life, his sexual interest metamorphosed into various activities which he pursued vigorously, including variations on the "instinct" to gaze upon and depict his erotic objects, whether they were smiling women or

Smiles, Leonardo da Vinci. See text for discussion.

beautiful boys. But at some point during his Milanese period, "his ability to form quick decisions began to fail," and "slowly there occurred in him a process which can only be compared to regressions in neurotics." In the service of the Duke of Milan, whose paternal influence finally proved double edged, he pursued studies of great breadth. "He became an investigator [producing one treatise after another 'with supreme confidence,' as Bramly says], at first still in the service of his art, but later independently of it and away from it," but the repression of a "real" sexual life, Freud says, "[did] not provide the most favourable conditions for the exercise of sublimated sexual trends."

In the evolution of this odd repression, Leonardo obsessively—regressively, neurotically—failed to complete anything. Like poet Emily Dickinson's complex lament that "'IT IS FINISHED' can never be said of us," Leonardo's inability to finish became a part of his art, just as Freud believes that the unconscious recollection of Ser Pietro played a role in Leonardo's conduct as a confident scientist. But in a grand mid-life crisis, about the time that someone named Caterina reappeared in his life, Leonardo produced the immortal paintings in his canon. He could still procrastinate to the point of annoying popes and other authorities, but Freud suggests (the insight is not original; it's mainly Walter Pater's), that Leonardo painted the same smile over and again, from the Giaconda's to the Virgin's and St. Anne's to the "treacherous" expression in *John the Baptist*, the last of his known works— "treacherous" (Pater's word), because the expression beguiles one into thinking about the meaning of a smile without providing one iota of certainty about that meaning. "I have shown," Freud writes, what justification can be found for giving this picture of Leonardo's course of development—for proposing these subdivisions of his life and for explaining his vacillation between art and science in this way. If in making these statements I have provoked the criticism, even from friends of psychoanalysis and from those who are expert in it, that I have merely written a psycho-analytical novel, I shall reply that I am far from over-estimating the certainty of these results. Like others I have succumbed to the attraction of this great and mysterious man.

Freud's disclaimer is not a throwaway comment: he absolutely cannot overestimate the certainty of his results. If personal history has absolutely nothing to do with who we are, then the premise and argument of books like *Leonardo da Vinci* amount to absolutely forgettable speculation. If, on the other hand, personal history has a great deal to do with who we are, then we are obliged to explain in what way this is so, even if we have to write a "psychoanalytical novel." The real problem in biography (biography is a subspecies of psychology in Freud's view) is how to provide some sense of the complexity of the subject beyond the mere description of events in a lifetime. Psychological description, in other words, has to achieve what we seek of any knowledge, a "depth" or "complexity" appropriate to the interest which the subject sustains. Freud sought a description that approximates what personal memory achieves, when the past revisits us in resurgent fullness and vivid strangeness. That kind of work amounts to sublimation, though we can only intuit (not delineate) how it works, based on our own personal familiarity with our own memories and their curious capacity to define exactly who we are.

As he ends his book, Freud asks whether Leonardo's fate as an artist was a function of accident: is it fair to say that his illegitimate birth, for example, had necessary bearing on the development of his genius? Freud's answer is both aggressive and evasive; we hear about chance *and* necessity, determining factors *and* uncertainty; the indelible first years of life *and* "countless aspects" that never enter experience (aspects which, we presume, were early, not registered in memory, but which still cast an influence on later life):

we are all too ready to forget that in fact everything to do with our life is chance, from our origin out of the meeting of spermatozoon and ovum onwards—chance which nevertheless has a share in the law and necessity of nature, and which merely lacks any connection with our wishes and illusions. The apportioning of the determining factors of our life between the "necessities" of our constitution and the "chances" of our childhood may still be uncertain in detail; but in general it is no longer possible to doubt the importance precisely of the first years of our childhood. We all still show too little respect for Nature which (in the obscure words of Leonardo which recall Hamlet's lines) "is full of countless causes ['*ragioni*'] that never enter experience."

In reading what sounds like a defensive and tempestuous Freud, does one think of the Prince of Denmark saying to his university chum, "There are more things in heaven and earth, Horatio,/Than are dreamt of in your philosophy," or do we think of a raging King Lear demanding that we reason not the need? I think the latter: we shouldn't be too proud of what Virginia Woolf sardonically called the "beautiful positivities of science." Freud doesn't confuse a psychoanalytical novel for a life; rather, the novel aspires to the intricacy of the life.

I think Freud is a bit stormy because he knows he will be misread: the chance occurrence of a child born out of wedlock, possibly raised by his biological mother in the absence of his father, doesn't explain the phenomenon of Leonardo da Vinci, but that is not to say that personal history is irrelevant to Leonardo da Vinci. Leonardo's artistic work, via Freud, gains in power and genius as we think of it as living memory, as a body of artistic and intellectual endeavor that can only be Leonardo's and no one else's. Freud's respect for genius, in the original sense of the word (genius as "inborn nature"), could not be greater, and he rails against those who would misappropriate psychoanalysis as some superficial gloss on uniqueness.

In the end, Freud responds to Virginia Woolf, as it were: it's not that a Freudian fiction is some stock plot; in the hands of some, it only becomes that way. By saying that psychosexuality is more than sex just as love is more than sex, the intent is to complicate—not simplify—a human story, for the simple reason that human stories are characteristically more complicated than they seem. One testament to Freud's love of art is his way of acknowledging, in *Leonardo da Vinci* more than in other places in his canon, how art achieves psychological representation better—with greater allusiveness and complex beauty—than any psychologist's portrait.

Seven

Moses

IN *Moses and Monotheism* (1939), religious sentiment, organized religion, and even religious history are subject to Freud's revisionist interpretation, which is grounded in his science of the mind. His approach begs a question. If belief has to do with the brain, then do we say that studying the brain through science can explain belief or faith? In recent years, we have seen the advent of "neurotheologists," who don't acknowledge any manner of debt to Freud—yet, they have presumed, as Freud did, to speak beyond their field of study:

> Most religious experience parallels ordinary experience. The religious senti-
> ments include religious joy, religious love, religious fear, and religious awe.
> These religious emotions are analogues of ordinary emotions of joy, love,
> fear, and awe, differing not in their emotional tone, but only in being direct-
> ed to a religious object. Their neural substrate is likely to contain nothing
> of a specifically religious nature, but instead to rest upon the same [neural]
> networks that support non-religious joy, love, fear, and awe.

Then again, maybe there is some discernable quality that distinguishes ordinary joy, love, and so on from the enthrallment of faith or revelation. Religious scholar Jaroslav Pelikan, attempting to define "Mystery" in theology,
has observed that the more we think we know of it, the harder it is to discuss.
"Mystery" refers to what he calls a "quality of the known" (a person knows
what he or she believes, for example); yet Pelikan contends, as many would,
that religious experience differs from ordinary experience, because there is
mystery in it. Can science address that alternate emotional reality in its otherness? Or, does science begin a supposedly objective study in the grip of a first
error–namely, that there is no relationship whatsoever between "religious"
joy and other secular pleasure?

Consider a related argument: among people who take hallucinatory drugs, it has been observed that a majority have some kind of religious experience, including seeing God. In one study, in which 206 people were directly observed to take hallucinogens, 96% experienced religious imagery of some type; 91% saw "religious buildings"; and 58% encountered religious figures. Even if 100% saw the face of God in a resplendent temple, is the experience (under some influence) religious in essence? The thought that an encounter with one's personal god amounts to nothing more than a hallucination (or, as scientists might otherwise claim, a brain seizure, a delusional psychosis, or some kind of near-death experience) isn't reductionist so much as it avoids an important question. Is there, in fact, a "parallel" for the religious experience?

Freud's career-long interest in religion culminates in *Moses and Monotheism* with a provocative analogy: the thought of god is a meditation on origins. Since we can't achieve self-knowledge without some reflection on where we came from (the Freudian interest in individual history being fundamentally a curiosity about our past), Freud thinks it shouldn't surprise us that our deepest spiritual sentiments are retrospective in nature. He makes the same point about human love, that it, too, is retrospective (as Leonardo's brush and pen depicted love for Leonardo), whether or not we care to acknowledge how driven by memory we are in everyday life.

A contemporary reader who opens *Moses and Monotheism* for the first time would do well to understand that the book is not just a speculation on who the historical Moses really was, because Freud's curiosity directs us elsewhere. He was interested in who *we* really are, even if we don't happen to believe in a covenant with the god of Moses.

Among Freud's direct and indirect critiques of religion spanning roughly from 1910 to his death, *Moses and Monotheism* is unusual in the risks it takes. Theologian Martin Buber was taken aback on reading it: "That a scholar of so much importance in his own field as Sigmund Freud could permit himself to issue so unscientific a work, based on groundless hypotheses, as his 'Moses and Monotheism' is regrettable." Peter Gay, for whom Freud is a hero of our time, agrees with Buber that *Moses and Monotheism* "is a curious production, more conjectural than *Totem and Taboo*, more untidy than *Inhibitions, Symptoms, and Anxiety*, more offensive than *The Future of an Illusion*." Why did Freud undertake a Moses project at all?

He offers two quirky hypotheses in *Moses and Monotheism*. We know from his correspondence that he worried about the historical veracity of both:

first, that Moses, the lawgiver, prophet, and leader of the Israelites out of Egypt, was not a Jew; and, second, that the Jews who followed Moses murdered him. The first was not an original argument; nineteenth-century German biblical scholarship routinely questioned the identity of Moses. Many sources contemporary to Freud, including sociologist Max Weber and others whom Freud directly cites in *Moses and Monotheism*, doubted the prophet's Hebrew ancestry. Peter Gay, in his *Freud: A Life for Our Time*, reports that even dating to the Enlightenment, Voltaire wondered aloud "Is it really true that there was a Moses?" And, in a conversation between Freud and Theodor Reik sometime before 1909, as reported by Reik, we have the testimony of a certain Itzig: "The boy Itzig is asked in grammar school: 'Who was Moses?' and answers, "Moses was the son of a Egyptian princess.' 'That's not true,' says the teacher, 'Moses was the son of a Hebrew mother. The Egyptian princess found the baby in a casket.' But Itzig answers, 'Says she.'"

Freud's second hypothesis is more problematic than the first. That a prophet's murder at the hands of his own people not only happened, but also perpetuated a religion based on guilt for all Jewish and Christian faiths after Moses, as he also argues, takes us beyond any tame mode of biography or history. A reviewer in *The New York Times* (in response to *The Future of an Illusion*, when it was translated into English) wrote, "[Freud's book] is warped by the limitation of his mind and the incompleteness of his knowledge of the better part of the human soul." When a self-proclaimed man of science presumes to know either the soul or the roots of sacredness, he courts outrage, as Freud knew well. Yet, he still published *Moses and Monotheism*.

The neurotheologists quoted earlier ask whether religious experience is different in degree, not in kind, from general experience. But the question can be reversed. If religious sentiment has to do with who we are neurologically, psychologically, and in terms of a relationship with divinity, then does it follow that human psychology is a variety of religious experience? In *The Varieties of Religious Experience*, William James, like Freud, examined the "larger" power of religious sentiment, only to conclude that for the common man as for the philosopher-scientist, sometimes it's eminently practical to believe in big things. More than that, writes James, "[a]nything larger will do, if only it be large enough to trust the next step. It need not be infinite, it need not be solitary. It might conceivably even be a larger and more godlike self, of which the present self would then be but the mutilated expression." I won't attempt a full comparison of Freud and James on religion here, but James's conception, which sounds Freudian, has implications for our discussion. An interest in that which is larger than ourselves is a common psychological phenomenon.

James implies that if religion didn't exist, someone would invent it out of pragmatic necessity, but we might ask: if any psychology discusses the human proclivity for transcendence as its proper and fitting subject matter, can it avoid becoming just a bit transcendental itself? In a person's small life, eventually something larger enters. If that is pragmatism, nevertheless James flirts with a force beyond pragmatism.

Freud's intention in *Moses and Monotheism* might originally have been to reveal the secret of the historical Moses, and to offer some speculation on the origins of monotheist belief, but the book that we have in front of us is more than parochially Jewish. As in his *Future of an Illusion* (1927), Freud is forever wary of the solace provided by religion. Maybe without religion, life would be too difficult to bear, but he cannot take its consolations at face value. He maintains that religion is an illusion, but, even if so, religion joins a club of innumerable consolations that we need and indulge in our lives. Freud will not sanctify the solace, and he certainly doesn't think that the problem of "an illusion" is just Jewish. In religious sentiment, he thinks that we rediscover much of human psychology. If religion is illusion, nevertheless it (like James's search for the larger matters in life) is human psychological experience. The inescapable influence of religion in the history of Homo sapiens demands a sophisticated explanation, especially if psychology intends to be a comprehensive science.

I

How accepting was Freud of religious transcendence? Both in his publications and private correspondence, we can safely say that he was curious about it on a regular basis. Critic Paul Roazen notes that in the last thirty years of his life, Freud stopped (almost piously) once per decade to write about religion—he refers to books like *Totem and Taboo* (1913), *The Future of an Illusion* (1927), and *Moses and Monotheism* (1938). Yet, whenever we read Freud about living or dead fathers (which is to say, at any point in his collected works), it's hard not to hear an overtone of religion in psychology. In "Obsessive Actions and Religious Practice" (1907), usually cited as his first foray into the psychology of religion, Freud invites us to think about religious practice as obsessive ritual—e.g., turning towards Mecca for a Muslim, a priest compulsively wiping down the chalice, or the act of nightly prayer.

To talk about how all ritual is ritualistic and how sacred practice is obsessive-compulsive is not Freud's insight, however.

"Obsessive actions are perfectly significant in every detail," he writes in "Obsessive Actions," "they serve important interests of the personality . . . they give expression to experiences that are still operative . . . either by direct or symbolic representation; and they are consequently to be interpreted either historically or symbolically." In these comments, Freud is curious about: "perfect" significance, the greater interests of the personality, and the nature of symbols and their interpretation by all sons and daughters who arrive late into a tradition.

In the later Freud, we need to read with special care at those moments when he seems most skeptical and godless. Here is his celebrated discussion of the "oceanic feeling," a quality of infinity in religious sentiment, from *Civilization and its Discontents*; he mentions a friend who had written a thoughtful letter to him:

> I had sent him my little book which treats of religion as an illusion, and he answered that he agreed entirely with my views on religion, but that he was sorry I had not properly appreciated the ultimate source of religious sentiments. This consists in a peculiar feeling, which never leaves him personally, which he finds shared by many others, and which he may suppose millions more also experience. It is a feeling which he would like to call a sensation of "eternity," a feeling as of something limitless, unbounded, something "oceanic." It is, he says, a purely subjective experience, not an article of belief; it implies no assurance of personal immortality, but it is the source of the religious spirit and is taken hold of by the various Churches and religious systems, directed by them into definite channels and also, no doubt, used up in them. One may rightly call oneself religious on the ground of this oceanic feeling alone, even though one rejects all beliefs and all illusions.

> These views, expressed by my friend whom I so greatly honour and who himself once in poetry described the magic of illusion, put me in a difficult position. *I cannot discover this "oceanic" feeling in myself.* [my emphasis]

Freud's correspondent was French author Romain Rolland, whose commentary regarding *The Future of an Illusion* is surprising in its claim that the ultimate source of religious sentiment is not quite belief.

A person can believe in the spirit of *credo quia absurdum* ("I believe because it is absurd"), but the oceanic feeling is not absurd. Freud complained in *Civilization* that *credo quia absurdum* leaves one wondering whether one is to believe every absurdity, and if not every absurdity, then why a particular one. But Rolland's feeling has little to do with religious faith as justification for anything. Like Yahweh's sublime comment in the Pentateuch "I am that I am," the oceanic feeling is what it is, no more and no less. The infinity is simply what we perceive at some private shoreline in the mental life. Freud's one-sentence response ("I cannot discover this 'oceanic' feeling in myself") could easily be his most disingenuous moment as an author. That *any* mention of an oceanic feeling finds its way into *Civilization and its Discontents* should clue us that there is absolutely no reason to believe that Freud never experienced a feeling of oceanic limitlessness.

Rolland's criticism is echoed in a letter, dated January 1, 1930, from Lou Andreas-Salomé to Freud. Salomé was his former patient who eventually practiced psychoanalysis herself. In her remarkable lifetime, she was the erotic love interest for philosopher Friedrich Nietzsche and poet Rainer Maria Rilke, but never for Freud, according to our best biographers. She reflects on Rolland's oceanic feeling, and, despite a qualification or two, sympathizes with it:

I have just read your *Civilization and its Discontents* with the greatest contentment, following your arguments with full assent, and enjoying it all the more for the free time vouchsafed me by the holiday. And yet, just as in the case of *The Future of an Illusion*, I was struck by the fact that despite this assent, my—how shall I put it—attitude to "religious" questions remains different from yours, in so far at least as you find it difficult to forgive the "common man" his religion, whereas to me this remains a subject of great interest in all its various forms. If we are going to find it "humiliating" when anyone enters into a pact with these religious infantilisms, then we must treat a person's culture and intelligence in precisely the same way—just as we now know how to assess moral indignation at its true worth. After all, infantile elements, alongside purely regressive or retarded elements, are closely allied to those powers of imagination which form part of all creative activity. And when, for instance, I read in your book of your friend with the "oceanic feeling" who is certainly far from accepting the religion of the common man, I would be prepared to wager that he would nevertheless in his inmost being admit that his oceanic feeling shares many elements which "elevate" the common man in his religion. Instead of the crude infantilisms which permit the old sensations towards the parents to express themselves in the form of delusions, he regresses still further to a quite vague and indistinct region of emotion, where he feels himself lulled into a kind of maternal embrace.

This may be the case with many of those people who so strangely maintain that what is "believed" by the common man and by the more enlightened man is at bottom one and the same thing (quite apart of course from the hypocrisy which makes a hotch-potch of all these things in order to get them accepted as "religious"). What interests me so much in this is the fact that all these people, from those suffering from the cruder delusions up to the oceanic mystics, should all be in the same boat, for the oceanic people can after all derive but little comfort from their "feeling."

Her language strikes me as gentle and beautiful when she isn't being too psychoanalytical. She wrote her letter in pencil (as Freud's wife often wrote him letters in pencil)—which makes her communication somehow lovelier and more fragile. Let me address the analytic language first, to put it deferentially to one side. In the last pages of *Civilization*, with phrasing that is both clinically cold and mordant in the extreme, Freud says that civilization or "culture" prides itself on how high it sets the bar for man—it "prates that the harder it is to obey [cultural demands], the more laudable the obedience." Moral indignation—at man's depravity, sexuality, or what have you—is what culture exists for. In such a world (Salomé summarizes Freud, using his terms), religion is an "infantilism," "regression," and so on.

A "pact with infantilism" refers, without much felicity, to covenant and belief. To take a current example, "Jesus loves me" is just such a pact, which isn't at all humiliating or infantile for the lucky person in question, who decides that a Jesus-loves-me bumper sticker belongs on his car, because Jesus really does love him. Conversion to Christ means many things to many people in the United States, yet "indistinctness" (Salomé's word) hardly describes its emotionalism, nor does calling it a delusion explain away the intensity of conviction that attends it. The strength of a conversion is the singular aspect: the stronger the conversion to Christ, apparently, the greater Christ's love seems in return. It hardly helps to call the conversion delusional or psychotic, since culture is also crazy in imposing standards on all humanity that people futilely strain to achieve. (Freud says humanity can't succeed vis à vis cultural standards, and therein lies man's great discomfort with culture.)

Far more usefully, Salomé observes that whatever the oceanic feeling might be, it happens in diverse contexts: creative activity might produce it, as can cultural and intellectual pursuit; common people and the self-anointed elite both can experience it. At its true worth, the oceanic feeling is the whole value of a number of important human activities–a kind of highest, not lowest, common denominator of mankind. All of us, including the delusional psychotics and the prophets, are in the same boat at infinite sea, Salomé suggests; "the boat" is not only our lot as humans, but also the somewhat tragic fate implied in her last sentence, which can't quite be predicted from what precedes it. Why should the entire spectrum of humanity up to the mystics derive "little" comfort from their feelings of transcendence?

Critic Lionel Trilling in *The Liberal Imagination* has wisely said that psychoanalytic language should never distract us from Freud's mode of judgment. By religion as an "infantilism," an orthodox Freudian could mean that religion is a throw-back to a time when an infant understands no separation between itself and the vast world, before the invention of the self or ego. The mode of judgment in such a statement is retrospective, but the terminology is clumsy. In the simplest terms, the oceanic feeling is not a new experience, whether or not it is a false comfort. To speak of a regression to infancy suggests retrenchment or retreat rather than progress to maturity, but, if there is one lesson to be learned from Freud, it is that the past occupies the present and the future, regardless of our supposed state of psychological advancement. A feeling of oceanic sublimity, which Rolland sees as a common if not universal experience, qualifies as a memory more than some novel mystical state, as occurs with hallucinogens. Freud and Salomé constitutionally will not acknowledge that Rolland's feeling is mystical or "beyond" the mind: its underpinning is a sometimes faulty memory of the joys (and discomforts) that constitute any psychological life.

In letters to Rolland during the summer of 1929, Freud spoke of the very different realms in which he and Rolland seemed to move. He spoke of the "closed book" of Rolland's mystical world view, and how Rolland's letter describing the oceanic feeling (dated December 5, 1927) left Freud mentally distracted, "without peace." I imagine that his consternation and his restlessness had to do with an inability to accept transcendence without attempting to explain transcendence psychologically. Freud articulated his views on "the oceanic" initially in letters to Salomé and, eventually, in book form—what Yosef Yerushalmi calls Freud's "first and only Jewish book," which in literal translation from the German would read "The Man Moses and The Monotheist Religion." Freud wrote back to Salomé that, regarding religion, all he wanted to do in *Civilization* was to articulate a basic theme; "I strike up a–mostly very simple–melody; you supply higher octaves for it." What harmonic resonance does Salomé provide? A first-pass answer is that Freud refers to the theme of religion as illusion, as in *The Future of an Illusion*, but Salomé forces a reconsideration. She writes (from the same letter quoted above), "I have often said to myself that when there is complete harmony in one's life, there is no necessity for [the oceanic] feeling and the need for religion is then eliminated. . . . When this harmony no longer exists, then those 'feelings' announce themselves: not only as 'wishes' . . . but also as a kind of dim memory of things having been different once upon a time." A *complete* harmony is an idealization, and if it existed, all psychological therapy would be obviated just as the need for religion would be eliminated. Salomé helps us to understand that religion isn't an illusion so much as an operation of memory. Religion so conceived is Freud's interest in *Moses and Monotheism*.

₿

When Salomé and Rolland discuss feelings of transcendence and the origins of religious sentiment, neither refers specifically to Jewish monotheism, since the oceanic feeling is not unique to a given faith. When we think about *Moses and Monotheism*, we sense that Freud's "theme" is Jewish or, at least, related in a complex way to his Judaism. Yosef Yerushalmi, in *Freud's Moses* (1991), helps me to correct that view. *Moses and Monotheism* is Freud's greatest religious meditation; the psychological idea of religion advanced in it is grander than Jewish history, the history of monotheism, or the shadowy biography of the historical Moses. With amendments, Freud's book could have been a treatise on Jesus or Mohammed, because his interest lies quite beyond the specifics of a single religion. Yerushalmi argues his point in the voice of a universalist rabbi:

> What readers of *Moses and Monotheism* have generally failed to recognize—perhaps because they have been too preoccupied with its more sensational aspects of Moses the Egyptian and his murder by the Jews—is that the true axis of the book, especially of the all-important part III, is the problem of tradition, not merely its origins, but above all its dynamics. "Only thus," Freud observes at the end of part II, "would an interest in our purely historical study find its true justification, What the real nature of tradition resides in, and what its special power rests on."

[A]s an historical essay *Moses and Monotheism* offers a singular vision of history as essentially a story of remembering and forgetting. To be sure, this is analogous to Freud's conception of the life of the individual. What has been overlooked is how strangely analogous it is also to the biblical conception of history, where the continual oscillation of memory and forgetting is a major theme through all the narratives of biblical events. Periodically, Israel forgets the God of the Covenant and lapses into idolatry; subsequently it remembers and is reunited with him. The primary biblical imperative is the command to remember, not to forget.

The twists of biblical narrative resemble the vicissitudes of memory and forgetting as anyone might experience them in routine life. Freud is more emphatic than Yerushalmi in his surmise that religion is not "strangely" analogous to psychology. In Freud's view, religion *recapitulates* psychology without strangeness at all. Memory, forgetting, "the problem" and "the dynamics" of tradition are processes inherent in human psychology. Memory, forgetting, and the dynamics of tradition are inherent in religion as well. As Freud will argue, the coincidence has meaning that we can barely fathom.

II

Freud wrote the three essays which comprise *Moses and Monotheism* from 1934 to 1938, under dire circumstances. He was dying from oral cancer; the Nazification of Austria, which some Austrian nationals believed could be forestalled, happened virtually without resistance; anti-Semitism was rife in Freud's Vienna. His personal assets were frozen; his children were interrogated by the Gestapo; and yet he resisted many entreaties from friends to leave the country. His exile to England in 1938 was subsidized by Princess Marie Bonaparte and made possible largely because of her political connections on the continent. Various others, particularly Dr. Ernest Jones, who enlisted the help of the British home office on Freud's behalf, expedited his departure from Austria, despite the fact that Freud, at age eighty-two, remained reluctant about exile almost to the day it happened. Perhaps at no other point in his life had Freud's Jewishness been so central and dangerous an issue for himself and his family. It makes sense, therefore, that *Moses and Monotheism* should be an elder's last perspective on what it means to be Jewish. Yerushalmi reads the book partly in that way, as a document suffused with strong and conflicted emotions about Jewish faith and identity. But he also suggests that Freud's Moses story was a pretext for a very encompassing discussion of man and transcendence, not just of one man and his Judaism.

Since Freud intended to write what he called an "historical novel" about Moses, it might be worth reviewing the basics of his plot. About 3,400 years ago, Egypt enjoyed military and cultural dominance throughout the Mediterranean. A young pharaoh, leader of a brave and new dynasty, promoted a religion of one universal god, but the priests of a more ancient and polytheistic faith rose up against him. The young pharaoh, Amenhotep IV (or Ikhnaton), was branded a criminal, and his dynasty ended, only to be followed by a period of anarchy after his death. A devout Egyptian follower of the pharaoh, who had once been governor of an outlying province, saw his future jeopardized because of the pharaoh's demise. The people whom he once governed had immigrated to Egypt; he entertained a plan to lead them in an exodus from Egypt. He chose his pharaoh's god as a rallying cause, but the religion he conceived was at once the same and different from pharaoh's. Among its idiosyncratic rituals, all males were circumcised as a testament of faith, as had been the case in pharaoh's religion. But at the center of the new religion was a god who was more mysterious and, so it seemed, more powerful than any previous god.

The plot then becomes a bit cloudy. We know that the times were dangerous, and that the new leader ruled over a contentious people, who had no real homeland. Uncertainty prevailed more than any one personage. There are hints that this former governor-turned-leader, named Moses, was murdered by his people. Circumstances surrounding the death are unclear, and writings attributed to Moses don't help to clarify the mystery of how he died. But Freud, borrowing very heavily from Ernst Sellin's *Moses and His Significance for the History of Israelite-Jewish Religion* (1922), believes that a murder did occur, and that the murderers joined forces with other wandering tribes, including a powerful group from Arab lands. The unification somehow worked, and together they occupied a place called Canaan. A very strange thing happened next, but only after much time: despite the fact that the disparate nomads with their various *Baalim* (or local gods) had no reason to unify behind a religion, they eventually subscribed firmly and irrevocably to one god only, whose name was difficult to pronounce (or the people didn't know exactly how to pronounce it).

The story agrees with a traditional conception of Moses as a leader of his people, but Freud (himself the embattled leader of the psychoanalytic movement) wonders what "leading a people" means. Commentator R. T. Herford (writing about *The Sayings of the Fathers*) has said that rabbinical Judaism never questions that Moses received Torah from God or that Moses led his people because he was chosen to do so. Freud departs from the notion of a submissive or passive Moses, and he almost completely ignores the "Chain of Tradition" in rabbinical teaching that "Moses received Torah from Sinai and delivered it to Joshua, and Joshua to the Elders, and the Elders to the Prophets, and the Prophets delivered it to the Men of the Great Synagogue."

Rather, Freud aligns himself with Jewish histories written under Hellenistic influence. In those histories, dating to the second century BCE, the identity of Moses became fused with that of the Egyptian god Thoth (whom Plato discusses in the *Phaedrus*) and the Greek Hermes. A personage of immense originality and brilliance, this fused Moses-Thoth-Hermes instructs man about the art of writing, as opposed to mere speech, and about science, as opposed to blind superstition. Martin Hengal in his definitive *Judaism and Hellenism* remarks that Moses *as teacher* dramatizes the passage of wisdom between generations—a characterization that "has its model less in the Old Testament, where it was not known in this strict form, than in Greece." Borrowing from Hengal, we could view Freud's Moses as a psychological hero in a Hellenistic mold.

How does the premise "Moses is an Egyptian" change one's view of Moses? One answer could be: it doesn't much, no more than saying that Moses as rabbi is a Hellenistic concept. But, there is another consideration: why is Freud so very bothersome; what good is there is in violating the sacredness of Moses as a traditional figure? Freud himself questioned Michelangelo's "blasphemy" in creating his image of the prophet at the Church of S. Pietro in Vincoli in Rome:

> But here it will be objected that after all this is not the Moses of the Bible. For that Moses did actually fall into a fit of rage and did throw away the Tables and break them. This Moses must be a quite different conception, a new Moses of the artist's conception; so that Michelangelo must have had the presumption to emend the sacred text and to falsify the character of that of that holy man. Can we think him capable of a boldness which might almost be said to approach an act of blasphemy?

Michelangelo's "new Moses of the artist's conception" is Freud's model for what he will produce with his Moses. Freud gives us every indication that he is concerned only with setting history straight, but he wants to be as flagrant as possible in rethinking who Moses was. He is more aggressively revisionist than either a skeptical Itzig or an artistically dominant Michelangelo.

Freud's irony about setting history straight compares to another patriarchal personification of a very different kind, by Franz Kafka: "To be sure, he would never get to be a patriarch," Kafka wrote regarding Abraham (not Moses). Abraham "would be prepared to satisfy the demand for a sacrifice immediately, *with the promptness of a waiter*, but would be unable to bring [the sacrifice] off because he cannot get away, being indispensable; the household needs him." The drama of Abraham's dark silence on the way to Moriah changes (to say the least) with Kafka's assumptions. The original Jewish patriarch *as a waiter* sounds like bad Yiddish humor, made slightly better when we think that Abraham can't leave for Moriah because he's needed at home as the irreplaceable domestic help.

The quandary of Abraham in Genesis is exactly what Kafka describes in household terms: en route to Moriah (in Genesis) or stuck at home (in Kafka's parable), Abraham is constrained absolutely, and we, as readers, feel the randomness of Yahweh's will visited upon him and us. In *Moses and Monotheism*, Freud thinks that received history errs on important facts. As in Kafka's parable, the premise is important for the psychological picture that results from it. Freud, too, will find himself utterly stuck with respect to both Abraham and Moses. The shock of Moses as an Egyptian and the shock of a murder, as hinted in fragments from the prophet Hosea, aren't quite so shocking when compared to what Freud has to say in the all-important last (and longest) section of his book—"all important," because it is Freud's summa about what psychology accomplishes. It is a science of the mind in which we fail to emend the largest truths.

⊜

The concluding section (Part III) is itself comprised of two parts. The first is remarkable for the bewildering movement in its argument (I will address the second part separately). First, Freud introduces a theme that religion isn't merely a consequence of sociopolitical forces. He talks about individual psychology—in particular, the concept that a psychological symptom complex represents a process with "latency" in its progression. In a presto of a conclusion, he details his insight, supposedly applicable to all religious doctrines and rituals, that the strength of a religion draws from what he calls the return of a forgotten history—what elsewhere he calls the return of the repressed. I would like to slow the pace of his associations, but part of the reader's experience of Part III is the feeling of rapid or breathless argument: Freud's alacrity invites one to be convinced without a moment's critical reflection.

"In Egypt, so far as we can understand, monotheism grew up as a by-product of imperialism: God was a reflection of the Pharaoh who was the absolute ruler of a great world empire." Freud's claim is plausible, but religion as an epiphenomenon of political hegemony simply could not have applied to a rag-tag of nomads. The rabbinical tradition that maintains an unbroken transmission of law and scripture from Moses to the modern sensibility "disavow[s] precisely what we have described as the most striking fact about Jewish religious history, namely that there is a yawning gap between the law-giving of Moses and the later Jewish religion." Freud says that inheritance of one's identity through religious tradition can't be seamless in the way that orthodoxy maintains. In counterpoint and comparison, he refers us to clinical experience—an experience which, let us admit, has essentially nothing to do with Judaism (as Freud himself admits, because he alludes specifically to the analogy of problems encountered in dealing with patients, not to an identity between the rise of monotheism and how clinical symptoms manifest in life).

Freud ranges far from his premise about the true identity and fate of Moses. He shifts our attention from ancient history to the fright of terrible accidents that occur every day:

> It may happen that a man who has experienced some frightful accident—a railway collision, for instance—leaves the scene of the event apparently uninjured. In the course of the next few weeks, however, he develops a number of severe psychical and motor symptoms which can only be traced to his shock, the concussion or whatever else it was. He now has a "traumatic neurosis." It is a quite unintelligible—that is to say, a new—fact. The time that has passed between the accident and the first appearance of the symptoms is described as the "incubation period," in a clear allusion to the pathology of infectious diseases. On reflection, it must strike us that, in spite of the fundamental difference between the two cases—the problem of traumatic neurosis and that of Jewish monotheism—there is nevertheless one point of agreement: namely, in the characteristic that might be described as "latency" . . . . We are thus prepared for the possibility that the solution of our problem is to be looked for in a psychological situation.

Readers who applaud the clarity, even the beauty, of Freud's prose mainly appreciate that at least they understand him, regardless of what outrageous associations he offers. Albert Einstein felt that even if he often strained to agree with psychoanalytic doctrine, he could always follow wherever a train of thought led Sigmund Freud. We should be clear that Freud is not saying that religion is a traumatic neurosis or an infectious disease. He is curious about whether the solution to the puzzle of religion lies in an extended analogy, which needn't be just the analogy between the consequences of a train wreck and Jewish monotheism. Any of a variety of clinical cases, even normal psychology, could serve as a thought experiment pertinent to religious experience.

An orthodox Freudian thinks, first and foremost, that our motivations in life are unconscious and, second, that psychoanalysis allows us to understand them better and, so too, ourselves to a greater degree. Yes, but: what do Moses and the Old Testament have to do with the insights of a talking therapy? The orthodox Freudian view is not quite what Freud himself advocates regarding religion as "a symptom." If one reads *Moses and Monotheism* to synopsize it, then fervent religious sentiment is most intelligible when we contemplate an original "trauma" (the murder of Moses or of Christ), the consequences of which we live out in our symptom-filled lives. Severe symptoms *equal* forgetting in one kind of easy formulation of Freud. After a stress or trauma, one develops symptoms (nightmares, for example); do we recognize the stress or trauma that gave rise to nightmares? Freud's perspective is different from such summary, especially if we think in clinical terms rather than religious ones, though I will admit the two worlds are brought so close to one another in Freud's argument that they infect each other completely. After a stress, one doesn't become symptomatic right away; one seems to deal with it quite well—for a time, one appears to "solve" the stress. Freud then asks, do we recognize the stress that gave rise to *the solution*? Why even bother with the hard work of recognition if the solution works well enough? Freud's insight is that people don't bother worrying about "recognition" for the compelling reason that they have no reason to bother. He acknowledges, even emphasizes, that religion—and beyond religion, spirituality—feels like the opposite of a symptom of disease.

For a normal person or for someone with a psychopathology, the work of recollection in therapy is unnecessary and quite undesirable unless one feels symptomatic, as Salomé said. And yet, as Freud maintains throughout his writing, we are all symptomatic. So, let's say that we do the work of memory and therapy, keeping in mind that the further back we go, the greater the likelihood of various false reconstructions. We realize that every memory of recent or distant experience is a reproduction with variable fidelity to the actual past. Whether or not a memory is true by some standard, Freud insists that our memories revisit us in time regardless—in the language just quoted, sometimes after a remarkable "latency." More than that, says Freud, "each portion that returns from oblivion [of forgetfulness] asserts itself with peculiar force, exercises an incomparably powerful influence on people in the mass, and raises an irresistible claim to truth against which logical objection is powerless: a kind of *credo quia absurdum*."

His language is insistent—*peculiar* force, *incomparable* power, *irresistible* claim. He describes a force which can neither be refuted nor evaded, whether memory is reliable or fantastical. A kind of absurd mandate applies to everyone, including the religious believer, the person incapacitated by some psychiatric condition, or the normal individual with a preserved capacity for work and love. The mandate is that memory works in a grand circle; it comes back relentlessly, whether or not we consider ourselves symptomatic in the first place. We can talk about how the return power can feel like the force of a spiritual conviction—which is to say, how memory can surprise us with its oceanic force—but we shouldn't confuse cause with consequence. The sense of one's conviction, says Freud, derives from an aspect of psychology, not (say) an awe before a god. For Freud, such conviction is evidence of what he calls the survival of memory-traces in archaic heritage. The first part of Part III ends with a strange statement about his belief that characteristics which develop at one point in time (like guilt over the distant murder of a prophet) can be passed to a subsequent generation: "I must admit that I have behaved for a long time as though the inheritance of memory-traces of the experience of our ancestors, independently of direct communication and of the influence of education by the setting of an example, were established beyond question. When I spoke of the survival of a tradition among a people or of the formation of a people's character, I had mostly in mind an inherited tradition of this kind and not transmitted by communication. Or at least I made no distinction between the two."

One begs to disagree: no, it is not as if we inherit the guilt over a murder that may not even have happened more than two millennia ago. Perhaps he means that memory and forgetting don't change, but his phrasing becomes oddly apologetic: "I must, however, confess in all modesty that I cannot do without this factor [the inheritance of acquired characteristics] in biological evolution."

Freud's awkwardly phrased insight belongs to Charles Darwin, *not* to Darwin's predecessor Jean Baptiste de Lamarck, who advocated the inheritance of acquired characteristics across generations. The structure of all organic being, Darwin said, is related in an essential yet hidden manner to all other organic beings. In quite Darwinian language, Freud suggests that the structure of all spiritual being is related in an essential yet hidden manner to all other human beings. The "structure" of spirituality, or of our search for transcendence and meaning, really refers us to the sometimes flimsy constructions of memory and the strange way in which the edifice of remembrance somehow continues to stand. Both factors also relate to secular psychology. Freud says he "can't do" without the inheritance of acquired characteristics—in his late *Outline of Psychoanalysis*, he even calls himself Lamarckian with respect to generational inheritance. But Freud's argument in *Moses and Monotheism* is essentially Darwinian, that who we *are* in the oceanic moments can't be much different from who we *were* a long time ago. In current vernacular, the very survival of a religious sentiment, perhaps even its hegemony in some quarters of the world, has always had "evolutionary significance" for the species.

To summarize up until the half-way point of Part III: we observe an interest in the commonality shared by religious people no less than purportedly godless ones. Freud searches for the mode of transcendence that he can call his own. He would protest if he heard us say that *Moses and Monotheism* was his oceanic meditation, but arguably it was. Rolland's thought of an oceanic infinity becomes, in Freud, what critic Walter Benjamin called the sense of "danger in history." Writing about the past as it seems to "flit" by, Benjamin spoke of history as the desperate activity of a man who tries to retrieve what he loses at the precise moment he starts to write history—"the good tidings which the historian . . . brings with a throbbing heart may be lost in a void the very moment he opens his mouth." To articulate the past historically does not mean to recognize it "the way it really was," Benjamin continues, "it means to seize hold of a memory as it flashes up at the moment of danger. . . . The danger affects both the content of tradition and its receivers." Just where this danger manifests (for Benjamin as for Freud, the danger is forgetfulness and the great emptiness of "the void"), Freud thinks we learn most about ourselves.

III

From the first pages of his book, Freud avoids all familiar aspects of the Moses story as it has been handed down to us: there is no burning bush, no plagues, frogs, lice—not even the stone tablets that preoccupied him in "The Moses of Michelangelo" (1914). He does, however, discuss idolatry as he begins the second part of Part III. As Moses does to his people, Freud chides us for our misapprehensions about the greatness of idols. How is it possible, Freud asks, that one personage can be so extraordinary? "Is not a hypothesis such as this a relapse into the mode of thought which led to myths of a creator and to the worship of heroes . . . ?" If Thomas Carlyle claimed that we learn history through the biographies of great persons in history, Freud says that greatness must be a function of more than the orthodox biography of a patriarch. His insight, which Freudians applaud as quintessential and original in *Moses and Monotheism*, seems to me perfectly traditional and still Carlylean, that Moses is vital because he is a paterfamilias deserving of worship as pure hero: "There is no doubt that it was a mighty prototype of a father which, in the person Moses, stooped to the poor Jewish bondsmen to assure them that they were his dear children." In concluding his book, Freud meditates at length on this statement.

Reading Freud's very next sentence on the "mighty prototype," my mind drifts to Abraham, the original patriarch for the Jewish people: "And no less overwhelming for them must have been the idea of an only, eternal, almighty God, to whom they were not too mean for him to make covenant . . . who promised to care for them *if* they remained loyal to his worship." The swap in question—if faith, then covenant—was certainly Abraham's transcendental transaction in the crucial twenty-second chapter of Genesis. Once Abraham demonstrates that he is willing to sacrifice his Isaac, the covenant becomes more secure. Commentator Everett Fox in *The Five Books of Moses* tells us that a great tension is lessened after Genesis 22: after Isaac's sacrifice doesn't happen in Moriah, "we can breathe easier, knowing that God will come to the rescue of his chosen ones in the direst of circumstances."

To be clear, Freud's mighty prototype is not Abraham, but why not? Fox talks about Abraham as the "biological father" of the Jews (a statement made problematic by scholarly observations that Abraham was Chaldean and not Hebrew), but it is trite, and possibly untrue, to maintain that Moses is more spiritual than Abraham and a mightier father as a consequence. If there is a story that captures the spiritual burden of a covenant, Abraham's near-sacrifice of Isaac seems paradigmatic, more so than the embattled, some-times just catty, relationships that Moses suffers both with his god and his people. Some chapters ago, I referred to Erich Auerbach's claim that Genesis 22 stands at one extreme of all western representations of reality (as opposed to the transparency of Homer), but for all its preoccupation with background and suggestion, Genesis remains an aching reminder that the God of Abra-ham was a very tough father-figure who, by the time of Moses and Exodus, became all the more demanding with Moses and just plain brutal with others, both Jews and Egyptians.

There are two major problems in tracing Freud's trajectory towards the thunderous conclusion of *Moses and Monotheism*, borrowed from Paul of Tarsus, that the reason we are unhappy is that we have killed God the father. Both problems relate to the very dangerous business of identifying a father. On the one hand, how can we speak meaningfully about the origins of tradi-tion without lapsing into some kind of received and tired wisdom—in other words, what is gained by calling Moses, as opposed to Abraham or Yahweh, the father that obsesses us? And, as a second problem, why is that fathers and children get so commingled (the Mosaic God becomes one with Moses, just as Paul's God is consubstantial with the murdered Christ)? Yerushalmi, whom I cite again with respect, says that Freud subscribes to a secular yet religion-obsessed view that tradition (and Jewish identity) is a privileged in-formation among the children of Abraham and Moses. But once we try to delineate the tradition and its filial indebtedness as Freud does, we irritate the keepers of the faith, says Yerushalmi: "Floating in their undefined yet somehow real Jewishness, they [Jewish people] will doubly resent . . . any at-tempt on the part of the surrounding society to define them against their own wishes. The worst moments are those in which, as a result of anti-Semitism, they are forced to realize that vital aspects of their lives are still determined by ancestral forces they may no longer understand and which, in any case, they feel they have transcended or repudiated."

Explicitly, it seems, Yerushalmi warns us against articulating the essence of Jewish tradition if we aren't Jewish ourselves—a point to which I will re-turn in a moment. But Freud clearly moves beyond Jewishness in his Part III, however indebted he might be to tradition. He generalizes to the point of los-ing (willfully forgetting?) much that is Jewish about his archaic past. "It may begin to dawn on us that all the characteristics with which we equipped the great man are paternal characteristics, and that the essence of the great man for which we vainly searched lies in this conformity." The identity of "the" father becomes muddled in Part III, and I suppose Freud intends for us to be confused: the Mosaic God, Moses, a Pauline Christ, and the first patriarch in Abraham all become vaguely one dad and we all become as children.

Regarding the Jewishness of Freud's approach, I think Yerushalmi identifies a problem made actually more vivid if one is not Jewish, because the last thing that helps me in understanding how I am determined by ancestral forces is to think about the historical reality of Moses. I am of Asian descent, but I can say with all earnestness that if my Jewish friends think they have problems with their past, then we should get together to share our tales. Yerushalmi nicely objects to the idea of someone—anyone—coming along to force a realization upon us: that we, as Asians, Jews, or what have you, are determined by our pasts might be true enough, but we don't want someone telling us how the process works, particularly since, as Yerushalmi says, we all have our own problems in understanding the nature and working of our respective determinisms. Theban tragedy and Shakespeare's Hamlet (as I have tried to argue in earlier chapters) are models for the complexity we want to describe in "our psychology." To say that we are variously Asian Oedipi or Jewish Hamlets in relationship to our immediate, biological parents—and, in a grossly theoretical extension, to very distant generations—is reductionist to be sure, but mainly such commentary reduces the richness of history to the platitudes of an exhausted psychology.

When in doubt, think about a story. Psychoanalyst Neville Symington relates that a patient came to see him in search of an explanation for a depression; the doctor considered offering this "little dissertation" to his patient:

> From what you have told me, I think your depression is due to unconscious aggression against your father and that when your father died when you were at the age of eight, you believed that your aggression had killed him. You believed this because of your unconscious omnipotence, and then you felt guilty and bad about what you had done. This guilt and badness is what you experience as depression.

Very wisely, Symington says nothing of the kind, because he knows, first, that the patient mainly wants to stop feeling depressed; second, that the explanation won't help because his dissertation is pretty depressing, especially if aggression is a universal force that persists long after dad is dead and gone. Why, then, should we be convinced by any dissertation on religious sentiment, whose origins, on Freud's view, aren't much different from the above

194 What to Read on Love, Not Sex

explanation? We need only make minor changes to Symington's commentary to make it good for Judaism (or Jewish memory from Freud's point of view): the persistence of religion relates to an old aggression against father Moses; guilt and badness change after much time into religious faith and adherence to traditions which have been transmitted from Moses. "Guilt and badness" in Symington's case amount to religious sentiment in Freud's *Moses and Monotheism*. When we think about *Moses and Monotheism*, we might do well not to regurgitate an Oedipal interpretation, just as Symington forebears delivering his little dissertation to his patient.

Theologian Hans Küng, to take another example of dissertation writing (from *Freud and the Problem of God*), "oedipalizes" Freud's arguments in *Totem and Taboo* and *Moses and Monotheism*. Here I quote Küng's conclusions in bullets:

> Thus religion is based entirely on the Oedipus complex of mankind as a whole. For Freud this is the psychological explanation of the origin of religion.

> The formation of religion is built on the father complex and its ambivalence.

> Unlike Judaism, Christianity admits parricide into religion.

> Paul reached the conclusion that we are unhappy because we have killed God the Father. We were released from this sin only when Jesus Christ as Son sacrificed his life. The Son even takes the place of the Father.

> Fear of the primordial father has been kept up in the most varied forms of Christianity.

In the first bullet, Küng's "Thus" is problematic. One can hardly accept a priori that religion is based on the Oedipus complex unless we subscribe to Freud's parricidal/patricidal view of Jewish history, and most informed readers disregard Freud's Moses story as historiographic poppycock. We probably will never know the historical truth of Moses, but if you subscribe to the Oedipus complex as doctrine, then you are more likely to see evidence for it everywhere, most especially in the leitmotifs of fathers, sons, murder, and sacrifice in religious history.

There is, however, another use of Oedipus, as suggested in Küng's second bullet, which is cleverer than the first. By "father complex," Küng refers to the hypothetical problem articulated in *Totem and Taboo*. If fathers had sexual monopoly over women in the "primal horde," as the argument of that book runs, it has always seemed to me that the women (not the sons) would want to kill the father out of an erotically pragmatic need for new partners. Freud says the sons wanted to kill the father. Either way, the father isn't popular, but he is formidable; he overwhelms one's thinking and action, just as Yahweh via Moses dominates the contentious rabble of idolaters. In *Moses and Monotheism*, Freud maintains that Moses was more complicated than just a medium of divinity, but to describe in what way he was more complicated (because he, too, was like a father) leads Freud down a path to a psychoanalytic dogma about the truth of the Oedipus complex.

He could have concentrated on the astonishing verbal exchanges between Yahweh and Moses or between Moses and his people to adumbrate the ambivalent relations between fathers and children, but he does not. Instead he relies on clinical material (specifically, a saga of a child who tries very hard not to be like his/her overbearing parent, who becomes just like his/her parent as life proceeds) to drive home the point that if we try to explain the power of religion, maybe we should contemplate our own intricate and usually conflicted relationships with parents (mothers or fathers).

In such psychological terms, Christianity, the subject of Küng's last three points, sounds like family therapy gone infinitely sour: the son of God, who was always one with his father, was killed in a sacrifice with tremendous implications for all later generations. But the son resurrects to become one with his father again after the murder. Fear (and awe) of God is a direct consequence. Over centuries, fear and awe continue to have legs. Those who arrive late in the Christian tradition are "released from sin" because of God's sacrifice, or as Freud dryly puts it, in the voice of a Christian, "[The Jews] will not accept it as true that they have murdered God, whereas we admit it and have been cleansed of guilt." The Oedipalism of Christianity, if it exists at all, manifests as a Pauline unhappiness over violent acts and thoughts. Personal acknowledgment of guilt is a liberation and salvation, in the same way that apologizing to one's parents seems to cure a thousand ills. Freud summarizes all of the above in his inimitably dour way: "Christianity, having arisen out of a father-religion, became a son-religion. It has not escaped the fate of having to get rid of the father."

I enjoy Küng's delicious understatement in bullet 3, that the son "even" takes the place of the father. Together with Freud, he acknowledges that in the transition from Judaism to Christianity, Abraham, Moses, and Christ are all paternal and filial figures. A tendency to conflation eventually progresses to the point, say after the Council of Nicea in the fourth century CE, of God as an image of an "entirety" of not two, but three parts—a tripartite image that (for me) is most moving in St. Augustine's *On the Trinity*, where trinity, he says, reflects the human mind, human experience, and human thought. Like Augustine, Freud looked to religion as a mirror of psychology and vice versa, no matter how many gods or reduplications of god are involved.

Küng in *Freud and the Problem of God* is not far from Freud in acknowledging that God is a problem for everybody (one recalls that the chief rabbi of Vienna, responding to Freud's religious criticism, remarked to Freud that the two of them were closer than they realized). Küng merely wants religion to be taken seriously:

> I am decidedly of the opinion that questions of religion, for the sake of the people—both the sick and the healthy—cannot be domesticated and relegated to a quasi-illegal garret existence in the great edifice of psychiatry, but rather that they should be included throughout as central questions of psychiatry, psychotherapy, and psychology. I plead not for a religious psychotherapy or a psychotherapy only for the religious, but rather for a therapy that takes the phenomenon of religion seriously as one of the specifically human forms of expression. I plead for a therapy that does not merely take note of the patient's confession of faith or denomination or inquire perfunctorily into his or her orthodox beliefs. Rather, therapy should try to explore in detail an individual's very personal, often very unorthodox religion, which usually undergoes great changes in the course of a lifetime: the patient's heart religion.

"Plead" is the central word in this passage ("quasi-illegal garret" is a nice phrase, but it is not central). What Küng wants is more or less what Freud attempts in *Moses and Monotheism*. Küng and many others of like mind recoil at the religion being examined as a scientific curiosity, but Freud's "heart religion" is a faith in everything but name. It is laced through with hopefulness about what his psychoanalytical science could achieve, namely, a respite from human misery.

IV

The concluding half of part III reads like a novel with two endings. Freud has prepared us for both of them. He has repeated his key points throughout his book, but at the end of part III, he writes as if there's a forgotten aspect of the Moses plot that needs to be followed through to a more momentous realization. Moses is not who we think he is—that is Freud's first summary observation, based on his reconstruction of various ancient clues. Then Freud balks: "There is an element of grandeur about everything to do with the origin of religion, certainly including the Jewish one, and this is not matched by the explanations we have hitherto given. Some other factor must be involved to which there is little that is analogous and nothing that is of the same kind, something unique and something of the same order of magnitude as what has come out of it, as religion itself." His second ending needs to be commensurate to the problem and the glory of religious sentiment, not just Judaic.

The murder of Moses (the Egyptian) did not mean that Moses died; a second Moses rose up in his place. Maybe this second Moses came from the land called Midian, just east of the Gulf of Aqabah in what is now Saudi Arabia. In Midian, the presumed locale of Mt. Sinai (although the Sinai peninsula has no volcanoes), Moses (II) essentially stole the idea of a local volcano God, and adopted it to the new religion. Yahweh worship (Yahweh is a volcano God, as Freud murmurs to us more than once), manifested late, flourishing in Kadesh (or Qadeš), well north of Midian and nearer to Canaan, perhaps a generation or two after the original Egyptian Moses. And then: "In the course of constant efforts over centuries, and finally owing to two great reforms, one before and one after the Babylonian exile [which occurred perhaps eight centuries after the first Moses lived] the popular [volcanic] god Yahweh transformed into a God whose worship had been forced upon the Jews by Moses." Moses (I) is dead, but Moses (II) replaces him: Freud has us fast-forward through Saul, David, Solomon, and more—at any rate, we bypass a good number of centuries. His narrative next deposits us around the time of the First Temple, just as the Babylonians are about destroy it, at the end of the sixth century BCE. What Freud calls "a peculiar psychical aptitude" allows the Jews to produce not one or two, but rather a series of leaders who take on the burden of Mosaic Yahwism. In the first (preliminary) ending to *Moses and Monotheism*, we learn that whoever fathered Judaism, he was never one father, but rather a pastiche of one.

Freud's second ending is unexpected. After telling us that we've gotten Moses all wrong in the past, Freud says that "Moses" is precisely the figure whom tradition has made him out to be, namely, the prophet (or multiple prophets) of a single *idea* of God. The idea passes from generation to generation, but with immense gaps. Like "generational law" as described by historian Marcus Hansen (that a grandson will want to remember what a son tries his whole life to forget), all vicissitudes circle back, and eventually we revisit origins, even if they lie buried or are in ruin.

When Freud speaks of the "peculiar psychical aptitude" of the Jewish people, he means that Jews uniquely conceived of God as an abstraction, by way of a prohibition against graven images. History has envied them for their "intellectuality" ever since. One could object, as Celsus did in about 200 CE, that maybe there is "no difference whether we call Zeus the Most High, or Zen, or Adonai, or Sabaoth, or Amoun like the Egyptians, or Papaeus like the Sythians." For good measure, Celsus intones that no one should invoke circumcision as evidence of particular Jewish holiness, since "the Egyptians and the Colchians did this before they did." After Moses, Freud says, we cannot forget God as a single God however much we try; and, in his surprising section entitled "The Advance of Intellectuality," Freud seems to equate Jewish brain power with chosen-ness. I personally don't know whether the claim about Jewish intellectuality is compliment or stereotype, but it's clear that Freud argues Judeo-centrically. For "Jewishness" we should read "psychology": Freud isn't saying that psychology is Jewish; he's saying that if the Jewish history teaches anything, it is the power of an idea, which is the idea of the mind.

We read that once Yahweh or YHWH, the name that defied pronunciation, became a divinity without an attendant "sensual" image of it, *the history of religion changed in the direction of psychology*: "Human beings found themselves obliged in general to recognise 'intellectual' forces—forces, that is, which cannot be grasped by the senses (particularly by the sight) but which none the less produce undoubted and indeed extremely powerful effects." And, a few sentences later: "All such advances in intellectuality have as their consequence that the individual's self-esteem is increased, that he is made proud–so that he feels superior to other people who have remained under the spell of sensuality." Writing his manuscript in the mid-to-late 1930s, there can be no question that Freud's Judaism was a horrible stigma on him, painted there by the hateful. His Moses becomes an artist's rendering of nothing but power, just as Freud viewed Michelangelo's horned statue adorning the tomb of a Pope an the expression of a limitless fight: "the giant frame with its tremendous physical power becomes only a concrete expression of the highest mental achievement that is possible in a man, that of struggling successfully against an inward passion for the sake of a cause to which he has devoted himself."

⊜

I do wish Freud had spent some time talking about the actual representation of Yahweh in scripture. If intellectual power comes in a package with brutal Yahweh, we might want to consider all other alternatives, religious or secular. The Yahweh in what we now read as *The Five Books of Moses* (and significantly more so in the writings of "J," or the Yahwist) is incarnate toughness. Not in graven image, but rather in the more striking word-pictures of scripture, Yahweh is interpersonally difficult and demanding to a point beyond Job's pain. Yahweh allows a man to understand His divine words—Moses hears every word Yahweh says—but Yahweh is inscrutable; Yahweh is like the father, mother, or love interest whom one would choose only if one had a penchant for quiet depression before that which simply will not yield. In what possible sense can Freud say that Yahweh is abstract, when descriptions compel us to think that an apt analogy for the relationship between God and man is a knock-down fight between formidable opponents, such as occurs between husband and wife, Lear and the storm, Oedipus and himself?

Here is Freud in what I take to be the coda of codas regarding his historical Moses, in his section entitled "What is True in Religion." He describes man and Mosaic religion in their intimate relationship:

> The religion of Moses . . . (1) . . . allowed people to take a share in the grandeur of a new idea of God, (2) . . . asserted that this people had been chosen by this great God and were destined to receive evidences of his special favour and (3) . . . forced upon the people an advance in intellectuality which, important enough in itself, opened the way, in addition, to the appreciation of intellectual work and to further renunciations of instinct.
>
> This is what we have arrived at. And, though we do not wish to take back any of it, we cannot hide from ourselves that it is somehow or other unsatisfying. The cause does not, so to speak, match the effect; the fact that we want to explain seems to be of a different order of magnitude from everything by which we explain it. May it be that all the investigations we have so far made have not uncovered the whole of the motivation but only a superficial layer . . . [?]

"The whole of the motivation" refers to the origin of "oceanic" sentiment, not just the origin of a religion, whether Judaism, Christianity, Islam, or other. We learn, as we learn so often in Freud, that origins refer to a past so distant in personal or collective memory that, by definition, we can only reconstruct it (imperfectly) out of fragments. To be generous, we might allow that psychoanalysis could reconstruct both memory and "the whole of the motivation," but Moses and Yahweh are not on the couch. Maybe God and man in their relationship are in need of intense couples therapy, but Yahweh won't come to the sessions, and he would cast endless plagues on all such psychotherapy anyway.

The "element of grandeur" or "order of magnitude" that Freud's analysis lacks, which the religious sentiment itself possesses as a virtue of being a powerful and personal experience, can't be achieved by analysis. If analysis did achieve it, then I doubt that Freudian psychotherapy of any type would ever have suffered a loss of popularity. Freud thinks he achieves the commensurate grandeur and magnitude of explanation when he speculates that our idea of god is the "superego," which he describes both in *Moses and Monotheism* and (I think more understandably) in his *New Introductory Lectures*. In the latter, we read: "a child's super-ego is in fact constructed on the model not of its parents but of its parents' super-ego; the contents which fill it are the same and it becomes a vehicle of tradition and of all time-resisting judgements of value which have propagated themselves in this manner from generation to generation." As we know from everyday experience, evidence for the superego is mundane and not divine–we are routinely hard on ourselves, often without knowing why. Freud says that as we think about the superego, we should be thinking about those "vehicles of tradition" that run over and through our egos. But the superego is not god.

Freud stands on firmer ground when he observes that god as an abstract idea is a fine accomplishment in the history of ideas. But there are other abstractions, such as numbers and physical laws and the axioms of logic—all are also excellent, and not all are Jewish. If a hierarchy of our abstractions exists at all, it would be strange to think that there is an abstraction greater than our own psychology, so the idea of God perhaps too facilely becomes the idea of our own psychology. There are readers who protest that Freud was just another atheist with another godless theory, but *Moses and Monotheism* simply suggests otherwise. Freud breaks the image of Moses into pieces of a *melitzah* as Jewish tradition describes it (the personal reconstruction of fragments), but the idea that lasts through time is an abstraction beyond all representations, call it mind, experience, thought, or God.

⊞

An ungracious correspondent from Boston, as quoted by Peter Gay, wrote of Freud and *Moses and Monotheism*, "It is to be regretted that you could not go to your grave without disgracing yourself, you old nitwit." The Jewish colleagues who advised Freud that he not publish *Moses and Monotheism* never understood Freud's motivation for writing it, and neither did the disgruntled Bostonian. Freud went to his grave with the idea that he had completed two novels, one regarding love of work (the book he might have called, along with Merezhkovsky, his "Romance" of Leonardo da Vinci) and the last regarding the love of higher things, including the idea of his psychology. Both "novels" return us to the problem of analogy. Wondering about the best analogy for religious experience refers us to a no less vexing concern about what the best analogy might be for psychological work. William James suggested in *The Varieties of Religious Experience* that, given the state of ignorance about mystical, sublime, or oceanic states, it was best just to take notes. For Freud, personal note-taking was a life-long exercise when it came to the story of Moses.

Yosef Yerushalmi usefully suggests that one recall a story from Freud's biography in any consideration of Freud's Moses. On the occasion of his thirty-fifth birthday, Freud received a gift from his father Jakob, the family's old Philippsohn German-Hebrew Bible that Sigmund had read as a child, now rebound in new leather. In his inscription, in a series of biblical allusions in Hebrew, Jakob the Father describes tablets with "new skin" on them now. Critic Jacques Derrida has observed that Jakob doesn't *give* Freud his bible, but rather *returns* it to him. In the figure of Moses, perhaps Freud saw nothing but intellectual returns, even if his speculation amounted to a bizarre psychological novel in the eyes of peers. Yerushalmi discusses Jakob's most important allusion in what he wrote to Sigmund, in Hebrew. If we read scripture strictly, Moses broke the original tablets, but none of the tablets' fragments were ever found. In Deuteronomy, however, Moses was instructed to produce new tablets on which the laws would be reinscribed. "The mandate lies here," Yerushalmi writes, "in the Hebrew inscription, the dramatic call to return to the Bible, to the originally shared values with the father, a 'memorial and reminder of love.'"

Lost fragments, reinscription (as Derrida would call it), and the gift of what was once part of us: whatever analogy we seek for religious experience, Freud in *Moses and Monotheism* suggests that it must contain those three aspects of recollection. Without that trinity, a psychological theory of religion loses authority, and it yields in defeat to what William James called the psychologist's fallacy.

Eight

Postscript

❝ THERE IS SCARCELY anything more difficult than to love one another . . . it is work, day labor, day labor, God knows there is no other word for it. And look, added to this is the fact that young people are not prepared for such difficult loving; for convention has tried to make this most complicated and ultimate relationship into something easy and frivolous, has given it the appearance of everyone's being able to do it. It is not so." That is poet Rainer Rilke, writing at age twenty-nine. He sounds older. His own love-life—which included marriage to sculptress Clara Westhoff, separation from her not long after he wrote the above in a letter (not to her), and a fierce lifelong attachment to Lou Andreas-Salomé, Freud's patient and correspondent—was an archetype of difficult love, but what he has to say applies not just to his particular circumstances.

The first sentence, "There is scarcely anything more difficult . . ." rings inevitably true (love isn't easy), but his counter-intuition in the last sentence is my interest: he denies the universal ability to love, because so few understand or even realize its cognitive and emotional demands. *It is not so* is made more disturbing when the poet observes that "at bottom, no one in life can help anyone else in life; this one experiences over and over in every conflict and every perplexity: that one is alone." Interpret a negation (e.g., love is not what one thinks it is), Freud believed, and you won't be disappointed, but you won't necessarily be comforted, either.

We tend to think that love is not "cognitively" difficult. We all need to give and receive love; what's so hard to understand? Yet I think Rilke describes what one learns after a few years of marriage (or in the second one), after a good amount of time working closely with people, or after enough disappointment that one begins to question how love is possible. The questioning is important, says our poet Rilke, who, many years later, would sound like a slightly exhausted veteran of psychological warfare:

> You are so young . . . I want to beg you, as much as I can, to be patient
> toward all that is unsolved in your heart and to try to love the questions
> themselves like locked rooms and like books that are written in a very for-
> eign tongue. Do not seek the answers, which cannot be given you because
> you would not be able to live them.

The pain of this advice (there is pain in it, because: why is the room locked?
Why the interest in otherness that will always be foreign?) returns us to the
shrewd vagueness of Rilke's word "difficulty."

Love "as difficulty" makes sense from the perspective of experience: the
reason why some people aren't prepared for "difficult loving" is because they
were critically misinformed at some point about what love means and entails.
Only experience teaches us to know love in both its joy and disappointment,
but sometimes, due to our own recalcitrance, we prefer to remain mystified
about it, thereby making love even more difficult than it always was. Mainly,
Rilke advises against overly simple answers, under the assumption that love
is too complex to be explained by them—or, as he puts it more enigmatically
and meaningfully, one might not be able "to live" the answers even if they
were simply given to us. There is scarcely anything more difficult than to love
one another, except the task of describing the difficulty, in Rilke's sophisticated sense of the word.

Some chapters ago, I quoted a question (J. H. van den Berg's) that deserves a last look: who can feel at ease with psychological explanation? Description and explanation are not equivalent, but when we think about Freud
on the subject of love, there is a tendency to assume that they are. Van den
Berg had a specific case in mind: a husband whose leg moved up and down, in
a kicking motion, as he spoke to his wife. At one point in the history of ideas,
before Freud's obsessive search for meaning in everything, the leg might have
meant nothing, but, to van den Berg's understated astonishment, he notices
that "we have different ideas now." Regarding the meaning of seemingly random events (a leg motion, a roll of the eyes, a sigh), we frankly don't need to
study Freud today to invent scenarios of meaning. Freud's usefulness, I think,
no longer has to do with stock explanations of intrapsychic or interpersonal
conflict, especially in an era predisposed to think about alternative scientific,
genetic, neurochemical, and many other types of explanation. One lesson
that we should gather from Freud is that one needn't feel at ease with any
type of explanation or description, certainly not with respect to human love,

unless it is "difficult" enough.

I am aware of a bias that simplicity is more compelling than complexity in any explanation. So, getting back to the leg, one says that husband wants to kick his wife out of the room—but, look, she sits there calmly, and she hasn't budged, so the leg movement is sublimely pointless. What does the gesture symbolize? Aggression or futility or nothing? While justifiable to indulge the bias for simple explanations in many contexts, the problem of love requires just the reverse. Simplification of what Rilke calls "this most complicated and ultimate relationship" is like a synopsis that mars the story.

It is very easy to fall into a language trap of saying that, for example, love is complicated knowledge, or that it is an "ultimate relationship," thus subverting, by way of platitudes, the whole point of referring to its intricate complexity. Many stories of love refer to what is unsolved in our hearts, but the greatest stories don't offer solutions so much as they capture the problem and the mystery better than other kinds of discourse.

Freud spent his entire psychological career interpreting the love between children and parents, siblings and each other, love within the same sex, between the sexes, love of intellectual and artistic pursuit, and even of one's god, but it's noteworthy that he largely avoided the word "love." When he did broach the subject directly, say, in his "Contributions to the Psychology of Love" (1910), he ambivalently deferred to the power of artistic representation:

Hitherto we have left it to poets and imaginative writers to depict for us the "conditions of love" under which men and women make their choice of an object, and the way in which they reconcile the demands expressed in their phantasy with the exigencies of real life. Writers indeed have certain qualities which fit them for such a task; more especially, a sensitiveness of perception in regard to the hidden feelings of others, and the courage to give voice to their own unconscious minds. But from the point of view of knowledge one circumstance lessens the value of what they tell us. Writers are bound to certain conditions; they have to evoke intellectual and aesthetic pleasure as certain effects on the emotions. For this reason they cannot reproduce reality unchanged; they have to isolate portions of it, detach them from their connection with disturbing elements, fill up gaps and soften the whole. This is the privilege of what is called "poetic license." They can display no great interest, moreover, in the origin and growth of those conditions of mind which they portray in being. It is inevitable, therefore, that science should lay hands on the stuff which poets have fashioned so as to give pleasure to mankind for thousands of years, although its touch must be clumsier and result in less pleasure. These contributions may serve to vindicate our handling of the loves of men and women as well as other things in a strictly scientific way. For science betokens the most complete renunciation of the pleasure principle of which are minds are capable.

How best to respond to such compromised praise of artists and imaginative writers? The phrase "from the point of view of knowledge" is a loaded one, and we might begin with it. By his account, the knowledge conveyed by art is dubious because it is staged like a play and artificial like a pose. Reality, the truth about origins and developments, distorts through the artist's lens, and clear-eyed science objects to such a mediated vision of how life operates. The subject of love needs an investigator prepared to renounce the pleasure principle in an effort to see without fantasy or distortion, and to arrive at a knowledge without delusion or self-mystification. To study love is work and knowledge, not pleasure, says Freud.

The "most complete renunciation of the pleasure principle of which minds are capable"—the phrase puts me in mind of faculty meetings at my university—is probably not what Freud wanted to accomplish through psychoanalysis. All kinds of day labor, including psychological insight, involve the renunciation of pleasure, but it's hardly the case that absence of pleasure and the psychology of love go together. In what Freud has to say, ostensibly a critique of poets as artificers, we are back to the theme of love (or the study of it) as a subspecies of work. Freud advocates for a "sensitiveness of perception" which is not without its profound pleasures. Freud always worked towards rigorous psychological explanation, while the poet Rilke, in contemplating love, tries to articulate how inexplicable its difficulties turn out to be. Yet both authors seem to agree on one critical point: since reality is always a bit hard to see, for both the artist and scientist, some work is necessary to appreciate (and to enjoy) love.

In seven separate instances in this book, Freudian insight and the privilege of poetic license couldn't be more akin. (There are more examples of Freud's indebtedness to art; I chose only seven.) He contemplates what critics call the representation of reality in each case; he runs the gamut of such contemplation, from allusion (Narcissus), to reinterpretation of plot (discovery of knowledge in *Oedipus*; choice of death in *Lear*), to psychoanalytical portraiture (Leonardo), to the novel recreation of a history of faith (Moses).

He quotes, interprets, defers to, but, most of all, *uses* these sources to achieve what Hamlet called "confounding the ignorant." That we remain largely ignorant and terribly confounded by human love is no mean conclusion to draw, especially if we think in terms of the stories Freud asked us to contemplate. A lover is a Narcissus who seeks like an Oedipus, and could mature into a Hamlet, but in certain acts of profoundest love and memory, could also achieve beauty in understanding, and redefine his relationship with that which is greater than himself.

In the opening paragraph from "Contributions" quoted above, Freud sounds less than exuberant about poets and the imaginative writers, though I think the conclusion can't be avoided that Freud is nothing but exuberant about them, if we read him with reasonable care. *From the point of view of knowledge one circumstance lessens the value of what they [the artists] tell us*: Freud says that the artist alters reality (the artist cannot reproduce reality unchanged); but he doesn't admit that, as a consequence, a great artist also introduces strangeness and surprise, qualities that were points of origin for Freud's own psychological work. A person can study patients in the clinical setting and call himself an empiricist, as Freud did on a regular basis; he can also study the language of poets, scripture, and visual art and be no less grounded in an exceedingly rich empiricism, in which, as Freud said of da Vinci, we recognize aspects of who we are. We shouldn't underestimate the significance of Freud's aside that it was inevitable that psychology would lay clumsy hands on the artist's "stuff." Why "inevitable"?

For thousands of years, the purpose of art, Freud says, was human pleasure, but Freud wrestled with reality and pleasure as dialectically related principles, as we have seen in our discussion of *Beyond the Pleasure Principle*. To speak of pleasure in art as a way to justify mankind's interest in it is rather like the argument, prevalent in the nineteenth century, that art was important because it gratified certain aesthetic instincts. Critic Kenneth Burke has nicely said that such self-fulfilling arguments reminded him of a desperate last stand: "against the accusation that art was 'useless,' . . . [the artist] pitted the challenge that art was important to those whom art was important." Far more generously, artistic representation for Freud had implicitly to do with the problematics of representing any human psychology, and therefore art related as much to truth, knowledge, reality, and even madness (à la Plato) as to pleasure. Just as Socrates relied on myth to describe a relationship, based in memory, to truth and the forms of truth, Freud's "point of view of knowledge" could hardly deprecate what Plato called the blessing of poetical madness. It is not merely that artists of genius have certain qualities which fit them for the representation of complex truths. It is more likely that the truth will always have plain sense and maddening obscurity built within it.

₿

Once upon a time, as I began medical training, I was under the impression that if one thought of some great novel, poem, or Shakespeare as the best use of one's reading time (better than, say, a book on biochemistry), then study of the brain recommended itself as a career. In the biochemical age of diazepams and citaloprams (among so many other drugs), it would appear that I was deluded.

But not entirely. Both before and after Freud, psychiatry has always confused mind-reading (in the clairvoyant or magical sense) and mere reading. Earlier in this book I quoted Freud's tongue-in-cheek claim that he invented psychoanalysis because it had no literature. But the man who resurrected *Oedipus the King* as a text of psychology, who quietly recommended *Hamlet* as an even-better textbook, who borrowed altogether liberally from Western literary and artistic tradition, was nothing but a reader and admirer of the imagination. In many ways, he read books and art better than people.

One of Freud's fundamental contributions to the study of the mind was that psychology as a science would have to contend—inevitably—with art. It is still a very striking hypothesis, one that we might reconsider at a time when biological notions of the inner life are so dominant. The story of the mind these days is very scientific, perhaps overwhelmingly so. I read the other day about a medical treatment to erase bad memories; I think about that report now, because if "mind editing" is in our future, it would do us well to understand basic reading before we go about editing. I personally doubt that erasing memory will have much success, because our personal fictions have an astonishing sticking power, far greater than the power of drugs to unstick them, provided that those drugs leave us at least partly conscious.

Freud, a powerful writer, was always opinionated. Psychology after Freud has held strong opinions that we should evaluate for ourselves. The Unconscious, perhaps Freud's singular contribution to the history of ideas, has sadly transmogrified into a false confidence that we can know it. "How do you know?" is the reasonable question that most patients ask, if they are critical types. J. H. van den Berg, whom we met early in this book, says that "[t]he discovery that every symptom has meaning *leads* to the separation of conscious and subconscious." One might rephrase his sentence to read that the discovery of meaning is always a less-than-tranquil recollection. If what the doctor has to say doesn't resonate with some phantom of the past somehow already known to us, then we probably won't pay for more psychoanalysis or therapy unless insurance covers it.

⊟

Freud's problem in interpreting other minds is still our problem: we are unable to read anyone's mind as effectively as we would like, because an individual psychology is stubbornly mysterious. The idea of truly knowing others (or ourselves)—which is the essential problem of love—remains one of our most cherished hopes and impossibilities. Psychiatric therapeutics, whatever form they may take, give doctors a sense that they do something powerful, and sometimes they do. But to "raze the written troubles of the brain," as Macbeth would have medicine do for Lady Macbeth, might be beyond the doctor's art in any age. That is not a statement of therapeutic pessimism: I merely observe that for thousands of years, the book of the mind has been a fascination for the precise reason that we cannot know it fully. The psychiatric reading of literature and art has served as a wish-fulfillment dream to know the mind better.

Someone has observed that, today, there are more people writing books than reading them. The surge in self-expression, if true, shouldn't surprise us. One reads to learn about things and people in a drive to satisfy curiosity, but most curiosities turn inward, and eventually everyone (all the people writing so many books) quietly writes an autobiography. Freud would say that those autobiographies, as diverse as they might seem, still read much the same. He would also say that we probably rewrite some key books over and over again. Such was his view of the mind, and we are still wrestling with that theory or perspective, whether or not we read literature, study art, or contemplate Freud.

⊟

Today, in the death throes of professional "talking therapies" (because taking pills is easier), the power of any theory or science doesn't consist in what it says about who we are. "I don't believe psychology explains one's self. . . . I don't pretend to know myself the way someone fresh from psychoanalysis would claim. I think that's silly," critic Alfred Kazin has said in an interview. Freud was not silly; but the author of "Analysis Terminable and Interminable" would have agreed with Kazin more eloquently.

Perhaps since ancient time, the study of the mind has been essentially Socratic insofar as we question, follow a line of thought with the best rigor we can, and usually find ourselves asking more questions. "Working through," one of Freud's favorite conceptions of psychology, leads to questions, not answers. An important corollary observation, which I have attributed to van den Berg (because I finally understood it by reading him, though the point is Freud's), is that the very existence of psychology, as a discipline and practice, underlines the separation between knower and known—it emphasizes and parades it. I wonder whether van den Berg's basic argument also applies to human science of any type, that the very existence and practice of a medical and psychological science, for example, emphasizes and parades an interpersonal distance that we so very much want to minimize.

Rather few people today are psychoanalyzed on the couch, and modern psychiatric training, however influenced by considerations of the Unconscious, cannot be called Freudian. We think that Freudianism has been assimilated into the way we think about love, particularly whenever we wonder about what we really, truly desire. Unfortunately, much of the assimilation has involved a vast misuse of Freud's method when he read books or looked at art. He re-read great literature, not for plot; he stared at the art he loved. For him, imaginative work was the representation of another mind in its magnificent strangeness. I fantasize that he thought reading and study could return him, as it were, to an early wonder, to an almost Greek appreciation of the plain sense of things or to an Hebraic appreciation of background and shadow—but, either way, back to the fascination of otherness.

A modern problem has been that, too often, we allow psychological thinking to get in our own way. At such times, we have what Virginia Woolf deftly chastised as "beautiful positivity."

☙

In his writing, Freud often engaged in question-and-answer dialogues with himself. By the end of his career, his Oedipal style of interrogation achieves a level of mastery not matched by many authors. In *The Future of an Illusion*, for example, he worries that his psychoanalysis is nothing more than occultism or bad religion. Perhaps religion is not so bad, he wonders:

I will moderate my zeal and admit the possibility that I, too, am chasing an illusion. Perhaps the effect of the religious prohibition of thought may not be so bad as I suppose. . . . *I do not know and you cannot know either.* It is not only the great problems of this life that seem insoluble at the present time; many lesser questions too are difficult to answer.

The "you" in this passage is his own best critic (Sigmund Freud on himself), and his italicized sentence describes a man at the precise intersection of ignorance and insight. The inner dialogue, part Sophoclean and part Socratic, is relentless; it questions even the primacy of intelligence:

What you have been expounding seems to me to be built upon errors which, following your example, I may call illusions, because they betray clearly enough the influence of your wishes. You pin your hope on the possibility that generations which have not experienced the influence of religious doctrines in early childhood will easily attain the desired primacy of the intelligence over the life of instincts.

This is surely an illusion . . .

His interlocutor dogs him; I think history has and will continue to dog Freud as well, since I think (as do others in American states, both red and blue) that religion will vastly outlive psychoanalysis and Sigmund Freud. But what should survive as Freud's legacy is the practice of reading for the sake of discovery. Reading Freud shouldn't make us Freudian so much as it should make us better readers of anything that we choose, including our patients, loved ones, and our books.

What I've called "talking therapies" (including psychotherapy, but not excluding our closest friendships) court two fundamental and related dangers. The first is banality or triteness. In the future, psychotherapy may never be reimbursed by payors, because talk as talk will be judged as valueless. There is a legitimate point in this view, because talk is often trite. The value of human communication should never be underestimated, but since that value can't be accurately estimated for any given encounter, a session of talk therapy floats in a vague estimation of its worth, at best. When Freud contemplated whether an analysis could be brief and terminable rather than extended and endless, he decided that, in the end, analysis is both. In the modern era, no one will pay forever for a brief treatment that doesn't end.

I said that psychotherapy courts the danger of banality, but perhaps I was being too cautious. I mean that achieving insight that is not trite could be the single longest exercise in delayed gratification known to man. But I anticipate my next and last point.

The second danger, related to the first, is dogmatism. A defense of psychotherapy is a loser's game even before the apology begins, because we enter into debatable assertions of validity and value. Therapists who prescribe medications are particularly guilty of this kind of argument, because they invoke studies to prove the validity of a profession. There are many important published reports that teach us about (a.) the value of drugs, (b.) the value of drugs prescribed along with talking therapies, (c.) how the talk helps the effects of drugs, and (d.) how the drugs don't help as well without the talk. Speaking as a clinical person, I certainly hope that we offer something with our drugs, talk, and empathy, because otherwise we would be complete charlatans. But it is a dangerous leap to say that we glean the human condition more profoundly because we have some incomplete idea about how our drugs and talk work. One sniffs unexamined dogma rather than truth in such claims.

Freud consulted powerful fictions to understand mental illness and health. The reason he did so, and why we should as well, is that the validity of psychology as a human discipline might well have to do with how and why certain fictions speak to us with a strange and powerful veracity, stronger than dogma and the often-reversed claims of any new psychological science. What fictions contain your own personal truth I cannot say; but, in reading Freud, I think we can be sure that he had his list.

Irving Singer, a philosopher who observed the ascendency of a new psychology at the beginning of this century (a psychology based on what we know of cognitive and brain science), lamented the insufficiency of its lexicon for the emotional or affective life: "When cognitive psychologists write about emotion, as they have started to do, they tend to think it can be explained in terms of the rationalistic concepts that science has on hand and that look as if they may suffice. . . . What one needs is a completely new lexicon and analytic approach to understand the nature of affect, which includes all of what we normally call feelings, emotions, sensations, 'intuitive' and 'instinctive' dispositions . . . hatred as well as love . . . For that job, we require a totally different type of methodology." Freud routinely asked whether his lexicon might not suffice; if he hadn't done so, we would have no such frontier concepts as narcissism or the life and death drives. He wanted to write a new and revolutionary science, but Singer rightly observes that "Freud is an especially interesting case study because his aspirations and achievements illustrate the more extensive question about the mission of science as a whole and its passionate pursuit of knowledge." Freud saw no need reinvent where mankind had been cognitively or rationally. His science depended for its ultimate authority on the words of poets and the nuances of portrait. He culled a lexicon from the history of creative production in the West.

Freud liked many artists I haven't discussed, including Germany's Goethe, Russia's Dostoevsky, and America's Mark Twain (by far, one of Freud's favorite authors), but I think debating Freud's list is an evasion and a waste of time. Some truths are so complicated that Freud sought elsewhere—to the Greeks, myth, Shakespeare, Scripture, and some remarkable representations of a human smile. In Freud's case, unlike any psychologist after him, *that* he invoked a pantheon of imagination is interesting in itself, not as the act of an anti-scientist, but rather as the habit of an ardent scientist.

When we encounter a new theory of mind in the future, whether next month or next century, we might welcome it to the club of psychological genius, *if* it invites us to ponder complicated and ultimate matters, especially that of love—and *only if* it strikes us as anything but easy and frivolous, because love is neither. How striking it would be, and how Freudian, to discover that the next new theory had been in circulation for a long time in our past, in other vernaculars, such as the lexicons of our art. If such a theory would appear, it would remind us that representation is not the sovereign domain of either science or art, and that, as we need to relearn repeatedly, truth is often both strange and familiar, like the profounder fictions about who we really are.

Acknowledgments & Sources

A SCHOLAR ONCE spoke of the responsibility and pleasure of acknowledging one's debts, and I undertake to do so in what follows, in that dual spirit. In personal terms, I am grateful in a way that I cannot repay to my wife and family—Karen, Brandon, Steven, and Kathryn—for their understanding of dad "upstairs," to David L. Cardozo in Boston and Patricia van der Leun in New York for their encouragement in this project, and, for my education at every turn, to those persons to whom the book is dedicated.

In academic terms, I have borrowed from diverse sources, and I want to credit as many of them as I can. Let me proceed along the lines of footnotes to whole chapters, if such a device might be indulged. Throughout this book, errors of omission and commission are, of course, entirely my responsibility.

EKM,

BOSTON AND KANSAS CITY, 2012

Introduction

Unless otherwise specified, all quotations from Freud are from *The Standard Edition of the Complete Psychological Works of Sigmund Freud*, edited by James Strachey (London: Hogarth, 1958 [Reprinted edition, with corrections]). I cite Freud's specific work, or the year from which I quote, or both. I cite other Freud references not translated by Strachey separately.

References to Freud's correspondence from October 8, 1895 (to Wilhelm Fliess) and to *Beyond the Pleasure Principle* (1920), are borrowed from Frank Sulloway's discussion of the early *Project for a Scientific Psychology* in his *Freud, Biologist of the Mind: Beyond the Psychological Legend* (New York: Basic, 1979), pp. 124-126.

The citation from "One of the Difficulties of Psycho-analysis" (1917) is taken from the anthology *On Creativity and the Unconscious: Papers on the Psychology of Art, Literature, Love, Religion*, ed. Benjamin Nelson (New York: Harper Colophon, 1958), pp. 4-9. Freud's historical synopsis of Copernicus-Darwin-Psychoanalysis can also be found in lecture 28 of *The Introductory Lectures on Psycho-analysis* (1917).

Frans de Waal is quoted from his *The Age of Empathy: Nature's Lessons for a Kinder Society* (New York: Three Rivers Press, 2009), p. 209.

Regarding the substitution of fantasy for reality, I quote from Peter Gay's brief introduction to *Totem and Taboo* in *The Freud Reader* (ed. Peter Gay, New York: W. W. Norton, 1989), p. 482. Even more than my reliance on Ernest Jones's three-volume *The Life and Work of Sigmund Freud* (New York: Basic Books, 1953, 1955, 1957) for biographical background and for vignettes that illuminate Freud's published writing, I am indebted to three of Professor Gay's books for inspiring "psychological thinking": *Freud: A Life for Our Time* (New York: W. W. Norton, 1988), especially its discussion of Freud's late-life departure from Vienna for London (as I discuss in chapter seven of this book); *A Godless Jew: Freud, Atheism, and the Making of Psychoanalysis* (New Haven: Yale University Press, 1987), though I disagree with Gay's depiction of Freudian godlessness; and *Reading Freud: Explorations and Entertainments* (New Haven: Yale University Press, 1990). The story about the man who "must find the switch" can be found on p. 135 of *Reading Freud*, in an essay entitled "Serious Jests."

1. Plato's Memory

I am grateful to J. D. McClatchy for his interest in publishing many of my previous essays, including a version of chapter one in *The Yale Review*, vol. 93, No. 4 (Oct. 2005), pp. 76-95.

Citations from William James–which center on the observation that when a psychologist tells you what's on your mind, possibly all you hear is what's on his–are from *The Principles of Psychology* in a powerful chapter entitled "The Methods and Snares of Psychology" (New York: Dover, 1950, vol. 1), pp. 196-197.

Karl Kraus's "kiss my ass" vignette is from his "Unauthorized Psychology" (1913), quoted by Jacques Bouveresse in *Wittgenstein Reads Freud: The Myth of the Unconscious* (trans. Carol Cosman, Princeton: Princeton University Press, 1995), p. 16. For a portrait of Kraus in his Vienna milieu, I have consulted "Karl Kraus: The School of Resistance" and "The New Karl Kraus" in Elias Canetti's *The Conscience of Words* (trans. Joachim Neugroschel, New York: Continuum, 1979). For Wittgenstein on Freud, in addition to Bouveresse's book, I think often about point 33 in his "Lectures on Aesthetics": "If you are led by psycho-analysis to say that really you thought so and so or that really your motive was so and so, this is not a matter of discovery, but of persuasion. In a different way you could have been persuaded of something different." For a single source of Wittgenstein's apothegms on psychology, I have used *Lectures and Conversations on Aesthetics, Psychology and Religious Belief* (ed. Cyril Barrett, Berkeley: University of California Press, no date of publication cited).

My quotations from Plato come from several translations. The first excerpt from book X of *The Republic* is from *The Collected Dialogues including the Letters* (eds. Edith Hamilton and Huntington Cairns, Princeton: Bollingen/Princeton University Press, 1961), p. 820, but my reading of book X is thoroughly influenced by Eric A. Havelock's personal translations, and by his interpretations of them, in *Preface to Plato* (Cambridge: Belknap/Harvard University Press, 1963). Havelock elaborates on the transition from oral to written communication in antiquity in *The Muse Learns to Write: Reflections on Orality and Literary from Antiquity to the Present* (New Haven and London: Yale University Press, 1986). For my citations from *Phaedrus*, I have also used Tom Griffith's translation, *Symposium and Phaedrus* (New York: Everyman's/Knopf, 2000) and, towards the end of the chapter, I quote Graeme Nicholson's translation of section 250 in *Plato's Phaedrus: The Phi-*

losophy of Love (West Lafayette: Purdue University Press, 1999), p. 99.

Erich Auerbach's *Mimesis* has been handsomely republished on its 50th anniversary of release; I quote from the chapter "Odysseus' Scar" (Princeton: Princeton University Press, 2003), pp. 3-23. Regarding the experience of Homeric poetry, including the matter of how long it would take to listen to an epic poem from start to finish (about 26 hours), see Danielle S. Allen's "The flux of time in ancient Greece" in *Dædalus* (Spring, 2003 issue), pp. 62-73, especially pp. 68-69.

In discussing the sacrifice of Isaac, I do not name the contemporary scholar who discusses Abraham's perplexity. He is Leon R. Kass—to do full justice to his discussion of "the meaning of patriarchy" in *The Beginning of Wisdom: Reading Genesis* (New York: Free Press, 2003), p. 339 ff. would have led me afield in my discussion. Here are some of his thoughts on "perplexity" in their context:

> [Yahweh's] test may be "perfectly rational" from God's point of view, and Abraham himself might even understand precisely the meaning of God's request. But not knowing that he is merely being tested, Abraham must be deeply perplexed, not to say distressed, by the contradiction between God's earlier promise, oft repeated, that it will be through Isaac that the covenant will be perpetuated.

Kass is reasonable, but he infers what Abraham thinks. In counterpoint, the silence on the way to Moriah simply is what it is: a suggestive silence.

Arthur Schopenhauer's speculation about a Jewish influence on Plato was a surprise for me; the source is *The World as Will and Representation* (trans. E. F. J. Payne, New York: Dover, volume 1), p. 487. Schopenhauer says that Plato was affectionately called, by Numenius (as quoted by Clement of Alexandria), *Moses graecizans*.

The Greek word *mania* is the subject of Josef Pieper's meditation in *Enthusiasm and Divine Madness: On the Platonic Dialogue Phaedrus* (South Bend: St. Augustine Press, 2000), which I found provocative and useful. For the description of Delphic experience, E. R. Dodds's landmark *The Greeks and the Irrational* (Berkeley: University of California Press, 1951) is cited by name in the chapter; the reader should consult "The Blessings of Madness" in particular, pp. 64-101. While I don't refer to Longinus's description of the Pythian Princess from "On the Sublime" (it postdates Plato), but it is has stuck in my mind for a long time:

For many men are carried away by the spirit of others as if inspired, just as it is related of the Pythian princess when she approaches the tripod, where there is a rift in ground which (they say) exhales divine vapor. By heavenly power thus communicated she is impregnated and straight-way delivers oracles in virtue of the afflatus.

The notion of a poetical Sublime is Longinian as much as it is High Romantic in the Western literary tradition (See "On the Sublime," translated by W. Rhys Roberts, in *Classic Writings on Poetry,* ed. William Harmon, New York: Columbia University Press, 2003), p. 93.

Regarding the Pythagorean influence on Plato and Plato's travels in Sicily after Socrates' death, see F. M. Cornford's *From Religion to Philosophy: A Study in the Origins of Western Speculation* (Princeton: Princeton University Press, 1991), especially section 126 in "The Mystical Tradition," and Cornford's "Mysticism and Science in the Pythagorean Tradition" in *The Classical Quarterly,* Vol. 16, no. 3/4 (Jul.-Oct. 1922), pp. 137-150.

On mystery in religion–a subject which I discuss again later in the book–one can turn and profitably return to Jaroslav Pelikan's *The Melody of Theology: A Philosophical Dictionary* (Cambridge: Harvard University Press, 1988). The lovely passage from Hebrews 11:1 regarding the certainty of realities we don't see is quoted in Pelikan's entry for "Faith" (pp. 86-89), and elsewhere in the book I use his entries on "Mystery" (pp. 167-171) and "Mystical" (pp. 171-174) in particular, but *Melody* as a whole is a pleasure far more than a reference book.

The unnamed religious scholar who discusses how the reality of divinity is neither subjective nor objective, but must be both, is Giovanni Filoramo in *A History of Gnosticism* (trans. Anthony Alcock, Cambridge: Basil Blackwell, 1990), p. 40. In the passage I cite, Filoramo discusses "the Gnostic self." I would refrain from saying that Freud was Gnostic, though the issue has been raised by David Bakan in *Sigmund Freud and the Jewish Mystical Tradition* (Boston: Beacon, 1975) and, more subtly, by Ken Frieden in *Freud's Dream of Interpretation* (Albany: State University of New York Press, 1990), pp. 47-71.

Freud's use of Plato is no novel thought. In a book like Gerasimos Santas's *Plato and Freud: Two Theories of Love* (New York: Basil Blackwell, 1988), for example, the *Symposium* is the focal point for discussion. Santas characterizes Freud as a worshiper of Diotima, but Santas respects a clinician's perspective, independent of Greek influence: "The aetiology of love turned into a sexual archeology of love," Santas writes (p. 177); "[Freud] was without doubt in a far better position than any man earlier to try to understand especially the mysteries and irrationalities of love." Plato's curiosity about madness and insight in the *Phaedrus* and *Symposium* anticipates Freud's patient-based study.

When Freud talks "clinically," one often senses that the Western tradition is part of his clinic, but the patient—in this case, Plato—teaches Freud in a kind of massive reversal of roles. As a medical doctor, if one believes such a strange turnabout, one starts to wander around where one probably doesn't belong—for example, in the world of Platonic scholarship. I am sincere about the word "wander." Among useful guides who prevented me from aimlessness, in this chapter I cite Nicholson, Havelock, and Dodds by name, though there were others (W. K. C. Guthrie, F. M. Cornford, U. von Wilamowitz-Moellendorf [usually as translated and quoted by others], R. Hackforth, and J. Gould). Nicholson's discussion of "loving something else all along" can be found in *Plato's Phaedrus: The Philosophy of Love* (West Lafayette: Purdue University Press), p. 208. I read and found useful, but did not quote, G. R. F. Ferrari's *Listening to the Cicadas: A Study of Plato's Phaedrus* (Cambridge: Cambridge University Press, 1987) and Charles L. Griswold's *Self-Knowledge in Plato's Phaedrus* (University Park: The Pennsylvania State University Press, 1986).

Søren Kierkegaard is another guide. His conflictedness regarding Socrates is interesting, as countless scholars have observed—he is like an expatriate whose attitude towards his home country is best revealed by being outside of it. The source I quote is from: *The Concept of Irony with continual reference to Socrates* (eds. and trans. Howard and Edna Hong, Princeton: Princeton University Press, 1989), p. 107.

I am indebted to J. H. van den Berg's *The Changing Nature of Man: Introduction to a Historical Psychology* (New York: Dell [reprint of the W. W. Norton & Co. edition], 1961). Regarding symptoms and meaning, see the chapter "Neurosis and Sociosis" in that book, especially pp. 119-121.

The bon mot "psychic-analysis" is Karl Kraus's.

2. OEDIPUS

In the Sophocles citations in this chapter, I consulted a translation which scholars seem to prefer, by David Grene, *The Complete Greek Tragedies: Sophocles I* (eds. David Grene and Richmond Lattimore, second edition. Chicago: University of Chicago Press, 1991). But certain moments in the plays make more sense to me in the language of Robert Fagles' translations of *Antigone*, *Oedipus the King*, and *Oedipus at Colonus*, published as *The Theban Plays* (New York: Penguin, 1984) and Bernard Knox's translation, intended for the modern stage, of *Oedipus the King* (New York: Washington Square Press, 1972). Quotations from Shakespeare throughout this book are from *The Complete Works* (general ed. Alfred Harbage, New York: Penguin, 1969) or from the Arden Shakespeare.

A reader might argue that Freud had only *Oedipus the King* in mind when he wrote about the Oedipus complex. Regarding the significance of *all* the Theban plays to the Oedipus idea in psychoanalysis, see Shoshana Felman's "Beyond Oedipus: The Specimen Story of Psychoanalysis," published in *Lacan and Narration: The Psychoanalytic Difference in Narrative Theory* (ed. Robert Con Davis, Baltimore: Johns Hopkins University Press, 1983). I would also cite Peter L. Rudnytsky's *Freud and Oedipus* (New York: Columbia University Press, 1987), which assumes, without need for justification, that all the Theban plays are fair game in understanding the Oedipus complex to the fullest degree. I have special respect for a moment in Rudnytsky's discussion of *Antigone* (p. 278) when he directly quotes from Kierkegaard's *Either/Or*: "When . . . Antigone in defiance of the king's prohibition resolves to bury her brother, we do not see in this so much a free action on her part as a fateful necessity, which visits the sins of the fathers upon the children. There is indeed enough freedom of action in this to make us love Antigone for her sisterly affection, but in the necessity of fate there is also, as it were, a higher refrain which envelops not only the life of Oedipus but also his entire family." That is Kierkegaard writing like Freud, and after reading the passage, one feels inclined to read *Antigone* at very least. What is the nature of that "higher refrain"?

Talk to an American (neuro)psychiatrist, and odds are that he/she doesn't bother much with the hegemony of French theoretical writing, a domination assumed by Professor Shoshana Felman. If a contemporary American psychiatrist has any identifiable theory at all, aside from some idea of being "scientific," principals other than French writers come to mind—H. S. Sullivan, M.

Klein, D.W. Winnicott, H. Kohut, O. Kernberg, inter alia. As much as possible in this book, I avoid direct discussion of ego-psychological, object-relationist, psycho-linguistic, historiographical, structuralist, post-structuralist, deconstructionist, and other theory. Instead, I advocate what Harold Bloom has called the Shakespearean reading of Freud in *The Western Canon: The Books and School of Ages* (New York: Harcourt Brace, 1994), pp. 371-394.

Harold C. Goddard's comments can be found in *The Meaning of Shakespeare* (Chicago: University of Chicago Press, 1951), p. 139. In thinking about necessity and tragedy, I did not mention Aristotle by name on the subject of catharsis, although the ghost of Aristotle's *Poetics* is present in what I say. The thought that we *need* tragedy rather than enjoy it as mere entertainment is Aristotelian. The specific passage from the *Poetics* that I have in mind is from part VI (See *Classic Writings on Poetry*, ed. William Harmon, New York: Columbia University Press, 2003), p. 38: "Tragedy, then, is an imitation of an action that is serious, complete, and of a certain magnitude . . . through pity and fear effecting the proper purgation of these emotions." What "proper purgation" means, of course, has been a curiosity and subject of critical debate for centuries.

The Freud quotation from 1915 is from "Observations on Transference Love." The often-cited letter to Fliess dated October 15, 1897 is from *The Complete Letters of Sigmund Freud to Wilhelm Fliess, 1897-1904* (ed. J. M. Masson, Cambridge: Harvard University Press, 1985), p. 272; Neil Hertz quotes and discusses it thoughtfully in his "Foreword" to *Sigmund Freud: Writings on Art and Literature* (ed. Neil Hertz, Stanford: Stanford University Press, 1997), pp. xii-xx.

I first encountered Jean-Pierre Vernant in his "Ambiguity and Reversal: On the Enigmatic Structure of *Oedipus Rex*," republished in *Modern Critical Interpretations: Oedipus Rex* (ed. Harold Bloom, New York: Chelsea House, 1988), pp. 103-126. A take-home point, that Oedipus has no obscure father-hate and mother-love, is from that essay. "Ambiguity and Reversal" comes from Jean Pierre Vernant and Pierre Vidal-Naquet, *Myth and Tragedy in Ancient Greece*, available in re-release (trans. Janet Lloyd, New York: Zone Books, 1990). In *Myth and Tragedy*, two additional essays were useful to my discussion: "Oedipus without the Complex" and "Tensions and Ambiguities in Greek Tragedy." The thought about a Clytemnestra complex as the unconscious wish to kill one's husband—upon which I elaborate—is from "Oedipus without the Complex," p. 93. Vernant discusses Sophocles' wordplay (two-foot, three-foot, and four-foot) in "Ambiguity and Reversal."

J. Laplanche and J.-B. Pontalis's *The Language of Psycho-Analysis* (trans. Donald Nicholson-Smith, New York: W. W. Norton, 1973) is a resource which I consulted from time to time in my reading. *Language of Psycho-Analysis* is a lexicon of psychoanalytic terminology, and while its definitions have much authority, one must guard against abuse of vocabulary and the condition of what, in German, would be called the *fachidiot*. (A *fachidiot* is someone whose arcane and obsessive professional interests and jargon get in the way of thought; see Gay, *Reading Freud*, p. 99). For those of us who are non-psychoanalytical psychologists, how we are to use Freud for our purposes is still an important question, as I maintain throughout the book.

Friedrich Nietzsche's comment regarding the origin of tragedy in Greece is from *The Birth of Tragedy* [or: *Hellenism and Pessimism. New Edition with an Attempt at Self-Criticism*] (trans. Douglas Smith, Oxford: Oxford University Press, 2000), p. 53.

Jonathan Lear had written thoughtfully about Freud and the philosophy of love in *Love and Its Place in Nature* (New York: Farrar, Straus, and Giroux, 1990) before his *Freud* (New York: Routledge, 2005), but the latter is especially useful for its simplicity and clarity on Freud's "meta-psychological" aspects. I quote from Lear's chapter in the latter book, "The Structure of the Psyche," p. 182.

Perhaps I am unnecessarily coy in referring to "a British writer," but I wanted to save the name Virginia Woolf for later effect (when she talks about "Freudian fiction"—see chapter six). The source of her description of "dangerous simplicity" is her review of John Galsworthy's novel *Beyond* in *Contemporary Writers: Essays on Twentieth-Century Books and Authors* (New York: Harcourt Brace Jovanovich, 1965), p. 63.

The Sphinx was the subject of a rich scholarly essay with interesting references: Elmer G. Suhr, "The Sphinx" in *Folklore*, Vol. 81, no. 2 (Summer, 1970), pp. 97-111. I borrow from it in discussing the Sphinxes of Thebes and Giza.

The 1928 essay in which Freud discusses Sophocles, Shakespeare, and Dostoevsky at the same time is "Dostoevsky and Parricide."

Regarding Tiresian prophecy and science, I paraphrase H. D. F. Kitto in *Sophocles: Dramatist and Philosopher* (London: Oxford University Press, 1958), p. 55: "Tiresias and the Astronomer Royal can each prophesy, for the same reason: the events with which they deal are not random ones; certain observable laws underlie them." Bernard M. W. Knox in *The Heroic Temper: Studies in Sophoclean Tragedy* (Berkeley: University of California

Press, 1964) offers an alternative view to Vernant's regarding Sophoclean heroism. Francis Fergusson, *The Idea of a Theater: A Study of Ten Plays; The Art of Drama in a Changing Perspective* (Princeton: Princeton University Press, 1949), pp. 25-27 discusses season-like cycles of death and rebirth in Greek tragedy. Regarding the misreading of the Greek mind, I quote C. M. Bowra, *Sophoclean Tragedy* (London: Oxford University Press, 1965), p. 8 and G. M. Kirkwood, *A Study in Sophoclean Drama* (Ithaca: Cornell University Press, 1994), p. 19. Vernant's comment is from "Oedipus without the Complex" in *Myth and Tragedy in Ancient Greece*.

Jacques Derrida's discussion of the *pharmakos/pharmakon* in Plato's *Phaedrus* informs what I say on the subject. Derrida's interest, different than mine, centers on the invention of writing as a dubious aid to memory—see "Plato's Pharmacy" from *Dissemination* (1972), excerpted in *A Derrida Reader: Between the Blinds* (ed. Peggy Kamuf, New York, Columbia University Press, 1991), pp. 124-139. René Girard—in *Violence and the Sacred* (trans. Patrick Gregory, Baltimore: Johns Hopkins University Press, 1977) and, especially, his discussion of *Romeo and Juliet* in "Levi-Strauss, Frye, Derrida and Shakespearean Criticism" (*Diacritics*, Vol. 3 No. 3 [Autumn 1973], pp. 34-38)—was more useful to me, so I mention Girard by name. The quote from Thomas Mann is from "Freud and the Future" in *Essays of Three Decades* (trans. H. T. Lowe-Porter, New York: Knopf, 1976), p. 414.

3. NARCISSUS

Christopher Lasch's disenchantment in *The Culture of Narcissism: American Life in an Age of Diminishing Expectations* (New York: Norton, 1978) rather misses the point of why and how Freud appropriated the Narcissus myth, in my opinion. Alain de Botton's *Status Anxiety* (New York: Pantheon, 2004) is a kinder and gentler, but merely updated *Culture of Narcissism*. If I had to choose between Lasch and de Botton on narcissism, I would read Ovid (de Botton, given his aestheticism, might agree). De Botton's "bubble" of self is described on p. 9 in his book.

The passage from Jorge Luis Borges that serves as an extended epigraph to the chapter is from "The Nothingness of Personality" in *Selected Non-Fictions* (ed. Eliot Weinberger, trans. Esther Allen, Suzanne Jill Levine, and Eliot Weinberger, New York: Penguin, 2000), p. 3.

The capsule of the Narcissus myth from *Essential Papers on Narcissism* is from Andrew Morrison's "Introduction," p. 1 (ed. Andrew Morrison,

New York: New York University Press, 1986). The case of the young girl is from "The Disorders of the Self and Their Treatment: An Outline," by Heinz Kohut and Ernest S. Wolf, in the same book, p. 184. Freud's August 3 comment is from *The Standard Edition (S.E.)*, vol. XXIII, p. 300.

Richard Wollheim's *Sigmund Freud* (Cambridge and New York: Cambridge University Press, 1981) is still the best one-volume summary of Freud's theory. I quote p. 114 regarding Freud's rejection of "pansexualism."

Mark Edmundson's comments come from his *Towards Reading Freud: Self-Creation in Milton, Wordsworth, Emerson, and Sigmund Freud* (Princeton: Princeton University Press, 1990), p. 82. For background on Paul Näcke and C. H. Hughes and a discussion of autoerotism, see Havelock Ellis, *Studies in the Psychology of Sex* (third ed.), vol. I: *The Evolution of Modesty, The Phenomena of Sexual Periodicity, Auto Eroticism* (Philadelphia: F. A. Davis, 1925), pp. 206-208. Later in the chapter, I refer to Havelock Ellis's "Conception of Narcissism," which is from *Studies in the Psychology of Sex* (no edition cited), vol. VII: *Eonism and Other Supplementary Studies* (Philadelphia: F. A. Davis, 1928), pp. 347-375. Also a bit later, I refer to Otto Rank, perhaps Freud's most literary follower; I would draw attention in particular to Rank's *The Double: A Psychoanalytic Study* (trans. and ed. Harry Tucker, Jr., New York: New American Library, 1971).

Herbert Fingarette's "Self-deception and the 'splitting of the ego'" can be found in *Philosophical Essays on Freud* (eds. Richard Wollheim and James Hopkins, Cambridge: Cambridge University Press, 1982). I quote from p. 214.

Ludwig Wittgenstein's off-the-cuff comment is from a letter written in 1945 to Norman Malcolm, quoted in Jacques Bouveresse, *Wittgenstein Reads Freud* (Princeton: Princeton University Press, 1995), p. xix.

All quotations from "On Narcissism" are from the *S.E.* vol. XIV; what I call the best of Freud's many side observations in the essay, regarding the impossibility of renouncing a satisfaction once enjoyed (*S.E.* XIV, p. 94), is repeated with a nuance of difference in "The Poet and Day-Dreaming," in *On Creativity and the Unconscious: Papers on the Psychology of Art, Literature, Love, Religion* (ed. Benjamin Nelson, New York: Harper Colophon, 1958), p. 46. Nelson uses a translation from Freud's *Collected Papers*, whose general editor was Joan Riviere: "anyone who knows anything of the mental life of human beings is aware that hardly anything is more difficult to them than to give up a pleasure they have once tasted. *Really we can never relinquish anything* [my emphasis]."

Regarding the Narcissus myth, I consulted a number of translations in this chapter: *Ovid: Metamorphoses* (trans. Rolfe Humphries, Bloomington: Indiana University Press, 1955); *Ovid's Metamorphoses: The Arthur Golding Translation* (ed. John Frederick Nims, with a new essay, "Shakespeare's Ovid" by Jonathan Bate, Philadelphia: Paul Dry Books, 2000); *Ovid: Metamorphoses* (trans. Charles Martin, introduction by Bernard Knox, New York: W. W. Norton, 2004); *The Metamorphoses of Ovid* (trans. Allen Mandelbaum, San Diego: Harcourt, 1993); *The Metamorphoses of Ovid* (trans. David R. Slavitt, Baltimore: Johns Hopkins University Press, 1994); Ted Hughes, *Tales from Ovid* (New York: Farrar, Straus and Giroux, 1997); and Pausanias, *Description of Greece*, Books VIII, 22-X (Loeb Classical Library, trans. W. H. S. Jones, Cambridge: Harvard University Press, 1935; see especially Boeotia, XXXI. 6-9, P. 311). I am indebted to Kenneth J. Knoespel's *Narcissus and the Invention of Personal History* (New York and London: Garland Publishing, 1985) and, particularly with reference to Conon's version of Narcissus and for her discussion of the Narcissus tradition in general, to Louise Vinge, *The Narcissus Theme in Western European Literature up to The Early 19th Century* (no publication city cited: Gleerups, 1967).

Dr. Samuel Johnson on marriage is from *Samuel Johnson: Selected Essays from the Rambler, Adventurer, and Idler* (ed. W. J. Bate, New Haven: Yale University Press, 1968), p. 93.

Jerry Fodor is the unnamed "contemporary psychologist trained in logic" (he might prefer the moniker of "cognitive psychologist and philosopher"). For reasons described in the chapter, I defer mentioning his name at first. His question about richness in formal systems is from *The Language of Thought* (Cambridge: Harvard University Press, 1975), p. 199, but the same question arises often in his works. Here are two (densely packed) additional sources: Fodor's lecture entitled "Fixation of Belief and Concept Acquisition," from a chapter entitled "On the Impossibility of Acquiring 'More Powerful' Structures," in *Language and Learning: The Debate between Jean Piaget and Noam Chomsky* (ed. Massimo Piattelli-Palmarini, Cambridge: Harvard University Press, 1980), pp. 143-149, and his chapter "Darwin Among the Modules" in *The Mind Doesn't Work That Way: The Scope and Limit of Computational Psychology* (Cambridge: MIT Press, 2001), pp. 79-100. The quip about a certain kind of speculative type being an embarrassment to academic deans is from *Language of Thought*, p. vii. Owen Barfield is quoted in Harold Bloom's introductory essay, "The Art of Reading Poetry," in *The Best Poems of the English Language* (New York: HarperCollins, 2004), p. 28.

4. CORDELIA

Jean Laplanche's comment about the death drive is from *Life and Death in Psychoanalysis* (trans. Jeffrey Mehlman, Baltimore: Johns Hopkins University Press, 1976), p. 107. John Crowe Ransom's passage is from "Freud and Literature," reprinted in *Twentieth Century Views: Freud, A Collection of Critical Essays* (ed. Perry Meisel, Englewood Cliffs: Prentice-Hall, 1981), p. 44. Maynard Mack on the Shakespearean Swiss-bank account of allusions is from *Everybody's Shakespeare: Reflections Chiefly on the Tragedies* (Lincoln: University of Nebraska Press, 1993), p. 4. The unnamed movie critic writing about two married couples exchanging partners en route to love and understanding is Stanley Kauffmann: he initially wrote on the theme in reviewing *We Don't Live Here Anymore* (*The New Republic*, September 13 & 20, 2004, Vol. 231, Issues 4,678 & 4,679, pp. 26-27). He revisited the theme in reviewing *Closer* (*The New Republic*, December 27, 2004-January 10, 2005,Vol. 231, Issues 4,693-4,695, pp. 28-29). I quote from the latter review, which is sardonically entitled "Conquests."

Quotations from "The Theme of the Three Caskets" come from *On Creativity and the Unconscious: Papers on the Psychology of Art, Literature, Love, Religion.*

Franz Kafka's "Resolutions" from *Collected Stories* (New York: Everyman's Library/Knopf, 1993), p. 11 is short and significant enough to be quoted in its entirety:

> To lift yourself out of a miserable mood, even if you have to do it by strength of will, should be easy. I force myself out of my chair, stride around the table, exercise my head and neck, make my eyes sparkle, tighten the muscles around them. Defy my own feelings, welcome A. enthusiastically supposing he comes to see me, amiably tolerate B. in my room, swallow all that is said at C.'s, whatever pain and trouble it may cost me, in long draughts.

> Yet even if I manage that, one single slip, and a slip cannot be avoided, will stop the whole process, easy and painful alike, and I will have to shrink back into my own circle again.

> So perhaps the best resource is to meet everything passively, to make yourself an inert mass, and, if you feel that you are being carried away, not to

let yourself be lured into taking a single unnecessary step, to stare at others with the eyes of an animal, to feel no compunction, in short, with your own hand to throttle down whatever ghostly life remains in you, that is, to enlarge the final peace of the graveyard and let nothing survive save that. A characteristic movement in such a condition is to run your little finger along your eyebrows.

Freud discusses Portia's "One half of me is yours, the other half yours" in "Slips of the tongue" in *The Psychopathology of Everyday Life* (*S.E.* VI) and in lecture II of the *Introductory Lectures* (*S.E.* XV and XVI).

Sir Karl Popper's parable about being run over by a car or bicycle comes from his *The Myth of the Framework: In Defense of Science and Rationality* (ed. M. A. Notturno, London and New York: Routledge, 1994 and 1996), p. 179. I paraphrase his argument that Freudian theory is impossible to falsify, and therefore can't be considered a science.

I happened on Jonathan Bate's essay "Shakespeare's Ovid," in which he discusses getting just what you seek in life, in *Ovid's Metamorphoses: The Arthur Golding Translation* (see full reference in my note to chapter three). J. W. von Goethe's protest about the oppression of Shakespeare's characters comes from "Shakespeare: A Tribute" (1771), anthologized in *Goethe: Essays on Art and Literature* (ed. John Gearey, trans. Ellen von Nardroff and E. H. von Nardroff, New York: Suhrkamp, 1986, p. 165). G. W. F. Hegel's possibly apocryphal remark about the one person who ever understood him is quoted by Roger Kimball in his "The Difficulty with Hegel," in *Lives of the Mind: The Use and Abuse of Intelligence from Hegel to Wodehouse* (Chicago: Ivan R. Dee, 2002), p. 120.

Bruno Bettelheim's exquisite book *Freud and Man's Soul* (New York: Knopf, 1983) can be read in one sitting. While on the subject of Bettelheim, his "How I Learned About Psychoanalysis" in *Reflections and Recollections* (New York: Penguin, 1992) is also a delightful read. Also from *Reflections and Recollections*, I borrow from his "Lionel Trilling on Literature and Psychoanalysis" elsewhere in this book. Regarding Freud "as writer," Patrick J. Mahony has written a book-length study, *Freud as a Writer* (New Haven: Yale University Press, 1987), which I found more insightful than his mixed treatments of Freud's case histories in *On Defining Freud's Discourse* (New Haven: Yale University Press, 1989) and *Freud and the Rat Man* (New Haven: Yale University Press, 1986).

Jerome Kagan's "The Pleasure Principle" is the third essay in his *Three*

Seductive Ideas (Cambridge: Harvard University Press, 1998); he discusses the ambiguity of pleasure in animal studies on pp. 152-153, and *passim* in his first essay, "The Passion for Abstraction."

One must never tamper with Lady Augusta Bracknell, from Oscar Wilde's *The Importance of Being Earnest*.

Paul Ricoeur's *Freud and Philosophy* (trans. Denis Savage, New Haven: Yale University Press, 1970) deals from start to finish with what he calls the "semantics of desire," and he invites us to consider that when we argue semantics, we might actually get closer to talking about "what we feel," although most of these arguments are inconclusive. The cited paragraph regarding the *fort-da* game is on p. 285.

I take some liberty with Freud's use of the eleventh-century Arabic poem *Maqâmât* ("The Seances") of al-Hariri of Basra. In a footnote, Strachey cites Freud's reference, a German version of the *Maqâmât* by Rückert. In the third chapter (of 50 total) in the *Maqâmât*, the character named Harith says: "I have feigned to be lame, not from love of lameness, but that I may knock at the gate of relief. For my cord is thrown on my neck, and I go as one who ranges freely. Now if men blame me I say, 'Excuse me: sure there is no guilt on the lame.'" A limp, feigned or not, as a testament of conflict puts one in mind of Genesis 32: 25-32 (Jacob's lameness after wrestling the angel), as certainly would have occurred to Freud. The passage I quote comes just a line earlier in Harith's speech. See *The Sacred Books and Early Literature of the East*, vol. VI (ed. Charles F. Horne, New York: Parke, Austin, and Lipscomb, 1917); the language in Horne's edition has been modernized by Jerome S. Arkenberg, and is available on-line at www.fordham.edu/halsallbasis/1100Hariri.html.

William R. Clark's chapter "The Nature of Cellular Senescence and Death" in *A Means to an End: The Biological Basis of Aging and Death* (New York and Oxford: Oxford University Press, 1999), especially p. 25, addresses the phenomenon of programmed death of cells–a subject of current interest in medicine, genetics, and biology.

Thomas Mann, in "Freud and the Future," the lecture he read on the occasion of Freud's 80th birthday (see previous citation in my note to chapter two), said that Freud "did not know Schopenhauer," but Mann was being rhetorical. The Schopenhauer passage cited is from *Complete Essays of Schopenhauer in Seven Books* (trans. T. Bailey Saunders, New York: Willey Book Company, 1942), in Book VII, entitled "The Art of Controversy," pp. 75-76.

Wilhelm Reich's late career was remarkable for his advocacy of cures by way of an individual's "orgone" or sexual energy, which somehow emanated from the body. He believed he could store up this energy by way of a telephone-booth-sized "orgone-energy accumulator." Federal authorities disallowed the manufacture and interstate distribution of these "medical" devices, but Reich persisted, leading to a two-year jail sentence. He died in the Lewisberg Federal Penitentiary. Early in his career, in his *Character Analysis* (trans. Vincent R. Carfagno, New York: Farrar, Straus and Giroux, 1972), he describes "character armor," a phrase I first learned from one of my supervisors in Psychiatry training, the late Dr. Doris Benaron in Boston. She told me not to read Reich, but rather to think about the term. In fact, I did read Reich. She was right: the phrase is a good one.

Regarding August Weismann, see his *Essays Upon Heredity and Kindred Biological Problems*, vol. I (eds. Edward B. Poulton, Selmar Schönland, and Arthur E. Shipley ["authorized translation"], Oxford: Clarendon Press, 1891), pp. 111-113 and 155-161. I am struck in particular by one sentence on p. 112: "Natural death appeared to me to be explicable on the principle of utility, as an adaptation." In reading biological theory contemporary to Freud, I ran into Herbert Spencer Jenning's lecture series given at Johns Hopkins, *Life and Death, Heredity and Evolution in Unicellular Organisms* (Boston: Bruce Humphries, 1920). I quote p. 23, from his "General Survey."

The redoubtable Steven Pinker is quoted from his *How the Mind Works* (New York: W. W. Norton, 1997), p. 419. He is perhaps the most strident contemporary spokesperson for evolutionary psychology. Jerry Fodor's *The Mind Doesn't Work That Way* (see reference in chapter three) responds heartily (and critically) to Pinker.

Quotations from *Civilization and Its Discontents* are from Joan Riviere's translation (Garden City: Doubleday, no publication date cited).

5. HAMLET

Ernest Jones included Freud's 1934 letter regarding *King Lear* (addressed to James S. H. Bransom, dated March 25) in an appendix to *The Life and Work of Sigmund Freud*, vol. III (New York: Basic, 1957), pp. 457-458. I have my obvious reservations regarding Jones's *Hamlet and Oedipus* (New York: W. W. Norton, 1949). Since I do not pursue a full reading of the book, I offer a little bit of it to clarify why I don't admire his argument:

> The explanation, therefore, of the delay and self-frustration exhibited in the
> endeavour to fulfil his father's demand for vengeance is that to Hamlet the
> thought of incest and parricide combined is too intolerable to be borne. One
> part of him tries to carry out the task, the other flinches inexorably from the
> thought of it. How fain would he blot it out in that "bestial oblivion" which
> unfortunately for him his conscience contemns. He is torn and tortured in
> an insoluble inner conflict.

If the assumption is that Hamlet is self-frustrated, then I suppose Jones (and
Freud) explain a frustration that *they* see in him. But if Hamlet had acted
promptly, he would be a kind of unthinking Fortinbras without particular
fascination, and we would have no play. If Hamlet were perceived not as a
frustrated person, but rather as an apotheosis of the contemplative person,
then psychoanalytic explanation falls short of explaining how well he thinks.
Regarding Freud and John Thomas Looney, see Peter Gay, "Freud and the
Man from Stratford" in *Reading Freud*, pp. 5-53, and Harold Bloom, "Freud:
A Shakespearean Reading" in *The Western Canon*, pp. 371-394. Bennett Simon offers a reading of *Hamlet* which extends beyond my use of him in his
"Hamlet and the Trauma Doctors," *American Imago*, Vol. 58, No. 3 (2001),
pp. 707-722. Simon maintains that Elsinore exudes an atmosphere of post-
traumatic stress syndrome and that Hamlet is the victim of trauma. Simon
diagnoses Hamlet. I try to dissect such diagnostic tendencies in this chapter.

Norman Holland's catalog of Freud's references to Shakespeare was published as "Freud on Shakespeare" in *Proceedings of the Modern Language
Association*, Vol. 75, No. 3 (Jun. 1960), pp. 163-173.

The unnamed philosopher speaking about "encircling" truth is Ortega
y Gasset in *What is Philosophy?* (trans. Mildred Adams, New York: W. W.
Norton, 1960), pp. 17-18: "The great philosophic problems demand a tactic
like that which the Hebrews used for the taking of Jericho . . . making no
direct attack, circling slowly around . . . holding live in the air the dramatic
sound of trumpets." I'm indebted to Ortega also (see pp. 216-217) for a
summary of the Egyptian Horus, whose representation in statuette stood in
plain view on Freud's desk in Vienna: "Isis, [Osiris's beloved], eager to bring
him back to life, makes him swallow the eye of the falcon, Horus. From then
on the eye appears in all of the hieratical drawings of Egyptian civilization,
representing the first attribute of life—the act of seeing oneself." In a caption
to plate 35 of Edmund Engelman's photography in *Berggasse 19: Sigmund
Freud's Home and Offices, Vienna 1938* (Chicago and London: University of

Chicago Press, 1976), p. 67, I read: "As in the *Hamlet* theme that so fascinated Freud, Horus, the falcon-headed god of Freud's childhood dream, avenged his father's death." An "avenger who knows–sees–himself" is a characterization of Hamlet with which I am sympathetic.

T. S. Eliot's comments are from "Hamlet" in *Selected Essays* (New York: Harcourt Brace, 1950), pp. 121-126. Jacques Lacan's comments are from Jacques Lacan, Jacques-Alain Miller, James Hulbert, "Desire and the Interpretation of Desire in Hamlet," *Yale French Studies*, No. 55/56 (1977), *Literature and Psychoanalysis. The Question of Reading: Otherwise*, p. 20.

In my discussions of Little Hans, Schreber, Ratman, and Wolfman, I have used translations from the Penguin Freud: *The "Wolfman" and Other Cases* (trans. Louise Adey Huish, New York: Penguin, 2003) and *The Schreber Case* (trans. Andrew Webber, New York: Penguin, 2003). For the Dora case, I used the *S.E.* VII. Schreber's book is available in translation: Daniel Paul Schreber, *Memoirs of My Nervous Illness* (trans. Ida Macalpine and Richard A. Hunter, New York: New York Review Books, 2000). In addition to the published case history of the Rat Man, one should also consult Freud's original notes on the case in the *Standard Edition*: see "Original Record of the Case" (vol. X, especially pp. 283-285, an example of Lanzer's all-too-open verbal exchanges with Freud).

F. A. Hayek is known mainly as an economic theorist, but he began his career as a psychologist. I quote from "The Primacy of the Abstract" (originally a talk given in 1968), reprinted in *New Studies in Philosophy, Politics, Economics, and the History of Ideas* (Chicago: University of Chicago Press, 1978), p. 45, and I am grateful to Richard Born in Boston for bringing my attention to that essay. On p. 46, in a line of thought that I try to follow in my discussion, he tries to describe what "primacy" means: "The point in all this which I find most difficult to bring out clearly is that the formation of a new abstraction seems *never* to be the outcome of a conscious process, not something at which the mind can deliberately aim, but always a discovery of something which *already* guides its operation."

I am indebted to Steven Marcus's analyses of the case histories from two sources: "Freud and Dora: Story, History, Case History" reprinted in *Freud: A Collection of Critical Essays* (ed. Perry Meisel, Englewood Cliffs: Prentice-Hall, 1981), pp. 183-210, and *Freud and the Culture of Psychoanalysis: Studies in the Transition from Victorian Humanism to Modernity* (New York and London: W. W. Norton, 1984). For a different point of view, see Frank J. Sulloway, "Reassessing Freud's Case Histories: The Social Construction of

Psychoanalysis" in *Isis*, vol. 82, No. 2 (Jun. 1991), pp. 245-275. Sulloway writes on p. 262: "During the seventeenth century a new way of knowledge production through scientific experiment had begun to oppose itself to the older, Scholastic tradition of learning from books and authorities." In this passage, I think he echoes his arguments in *Freud, Biologist of the Mind: Beyond the Psychoanalytic Legend* (New York: Basic, 1979), but I find it difficult to comprehend how "a new way of knowledge production" supercedes other modes of knowledge production, if we are all in search of complex knowledge. Sulloway (in 1991) quotes and discusses Karin Obholzer's *The Wolf-Man Sixty Years Later: Conversations with Freud's Controversial Patient* (trans. Michael Shaw, London: Routledge and Kegan Paul, 1982), which I mention in passing.

I use the word "mysterian" in drawing a contrast to Hamlet's skepticism. The term and concept comes from Owen Flanagan, *The Science of the Mind* (second edition, Cambridge and London: MIT Press, 1991), p. 313. Flanagan says that some philosophical types dismiss the scientific study of the mind and consciousness out of a belief that consciousness will never be understood. He got the name "mysterian," he says, from "a forgettable 1960s pop group called "Question Mark and the Mysterians"; he proceeds to describe two types of mysterian:

> old mysterians were dualists who thought that consciousness could not be
> understood because it operates according to nonnatural principles and has
> nonnatural properties. The new mysterians are naturalists. They believe that
> mind and consciousness exist and are comprised of natural properties. But
> the new mysterians are a postmodern group, naturalists with a kinky twist.
> The are trying to drive a railroad spike through the heart of scientism, the
> view that science will eventually explain whatever is natural.

Many of the best scientists I know are quintessentially Hamletian in their view that there is a great deal that is never dreamt of in our philosophy. Hamlet in Elsinore actually hones a scientific skepticism without submitting to either an old or new mysterianism. Flanagan believes that philosopher Thomas Nagel (to be mentioned in a moment) was one of the original mysterians—a harsh judgment, given what Flanagan has to say about them as a group. "Kinky" is an absurd adjective that doesn't apply to Nagel.

Juliet Mitchell's *Psychoanalysis and Feminism* (new edition, with a new introduction by the author, New York: Basic, 2000), particularly her Part

I, is immensely thoughtful. Her book was originally published in 1974; she intended "not to augment our understanding of sexual difference through sexuality, but to map an area where we might begin to chart the transmission of unconscious 'ideas' of sexual difference" (from her new introduction, p. xxv). She makes a delicate and important point. In Freud, the most important "ideas of sexual difference" don't necessarily have to do with the biological differences between men and women. Men and women could be much the same, at least when it comes to fulfillment—and, more importantly, the lack of it—in love. In the chapter, I cite Mitchell on the Oedipus complex, from pp. 63-64.

With admiration, I quote from Thomas Nagel's addendum to "Freud's Permanent Revolution," reprinted along with other of his formidable studies of Freud, in *Other Minds: Critical Essays 1969-1974* (New York and Oxford: Oxford University Press, 1995), p. 44.

6. Leonardo

I use *S.E.* XI's *Leonardo da Vinci and a Memory of His Childhood* throughout this chapter, but Brill's translation (as well as his rather-too-clinical introduction) has had a way of sticking or cloying in my head over time. See *Leonardo da Vinci: A Study in Psychosexuality* (trans. A. A. Brill, New York: Vintage, 1947). I allude passingly to Karen Horney's *The Neurotic Personality of Our Time* (New York: Norton, 1933).

Passages from Virginia Woolf are from her review "Freudian fiction" in *Contemporary Writers* (New York: Harcourt Brace Jovanovich, 1965), pp. 152-154.

The first of Malcolm Bowie's comments is taken from "Freud and Art" in *Psychoanalysis and the Future of Theory* (Oxford: Blackwell, 1993), p. 68. A bit later, I quote from "Freud and the European Unconscious," also from *Psychoanalysis at the Future of Theory*, p. 125. Donald P. Spence's best articulation of "narrative truth" can be found in *Narrative Truth and Historical Truth: Meaning and Interpretation in Psychoanalysis* (New York: W. W. Norton, 1982).

Serge Bramly's *Leonardo: The Artist and the Man* (trans. Sian Reynolds, New York: Penguin 1994) is my source for a great deal of this chapter's biographical information. Reading a vast and thoughtful biography like Bramly's against Kurt R. Eissler's *Psychoanalytic Notes on the Enigma* (New York: International Universities Press, 1961) convinces one that the difference between biography and bad psychohistory is wider than a chasm, as I try to explore. Regarding Eissler's contention about who raised baby Leonardo, see his chapter "Selected Problems of Leonardo's Childhood," pp. 77-85. I consulted Sherwin Nuland's short biography, *Leonardo da Vinci* [A Penguin Life] (New York: Lipper/Viking, 2000) during my research. A thoughtful, recent short treatment is Martin Kemp's *Leonardo* (Oxford: Oxford University Press, 2004), which is a handbook-sized version of his extensive scholarship in *Leonardo da Vinci: The Marvellous Works of Nature and Man* (London: J. M. Dent, 1981). Recently as well, Charles Nicholl has weighed into the melee of Vinciana with his substantial *Leonardo da Vinci: Flights of the Mind* (New York: Penguin, 2004); I quote from p. 35 regarding kites, birds, and swans, and I appreciate his sotto-voce recommendation: "In the matter of Leonardo's childhood we have only nuances of knowledge, and the speculations of Dr Freud seem to me worth listening to" on p. 34.

Jacques Barzun's *Clio and the Doctors: Psycho-History, Quanto-History, and History* (Chicago: University of Chicago Press, 1974) is a historian's unapologetic apology for History without prefixes of any kind. The sentences I quote are on p. 62.

Kenneth Clark's *Leonardo da Vinci* (New York: Penguin, 1989) examines what, in German, would be *geist* and *bildung* rather than biography—"mind" and "spiritual education," as opposed to events in a life. But the differences between mind, education, and chronology blur quickly in Leonardo's case, as Freud, Bramly, Kemp, and Clark would all maintain. To the list on da Vinci, I would add Ernst Gombrich, based on one article in which he applies his argument in his *Art and Illusion* to da Vinci: "The Trattato Della Pittura [The Treatise on Painting], Some Questions and Desiderata" in *Leonardo E L'Eta' Della Ragione* (eds. Enrico Bellone and Paolo Rossi, New York, Lucerne, Florence: Scientia/McGraw Hill, 1982), pp. 141-158. The passage from Kenneth Clark's *Leonardo da Vinci* regarding *Ginevra de' Benci* is on p. 59.

Bramly discusses the passage from Manuscript A and Leonardo's sexual humor on pp. 123-124 of his biography. Eissler's (frankly) weird response is from chapter 12, "The Problem of Homosexuality and Trauma," in *Psychoanalytic Notes on the Enigma*. I still wonder what possessed Eissler to write the following, a bit further on in his discussion: "Yet Leonardo expresses here, in the form of a scientific statement, a consternation that is often encountered clinically in men–that penile reactions are not accessible to the will" (p. 152). Forget, for a moment, about a body part having a mind of its own; why does Eissler think Leonardo is being "scientific" in the Manuscript

A passage? I think, as Bramly does, that Leonardo tells a joke that we still tend to enjoy today, because it says something believable to both men and women. As Leonardo suggests, if we want to see humor in sexual behavior, all we have to do is pay attention.

I use Meyer Schapiro's "Leonardo and Freud: An Art Historical Study" from *Journal of the History of Ideas,* Vol 17, No. 2 (Apr., 1956), pp. 147-178 in counterpoint to Freud throughout this chapter. Schapiro discusses the gaff about the kite as a vulture with relish (he cites Maclagan's first observation of the error).

Chapter three of Volney P. Gay's *Freud on Sublimation: Reconsiderations* (Albany: State University of New York Press, 1992) is entitled "Sublimation and the Mystery of Transformation." Perhaps there is a trick in the chapter's title: a sublimation is not a mystery to the person who sublimates. He or she merely sublimates; so, an interesting chapter like V. P. Gay's (merely) refers us back to a contemplation of the work, life, and mystery of a da Vinci.

Norman O. Brown has an honest complaint in his *Life Against Death* (Middletown: Wesleyan University Press, 1959). It can be phrased in this way: So, what about the rest of us, who are not geniuses? His Part Four, on sublimation, is the pertinent portion of his book for my purposes, but consider this one-liner from p. 307 as a summary of his un-sublimated discontent: "The path of sublimation, which mankind has religiously followed at least since the foundation of the first cities, is no way out of the human neurosis, but, on the contrary, leads to its aggravation."

Passages from Giorgio Vasari are from *The Lives of the Artists* (selected and trans. George Bull, Harmondsworth and New York: Penguin, 1965), pp. 255-271. Freud had certainly read Vasari, but his greater debt is to a later tradition of aesthetic biography. He stole outright from Walter Pater. For my Pater quotations, I have used *Selected Writings of Walter Pater* (ed. Harold Bloom, New York: Columbia University Press, 1974), pp. 31-51.

The passage from Steven Rose, a scientist and theorist of memory, is from his *The Making of Memory,* anthologized in *The Anatomy of Memory* (ed. James McConkey, New York: Oxford University Press, 1996), p. 57. In discussing Rose, the Nietzsche passage I have in mind, from "The Utility and Liability of History," in *Unfashionable Meditations, vol. II The Complete Works of Friedrich Nietzsche* (trans. Richard T. Gray, Stanford: Stanford University Press), pp. 87-88, is worth quoting more fully: ". . . the animal lives *ahistorically*, for it disappears entirely into the present, like a number that leaves no remainder . . . The human being braces himself against the great and ever-greater burden of the past."

Eric Berne, perhaps most famous for writing *Games People Play*, offers us a definition whose virtue is its accessibility; it is from *A Layman's Guide to Psychiatry and Psychoanalysis* (New York: Grove Press, 1947 and 1957), p. 48. I particularly like his observation that the artist could choose fruit, a landscape, *or* a face to draw: the subject matter would seem to have nothing to do with the displacement of libido—which is a displacement onto generic "art." Freud argues slightly differently. His emphasis is Paterian and not generic: the smile is the focus, no matter the ostensible subject of Leonardo's later artistic work.

Anna Freud's *The Ego and the Mechanisms of Defense* (revised edition, New York: International Universities Press, 1966) discusses the psychological defenses—repression, reaction-formation, sublimation, etc. more systematically than her father did. I quote from p. 32.

Regarding the recording of accounts, Leonardo often did so, to the unending fascination of scholars. In one year (1490), for example, he recorded clothing expenses for the boy Salai, who had come to live with him: "One cloak: 2 lire; 6 shirts: 4 lire; three jerkins: 6 lire; 4 pairs of hose: 7 lire 8 soldi; a lined suit 5 lire; 4 pairs of shoes: 6 lire 5 soldi; a cap 1 lira; thongs for belts 1 lira"—Bramly adds (p. 224), "Oddly, he does not work out the total. . . ." Bramly's comments regarding Leonardo's productivity in Milan are from p. 245.

I tend to agree with poet Rainer Rilke that Merezhkovsky is "bad and boring." I read Bernard G. Guerney's translation from the original Russian, entitled *The Romance of Leonardo da Vinci* (New York: Heritage, 1938). Freud borrowed from Merezhkovsky on two counts. The idea that Leonardo's mother returned in 1493 is Merezhkovsky's, as Freud says. Peter Gay tells us that, in addition, it was Merezhkovsky who drew Freud's attention to the Leonardo's bird memory or fantasy. In the Freud Museum (London), on p. 382 of Freud's copy of a 1903 German translation by Carl von Gütschow, Merzhkovsky's discussion of the cradle memory is emphatically double underlined, says Gay. See "Reading Freud through Freud's Reading" in *Reading Freud*, p. 106, n. 26.

Richard Wollheim's central question about the explicitness of understanding is from "Freud and the Understanding of Art" in *Modern Critical Views: Sigmund Freud* (ed. Harold Bloom, New York: Chelsea House, 1985), p. 91.

7. MOSES

The neurotheological scientists whom I quote at the start of the chapter are Jeffrey L. Saver and John Rabin, from "The Neural Substrates of Religious Experience," in *The Journal of Neuropsychiatry and Clinical Neurosciences*, Vol. 9 (1997), p. 499. Saver and Rabin refer to *The Varieties of Psychedelic Experience* by R. E. L. Masters and J. Houston (New York: Holt, Rinehart, and Winston, 1966)—the latter is the source for the survey of 206 individuals regarding the content of their hallucinatory experiences.

I have cited Jaroslav Pelikan's *Melody of Theology* previously (see note to chapter one). I've mentioned Peter Gay's treatment of Freud's late career in *Freud: A Life for Our Time* also in chapter one. In this chapter, I rely on Gay's chapter 12, "To Die in Freedom." Martin Buber, of course, wrote on Moses himself in his *Moses* (Oxford: Oxford University Press, 1946). C. Johnston's review of *Future of an Illusion* from *The New York Times* (Aug. 12, 1928) is quoted in *Book Review Digest* 1928, p. 277. Quotations from Freud's "The Moses of Michelangelo" are from *On Creativity and the Unconscious. Papers on the Psychology of Art, Literature, Love, Religion*, p. 34 and, later, p. 37.

For me, William James's *The Varieties of Religious Experience: A Study in Human Nature* (New York: Barnes and Noble Classics, 2004), particularly its "Postscript" (pp. 445-450), is a good companion text to *Moses and Monotheism*. Lou Andreas-Salomé's letter and Freud's response come from *Sigmund Freud and Lou Andreas-Salomé: Letters* (ed. Ernst Pfeiffer, trans. William and Elaine Robson-Scott, New York: Harcourt Brace Jovanovich, 1972), pp. 182-185. In addition to the "oceanic-feeling" letter of December 27, 1927, see Freud's letters to Rolland on July 14 and 20, 1929 in *Letters of Sigmund Freud* (ed. Ernst Freud, trans. Tania and James Stern, New York: Basic, 1960), pp. 388-389. An entire book has been written on the exchange between the two men which I found interesting and helpful: William B. Parsons, *The Enigma of the Oceanic Feeling: Revisioning the Psychoanalytic Theory of Mysticism* (New York and Oxford: Oxford University Press, 1999). Paul Roazen's observation that Freud wrote about religion in each of the last three decades of his life is from *Freud: Political and Social Thought* (New York: Knopf, 1968), p. 125.

I am indebted to Yosef Hayim Yerulshalmi's *Freud's Moses: Judaism Terminable and Interminable* (New Haven: Yale University Press, 1991) throughout my discussion. I quote him in several places, beginning with his reference to Freud's Itzig story (on p. 1 of *Freud's Moses*) and then, in longer citations, from p. 29, p. 34, p. 10, and p. 74, in order of appearance in my chapter. Jacques Derrida responds to Yerulshalmi's book in his *Archive Fever: A Freudian Impression* (trans. Eric Prenowitz, Chicago and London: University of Chicago Press, 1995); I borrow from Derrida's p. 38. R. Travers Herford's commentary to the *Pirke Aboth* or *The Ethics of the Talmud: Sayings of the Fathers* (ed. and trans. R. Travers Herford, New York: Shocken, 1962) begins with what he calls "a fundamental axiom of Rabbinical Judaism" which I recite. For background regarding Hellenistic influence on the personification of Moses, see Martin Hengal's *Judaism and Hellenism: Studies in their Encounter in Palestine during the Early Hellenistic Period* (trans. John Bowden, Philadelphia: Fortress, 1974), especially pp. 81-83, 92f., 255 ff. I quote first from page 81; later in the chapter, I borrow from Hengal's discussion of Celsus, a writer in the second century CE, p. 262.

Walter Benjamin quotes and discusses Franz Kafka's variation on the Abraham story in "Franz Kafka: On the Tenth Anniversary of his Death" in *Illuminations* (ed. Hannah Arendt, trans. Harry Zohn, New York: Shocken, 1969), p. 129. In my chapter a bit later, I quote from Benjamin's "Theses on the Philosophy of History," also from *Illuminations*, p. 255.

Freud has been criticized for his Lamarckianism (because of the claim implicit to psychoanalytic theory that a later generation inherits knowledge or memory that an older generation possesses, however modified or "repressed" that memory might be), but I wonder whether Freud aspired, primarily, to Darwinism in one specific regard. I paraphrase from *On Natural Selection*, excerpted from *The Origin of Species*, and recently re-published as part of Penguin's "Great Ideas" Series (New York: Penguin Books/Great Ideas, 2005), p. 17.

The Five Books of Moses: Genesis, Exodus, Leviticus, Numbers, Deuteronomy (trans. and commentary Everett Fox, New York: Shocken, 1995) offers us Fox's sometimes surprising commentary regarding the Pentateuch. I quote his comments regarding Genesis 22 (p. 92), but I do wonder: in what sense, knowing what Yahweh is capable of, does one ever feel that one can "breathe easier" once and for all?

Neville Symington's "dissertation" is from "Is Psychoanalysis a Religion?" in *The Blind Man Sees: Freud's Awakening and Other Essays* (London and New York: Karnac, 2004), p. 159. Hans Küng's summary of Freud on religion (I offer a cento of quotes) is from *Freud and The Problem of God* (enlarged edition, trans. Edward Quinn, New Haven: Yale University Press, 1979), pp.

39-40. I also quote Küng's plea regarding religion and psychology from the same book, pp. 155-6. Symington thought about "oedipalizing" his patient's depression, but he didn't: he decided that theorizing helps the doctor more than it helps the patient. Whether theory really helps anyone is a function of how we use theory.

The correspondent from Boston, as quoted by Peter Gay (*Freud: A Life for Our Time*, pp. 646-647), descends into gross anti-Semitism as his letter goes on: "We have renegades like you by the thousands, we are glad we are rid of them and we hope soon to be rid of you. It is to be regretted that the Gangsters in Germany did not put you into a concentration camp, that's where you belong." The malice in the above sentences was omnipresent in Vienna as Freud approached his death.

8. POSTSCRIPT

My source for the poet Rilke is *Rilke on Love and Other Difficulties* (trans. John J. L. Mood, New York: W. W. Norton, 1975), pp. 3, 28-29. There's a problem with Mood's edition, which nevertheless remains very lovely to read from page to page: the reader bounces around in Rilke's life from excerpt to excerpt without being told about the leaps in chronology. The impression is that the poet writes a sustained (younger man's) meditation on love, when, in fact, Mood's selection amounts to a career's reflection on the subject. The younger Rilke (in his late twenties) writes the first and second passages I quote, but, in the third, Rilke is older (about forty-five), writing about "locked rooms."

The translation from "Contributions to the Psychology of Love" (Joan Riviere's) is from *Sigmund Freud: Sexuality and the Psychology of Love* (ed. Philip Rieff, New York: Touchstone, 1997), p. 39.

Kenneth Burke on art for art's sake is from *Counter-statement* (second ed., Chicago: University of Chicago Press, 1953), p. 63. The possibility of medical treatment to "erase" memory is an overstatement on the part of Robin Marantz Honig in *The New York Times Magazine* (April 4, 2004, p. 32 ff.); she refers to work by psychiatrist Roger Pittman, who has studied post-traumatic stress disorder at my medical school. Pittman's interest is that people do not forget, no matter what happens. Critic Alfred Kazin was interviewed about a selection from his journals, entitled *A Lifetime Burning in Every Moment* (New York: HarperPerennial, 1997), as recorded on a website that may long since have been updated: www.bookpage.com/9608bp/

nonfiction/alifetimeburning.html.

The observation about more people writing books than reading them is from Gabriel Zaid, *So Many Books: Reading and Publishing in an Age of Abundance*, (trans. Natasha Wimmer, Philadelphia: Paul Dry, 2003).

Quotations from Irving Singer are from his monograph *Philosophy of Love, A Partial Summing Up* (Cambridge and London: MIT Press, 2009), pp. 56-58. Singer "sums up" his vaster work in three volumes, *The Nature of Love*, also published by MIT Press, 2009.

Index of Authors or Works

www.ingramcontent.com/pod-product-compliance
Lightning Source LLC
Chambersburg PA
CBHW031245090426
42742CB00007B/320